D1416737

A Treasury of Great Christians' Correspondence

VOLUME 2

Letters OF *Faith*

THROUGH
THE

Seasons

James M. Houston

HONOR **HB** BOOKS

Inspiration and Motivation for the Seasons of Life

COOK COMMUNICATIONS MINISTRIES
Colorado Springs, Colorado • Paris, Ontario
KINGSWAY COMMUNICATIONS LTD
Eastbourne, England

Honor Books® is an imprint of
Cook Communications Ministries, Colorado Springs, CO 80918
Cook Communications, Paris, Ontario
Kingsway Communications, Eastbourne, England

LETTERS OF FAITH THROUGH THE SEASONS VOL. 2
© 2007 James M. Houston, Editor

First Printing, 2007
Printed in the United States of America

1 2 3 4 5 6 7 8 9 10

Cover Design: Greg Jackson, Thinkpen Design, llc
Cover Photo: © iStockphoto

All Scripture quotations, unless otherwise noted, are taken from the *Holy Bible: New International Version®. NIV®.* Copyright © 1973, 1978, 1984 by International Bible Society. Used by permission of Zondervan. All rights reserved. Scripture quotations marked KJV are taken from the King James Version of the Bible. (Public Domain); and marked MSG are taken from *THE MESSAGE.* Copyright © by Eugene H. Peterson 1993, 1994, 1995, 1996, 2000, 2001, 2002. Used by permission of NavPress Publishing Group.

[Editor's comments appear in brackets throughout the text.]

ISBN 978-1-56292-834-6
LCCN 2006932519

Dedicated to "the elect ladies":

Elisabeth Bockmuehl, Gail Stevenson, and Julie Gay, for their vision and initiatives

in the endowment of the Professorship of Spiritual Theology at Regent College

CONTENTS

INTRODUCTION

*The chief interest of a study of the great letter writers is that it
introduces us not to literary works, but to persons. This is the
triumph of letter writing, that it keeps a more delicate image
alive and presents us with a subtler likeness of the writer than
we can find in the more formal achievements of authorship.*

—*Sir Walter Raleigh*

*D*ear Reader,

In my introductory letter to *Letters of Faith Volume I*, I outlined the
purpose of these collections of letters. It is to communicate in both a
more historical, and a more personal way the wide-ranging vicissitudes
of what has shaped our Christian faith, as well as what keeps on challenging it. The first volume, which covers the months from December
through May, is fundamentally shaped by the events of the Incarnation,
beginning with the season of Advent and closing with the fifty days
between the Resurrection and the Ascension, followed by Pentecost.
These historical events then challenged the early Church to celebrate
Trinity Sunday, bringing the final and full disclosure of the nature of God
as Father, Son, and Holy Spirit.

After this disclosure of the mystery of the triune God of grace, what
else is there to celebrate in the Church's sacred calendar? For the next
twenty-five Sundays, there is the simple nomenclature, "The first to the
twenty-fifth Sunday(s) after Trinity." In speaking of "twenty five Sundays
after Trinity," the new revised common lectionary now speaks of "twenty
nine Proper Sundays," including All Souls and the three Sundays following. This time period embraces the whole Season after Pentecost, which
is technically called "Ordinary Time." Ordinary Time begins with Trinity
Sunday and ends the last Sunday of November before the season of
Advent begins. This is the period covered in this volume.

Yet there is one sacred focus of this second half of the Christian year,
All Saints' Day, celebrated on November first or on the first Sunday of
November. It has been argued that this day is the climax of the entire
Christian calendar, since it celebrates the unity of the Body of Christ and
the fulfillment of our Lord's prayer before his Passion: "that all of them
may be one, Father, just as you are in me and I am in you. May they also

7

be in us so that the world may believe that you have sent me" (John 17:21).

The format of this second collection of letters changes, not to celebrate festal seasons of the Church, but to illustrate as universally as possible how the Christian revelation of the Gospel has been received in diverse cultures, political and social circumstances, as well as in the vicissitudes of the human condition. The various subheadings of groups of letters illustrate how varied they have been and still are. But as Sir Walter Raleigh reminded us, letters are ideally very personal, so we need to remember that twenty-one of the twenty-nine books of the New Testament are letters. In addition, the book of Revelation is comprised of one long letter containing within it seven others to the seven groups of churches in Asia Minor. So the communication of our faith is primarily in the epistolary genre. This genre is focused within the central part of this volume, to remind us how deeply personal our faith should always be. As Francis Bacon is said to have been impressed, "Letters, such as written by wise men, are, of all the words of men, in my judgment, the best." How much more then we should listen to the Word of God when he deigns to write to us in letters too!

The remaining collections of letters are more directive, both illustrating the wide range of human circumstances, calling for help, even rescue, as well as seeking spiritual direction through many traditions and schools of guidance, both Roman Catholic and Protestant. As Samuel Johnson observed, our human letters "are only the mirror of his [or her] heart. Whatever passes within him [her], is there shown in its natural progress; nothing is invented, nothing distorted; you see systems in their elements, you discover actions in their motives." If others then have so bared their soul, such as we can now profit across the years or even centuries since they did so, by how much more we should be willing to open our hearts today to their continuing ministry. This then should be a personal sphere where doubt and distrust, even depression and despair, can be evacuated to celebrate the friendship of God and the friends of God too.

I hope you will be as blessed and inspired in reading these further letters as I have been in sharing them with you.

ACKNOWLEDGMENTS

I am indebted to my editors: Craig Bubeck, who shared the vision to publish this anthology of letters; and to Ingrid Beck, who completed the process of bringing this manuscript to press. I am grateful to David Dobson and David Chao, earlier editors who gave the initial help to launch the project. Anita Palmer assisted in the early editing, and her enthusiasm encouraged me in the task ahead. I owe warm thanks to two assistants, Diane Krusemark and Paul Philatreau, who collected and typed out some of the letters, while Paul Fiber nobly established a system for obtaining copyright permissions. Corinna Rogge also helped me in the late stage of editing. My family, Christopher, Lydele, Claire, and Penelope cheered me on with the overall shaping of the anthology, while my wife Rita endured with infinite patience my immersion in the task, which proved far greater than I had originally anticipated. Above all, my warmest thanks go to the many correspondents whose letters give strong and profoundly honest, contemporary perspectives to balance the widely historical and ecumenical approaches selected. For me this has been a wonderful experience of the communion of saints.

SEASONS OF CHRISTENDOM

*W*e move now from the sacred calendar of the events of our Lord's earthly ministry, as reflected upon in the first volume, to the historical, political, and social vicissitudes of the Christian church since Pentecost. Likewise, we trace the extraordinary range of human circumstances that we may encounter individually within the nominal religious life we call "Christendom."

THE EARLY CHURCH FATHERS

JUNE 1: POLITICAL EXPEDIENCY CAN TRY TO
DICTATE DOCTRINAL COMPROMISES

In this letter, the emperor Constantine urged Alexander, bishop of Alexandria,
for the sake of the political unity of the empire, to "accept peace doctrinally at
any price," urging him to make a compromise with the heretical priest Arius.
Yet later it was the spread of Arianism—denying the deity of Christ—that
prepared the way for all "natural religion" within Christendom.

Victor Constantinus Maximus Augustus to Alexander and Arius.

God is my witness, who is the help of all my endeavor, and the preserver of all men, that I had a twofold reason for undertaking that duty which I have now performed.

It was my purpose in the first place to bring the diverse opinions of all nations respecting the Deity to a settled condition and a single form, and secondly, to restore health to the body of the world, then suffering as it were under a malignant power, stricken as with a grievous disease. With this end in view, I sought to accomplish the one by the secret eye of thought, while the other I tried to establish by military forces and authority. For I perceived that if I could succeed in establishing, according to my hopes, a harmonious agreement amongst all the servants of God, the State itself would also undergo a change consonant with the pious desires of all men....

I find that your present controversy originated thus. When you, Alexander, inquired what each of your presbyters thought on a certain obscure passage of Scripture, rather, on a passage which it was idle to investigate; and you, Arius, rashly gave an opinion which you ought never to have conceived, which having been conceived ought never to have been expressed, the whole question should have remained buried in silence. And by reason of this dispute which has arisen amongst you, communion has been denied and the most holy people of God have been rent into two factions, and have betrayed the unity of the common body.

Wherefore, let each of you show forbearance the one to the other, and listen to the impartial exhortation of your fellow servant. What then does he counsel you? It was indecorous in the first place to raise such a question, and in the second, to reply to such a question when proposed. For discussions such as these, which are enjoined by no precept of the law, are induced by the vain talk of idleness. And even if they should arise, for the exercise of our natural faculties, yet ought we to confine them to our own meditations, and not indiscreetly propound them in public assemblies, nor thoughtlessly confide them to the ears of everybody....

The controversy between you does not rest on any difference about an important principle contained in the Law; nor does it involve any heresy in connection with the worship of God. You both hold the same view on these points; you may join without hindrance in communion and fellowship together. Moreover, so long as you thus stubbornly contend with one another about these small and insignificant questions, it is unsuitable for you to have charge of so many people of God, since you are divided in opinion among yourselves. Not only is it unbecoming, but it is plain wrong!

Scripture Meditation

Fight the good fight of the faith. Take hold of the eternal life to which you were called when you made your good confession in the presence of many witnesses.

— 1 TIMOTHY 6:12

Thought for the Day

Peace is not bought at the price of truth; it is only valid when it is being held by the truth.

Prayer

Almighty God, whose Son, our Savior Jesus Christ, is the light of the world: Grant that thy people, illumined by thy Word and Sacraments, may shine with the radiance of Christ's glory, that he may be known, worshiped, and obeyed to the ends of the earth.

— COLLECT FOR THE SECOND SUNDAY AFTER EPITHANY,

THE BOOK OF COMMON PRAYER

JUNE 2: RATIONAL EXPLANATIONS OF GOD TEND TOWARD THE ABSTRACTION OF MONOTHEISM

We forget that the spread of Arianism (the denial of the divinity of Jesus Christ)
from the fourth century onward prepared the way for the rise and spread of
Islam later, within the Near East. Here Athanasius (293–373) wrote to Serapion,
an Egyptian bishop, in defense against the Arian persecution of the Christians.

A letter of your Piety was given to me in the desert [i.e., while in exile]. A bitter issue arose when we were being persecuted, and many attempts to find us were made by those who sought to kill us. But "the God of mercies and Lord of all comforts" assured us by your letter.... The Arians in their blasphemies against the Son of God, declare him only to be human, and see the Holy Spirit to be merely one of other ministering-spirits; only by degree superior to the angels.... Denying the Son, they also deny the Father, and thus blaspheme against the Holy Spirit.... Because of their false conception of the Holy Spirit, the Trinity is no longer one being, but composed of two differing natures.

So what kind of theology is this amalgam of Creator and creature? No longer is it the divine Trinity; it is only a human make-up. All the result of this is a profound denial of the deity of the Holy Spirit. So the challenge is where in the divine scriptures is the Holy Spirit merely called "a spirit," without the additional link, as being "of God," or "of the Father," or "my," or "his," or "of Christ" and "of the Son," or "from me," that is, from God.... Does not the article appear "the Spirit," not just "spirit," or else as "the Holy Spirit," or "the Comforter," or "of Truth," that is, of the Son, who says, "I am the Truth"?

For the Savior in the Gospels is always referred to by their writers in the context of the Holy Spirit. So "Jesus, full of the Holy Spirit, returned from the Jordan," or again "Jesus was brought to the desert by the Spirit," or as Luke states: "When Jesus was baptized, and while he was in prayer, the heavens opened and the Holy Spirit descended with a bodily appearance like a dove upon him."

From all such passages, it is clear the mention of "the spirit" means the Holy Spirit. Similarly, it is the presence of the Holy Spirit with human beings which has been promised to be our "Comforter."

Scripture Meditation

When the Counselor comes, whom I will send to you from the
Father, the Spirit of truth who goes out from the Father, he will
testify about me.
—JOHN 15:26

Thought for the Day

Translating "same as" and "of similar substance" from the Greek into
theological language about the three Persons of the Trinity has spawned
major heresies.

Prayer

Spirit of God, descend upon my heart:
Wean it from earth, through all its pulses move.
Stoop to my weakness, mighty as Thou art,
and make me love Thee as I ought to love.
—GEORGE CROLY

JUNE 3: CHRISTIAN BAPTISM IS IN THE NAME OF THE TRIUNE GOD

---

*Athanasius wrote again to Serapion against the further
consequences of Arian heresy.*

Whoever takes away something from the Trinity, and is baptized only
in the name of one person of the Trinity, is false and incomplete. For only
in the Trinity is there divine fullness. Likewise, whoever divides the Son

from the Father, or lowers the Spirit to the level of the creatures, has neither the Son nor the Father but is godless, and is worse than the unbeliever.

As the apostle states: "There is one faith and one baptism," so there is baptism only as it has been by the Father *and* the Son *and* the Holy Spirit, and they are one. So such faith is also one. For as the Trinity are united as one, faith in the triune God is also one faith. But according to the spurious talk of you heretics, it is not this.

Having dreamed up that the Holy Spirit is only a creature, your faith is no longer one, nor is your baptism. For one is in the Father and the Son, and the other in an angel, considered now as a creature. So you end up with no certainty, with a mix-up of communion with both a creature and the Creator....

Knowing of this heresy, the blessed Paul does not divide the Trinity as you do. Rather he teaches its unity when he writes to the Corinthians ... summing up everything in one God, saying: "Although there are divisions of graces but the Spirit is the same, and although there are divisions of operations but God is the same, he operates all in all." Whatever is given by the Spirit, is distributed from the Father through the Word; for all things of the Father are of the Son.... Whatever is given by the Son, is through the Spirit, as graces of the Father. And when the Spirit is in us, the Word is also the giver of the same is in us, and the Father is in the Word.

And so it is written, "I and the Father will come and will make a dwelling with him." Just as where there is light, there also is radiance, and where there is radiance, there also is its activity and clear grace. So Paul concludes his teaching in the second letter to the Corinthians: "The grace of our Lord Jesus Christ, the love of God and the communion of the Holy Spirit shall be with you all." For the grace and gifts which have been given are distributed by the Trinity, from the Father, through the Son, by the Holy Spirit.

Scripture Meditation

Therefore go and make disciples of all nations, baptizing them in the name of the Father and of the Son and of the Holy Spirit, and teaching them to obey everything I have commanded you.

—MATTHEW 28:19–20

Thought for the Day

Heresy divides, truth unites, since all truth is the truth of the triune God of grace.

Prayer

My prayer is not for them alone. I pray also for those who will believe in me through their message, that all of them may be one, Father, just as you are in me and I am in you.

—JOHN 17:20–21

JUNE 4: THE FULL DIVINITY OF GOD AS FATHER, SON, AND HOLY SPIRIT

Following Athanasius, Basil the Great (329–79), bishop of Caesarea, further defended the Christian faith against Arians and other heretics. With his brother Gregory of Nyssa, and friend Gregory of Nazianzen, he defended the mystery of the Holy Trinity. Basil wrote many letters in defense of the deity and person of the Holy Spirit, of which this is one, date unknown.

It is clear that while some denied that the Son was of the same substance with the Father, and some asserted that He was not of the substance and so was of some other *hypostasis* or identity, both views were condemned officially as not those held by the Church. When they thus speculated, declaring the Son to be of the substance of the Father, they withheld the phrase "of the *hypostasis*." The former clause stands for the condemnation of the faulty view; the latter plainly states the dogma of salvation.

We are therefore bound to confess the Son to be of one substance with the Father, as it is written; but the Father to exist in His own proper *hypostasis*, the Son in His, and the Holy Ghost in His, as they themselves have clearly declared the doctrine. Indeed, they clearly and satisfactorily declared in the phrase "Light of Light" [i.e., God], that the Light which originated and the Light which was begotten, are distinct, and yet "Light and Light"; so that the definition of the Substance is one and the same. I will now add to the actual creed as it was drawn up at [the Council of] Nicea....

The doctrine of the Spirit, however, is merely mentioned, as needing no elaboration, because at the time of the Council no question was raised on the issue, and the opinion on this subject in the hearts of the faithful was not under attack. Little by little, however, the growing poison-germs of impiety first sown by Arius, the champion of the heresy, and then by those who succeeded to his inheritance of mischief, were fertilized to the plague of the Church, and the poplar growth of the impiety resulted in blasphemy against the Holy Ghost.... They must be all condemned, who think or call the Holy Ghost a creature; all who do not confess that He is holy by nature, as the Father is holy by nature, and the Son is holy by nature; and refuse Him His place in the blessed divine nature.

By not separating Him from the Father and the Son is proof of sound doctrine. For we are bound to be baptized in the terms we have received, as professing belief and this giving glory to Father, Son, and Holy Ghost....

We are also bound to condemn all who speak of the Holy Ghost as ministerial, degrade Him to the rank of a creature, by such a term. For ministering spirits are creatures, as Scripture states: "they are all ministering spirits sent forth to minister." By not keeping Gospel doctrine, they confuse the Christian public. So they must be shunned, as plainly hostile to true religion. For they invert the order given us by the Lord, putting the Son before the Father, and the Holy Spirit before the Son. So let us maintain the very words of the Lord: "Go ye therefore, and teach all nations, baptizing them in the name of the Father and of the Son, and of the Holy Ghost."

Scripture Meditation

This salvation, which was first announced by the Lord, was confirmed to us by those who heard him. God also testified to it by signs, wonders and various miracles, and gifts of the Holy Spirit distributed according to his will.
—HEBREWS 2:3–4

Thought for the Day

As Jesus Christ did not forfeit his deity in becoming man, no more is the Holy Spirit only a ministerial spirit by indwelling Christian believers.

Prayer

Make us eternal truth receive,
And practice, all that we believe:
Give us thy self, that we may see
The Father and the Son, by Thee.
—*Veni Creator Spiritus*, translated by John Dryden

JUNE 5: THE UNITY IN ALL ACTIONS OF THE THREE PERSONS

Basil the Great continued with another pastoral letter on the same theme.

United as One, the Father, the Son and the Holy Ghost hallow, quicken, enlighten, and comfort. The Spirit does not "hallow" without the other Persons being involved. As Jesus prays to the Father about His disciples, "sanctify them in Thy name." Likewise, all other divine actions who are worthy of them, by the Father, by the Son and by the Holy Ghost; that is every grace, guidance, life, consolation, change into the eternal, the way into freedom and all other things [are] gifts of God....

Nothing that comes to us from God is constituted apart from the operation and power of the Holy Ghost, every individual sharing His help in proportion to the dignity and need of each. What lies beyond our knowledge is bound to be obscure to our perception; nevertheless any one, arguing from what is known to us, would find it more reasonable to conclude that the power of the Spirit operates even in those beings, than that He is excluded from the government of mysterious realities.

So to limit the character and power of the Spirit is blasphemy, plainly so, for it has no evidence of truth. On the other hand, to accept that even the world beyond us is governed by the power of the Spirit, as well as by the Father and the Son, is supported on the plain testimony of what is seen in human life. Identity of operation in the case of the Father, the Son and the Holy Spirit, clearly proves the divine nature. So if the name of "God" denotes divinity, the community of Trinitarian essence is very properly applied to the Holy Spirit.

Scripture Meditation

If you love me, you will obey what I command. And I will ask the Father, and he will give you another Counselor to be with you forever—the Spirit of truth.
—JOHN 14:15–17

Thought for the Day

If Christ can do nothing of himself but by the Father and the Spirit, no more can we live the Christian life without the Father, Son, and Holy Spirit.

Prayer

We beseech you, O Lord, let the power of the Holy Spirit come upon us: that it may mercifully cleanse our hearts, and defend us from all adversities.
—COLLECT, THE BOOK OF COMMON PRAYER

JUNE 6: THE UNIVERSAL CLAIM OF THE HOLY SPIRIT OVER
THE WHOLE CHURCH OF GOD

*Leo the Great continued his pastoral circulars for the season of Pentecost. He
had been a leading theologian of the Council of Chalcedon.*

By these and other innumerable proofs, shining forth among the
authoritative and divine utterances, let us revere unitedly the celebration
of Pentecost. Let us rejoice to honor the Holy Spirit, who sanctifies the
whole Catholic Church, and who enters into all our minds. For he is the
Inspirer of faith, the Teacher of knowledge, the Fountain of love, the Seal
of chastity, and the Cause of all virtue. Let the faithful rejoice, because
throughout the world One God—the Father, and the Son, and the Holy
Spirit—is praised in all languages.

For that mystery, which appeared in the form of fire, endures both in
operation and in bestowal. For the Spirit of Truth Himself glorifies his
house, shining with the radiance of his own light, to remove from his temple whatever is dark or lukewarm. This teaching cleanses the fasts and
alms we practice. For, if in the days preceding the Feast any stain has
been contracted through careless negligence, it may be dealt with fasting
and renewed devotion. So on Wednesday and Friday, let us fast; on the
Sabbath, let us all join in keeping vigils with our accustomed devotion;
through Jesus Christ our Lord, Who lives and reigns with the Father and
the Holy Spirit, one God, forever and ever. Amen.

Scripture Meditation

*Do you not know that your body is a temple of the Holy Spirit,
who is in you, whom you have received from God? ... Therefore
honor God with your body.*

—I CORINTHIANS 6:19–20

Thought for the Day

Because of Pentecost, "holy places" have now become "holy people"!

Prayer

Enrich my heart, mouth, hands in me,
with faith, with hope, with charity;
that I may run, rise, rest with Thee.

—GEORGE HERBERT, POEM FOR TRINITY SUNDAY

JUNE 7: THE HOLY SPIRIT REVEALS THE TRIUNE GOD OF GRACE

Leo the Great continued his series of pastoral reflections of Pentecost.

Dearly beloved,

The appearance of Pentecost was wonderful indeed. Nor can it be doubted that the majesty of the Holy Spirit was present in the exultant choir of so many languages spoken. Yet don't imagine His Divine substance was made visible to human eyes. For His invisible nature, which He shares with the Father and the Son, revealed in this way the character of its own gift and work, while retaining within its Divinity what belonged to its essence.

For is as the Father and the Son, so also the Holy Spirit is inaccessible to human sight. For in the divine Trinity there is nothing dissimilar, nothing unequal; and all that can be thought of as pertaining to that substance, admits of no difference in respect to power, glory, and eternity. But in regard to the distinctness of Person, the Father is one, the Son is another, the Holy Spirit another. Yet it is not another Godhead, nor a different nature: seeing that, while the Only-begotten Son also is from the Father, the Holy Spirit likewise is the Spirit of the Father and of the Son, the living and mighty One together with the Two, eternally subsisting from the Father and the Son.

So our Lord promised his disciples before his Passion: "I have many things to say to you, but you cannot bear them now. When He, the Spirit of truth is come, He will guide you into all truth. For He will not speak from himself, but whatever He will hear, He will speak, and will announce to you things to come. All things that the Father hath are Mine: therefore said I, that He shall take of Mine, and shall show it unto you." It is not then that some things belong to the Father, some to the Son, some to the Holy Spirit, for whatever the Father has, the Holy Spirit has also in an eternal communion.

Scripture Meditation

Exalted to the right hand of God, he [Christ] has received from the Father the promised Holy Spirit and has poured out what you now see and hear.
—ACTS 2:33

Thought for the Day

Occasioned by the incarnation of Christ, the revelation of the Trinity invites us to share in the filial relationship the Son has with the Father.

Prayer

Come, Holy Ghost, Creator blest,
vouchsafe within our souls to rest;
come with Thy grace and heavenly aid,
and fill the hearts which Thou has made.
—VENI CREATOR SPIRITUS

June 8: A Trinitarian Text Commonly Misinterpreted

Leo the Great further responded to a scriptural text falsely interpreted by heretics, which is still used by Mormons, Jehovah's Witnesses, and other cults.

It is true that the Lord Jesus said to His disciples, as has been recited in the Gospel reading, "If you loved me, you would be glad that I am going to the Father, for the Father is greater than I" (John 14:28). But this passage is eternally understood by those ears which have often heard, "I and my Father are One" (John 10:30), and "Anyone who has seen me has seen the Father" (John 14:9), as implying no difference of Godhead. Nor do they refer it to that essence which they know to be everlasting with the Father, and of the same nature.

It was given to assure them ... for they were disturbed when the Lord announced his departure from them ... "If you loved Me," he says, "you would be glad that I am going to the Father," meaning "if you only knew perfectly what glory is now bestowed on you because I, begotten of God the Father, have also been born of a human mother; that I, the Lord of things eternal, have willed to become one with human mortals. Then, indeed, you would rejoice that I go to the Father. Further, reminded that although everlasting God, yet taking the form of a servant, you should rejoice indeed, because I go back to the Father.

"For the doctrine of the Ascension is something for us to experience personally. It is your lowliness in me, which is exalted above the heavens, to be seated at the Father's right hand.... For I, remaining indivisibly one with the Father, yet never leave you in returning to the Father, as in coming to you from him, I never departed from the Father. Rejoice, then, that I go to the Father, for the Father is greater than I. I have united you to Myself, becoming the Son of Man, that you may become sons of God. Wherefore, although I am One in both [natures], in being conformed to your nature, I am inferior to the Father; but never divided from the Father, I am greater than Myself."

So let us, dearly beloved, condemn the vain and blind craft of heresy, which interprets perversely this biblical verse.... Mercy in God does not lessen power; nor is the reconciling of a beloved creature a defect of everlasting glory. What the Father has, the Son has also. What the Father and the Son have, the Holy Spirit has also. For the whole Trinity together is One God, which as an article of faith is no mere discovery of human wisdom, for the Only-begotten Son himself has taught it, and the Holy Spirit himself has inculcated it—the Spirit which is no other than of the Father and the Son.

Scripture Meditation

If you loved me, you would be glad that I am going to the Father, for the Father is greater than I.
—John 14:28

Thought for the Day

The Holy Trinity alone assures our existence as persons, rather than pantheists, individualists, or aliens.

Prayer

May *the grace of the Lord Jesus Christ, and the love of God, and the fellowship of the Holy Spirit be with you all.*
—2 Corinthians 13:14

June 9: The Ongoing Significance of the Council of Chalcedon

Dr. Gerald Bray (b. 1948) is professor of Historical and Anglican Theology, Beeson Divinity School, Samford University, Birmingham, Alabama. He wrote to the editor about the Council of Chalcedon that took place in 453.

ear Jim,

It seems to me that the supreme importance of the Chalcedonian Definition for the faith of the church is the fact that it succeeded in attaining the right balance between the divinity and humanity of Christ. Not everyone agrees with this, of course, and the Definition has never been accepted in large parts of the Eastern Church. But the reasons for that were mainly to do with difficulties over the technical terminology, and it is now accepted that what Chalcedon was trying to affirm was in fact believed on both sides of that debate.

Chalcedon wanted to affirm both the full divinity and the full humanity of Jesus Christ, without losing his identity as a single person. It [the Chalcedonian Definition] did so in the only way possible, which was to say that the Son of God, a divine person, took on a human nature in addition to the divine nature, which he already had. Moreover, he did this by entering the womb of the Virgin Mary and undergoing a normal human birth. In other words, he inserted himself in the regular pattern of human descent and so shared our humanity in all its formative stages.

How can a divine person be a human being? One simple way of looking at this is to think of a child who has two nationalities. The child will speak one language to its father and another to its mother, without confusing them. This is a mystery to others who do not have this ability, but to the child it is perfectly natural and normal. Jesus communicated with both his parents in different modes, but was not any less "normal" for that!

Another way to look at it is to remember that, in a sense, all persons are divine. We have been created in the image and likeness of God, and it is that which defines the significance of our humanity. In other words, we cannot understand ourselves without taking the divine dimension of our being into account—the part of us which we call our personhood. So the fact that Jesus was a divine person does not compromise his ability to be fully human. If anything, it gives him the power to be even more human than we are!

The Chalcedonian Definition got the balance right—Jesus Christ was God and man, without change, without confusion, without division, without separation. Side by side, indissolubly united, but each nature performing its own functions in that harmony which is meant to be shared between God and us as well. What we experience imperfectly, he demonstrates in fullness and in power.

This is the model for our life, the promise for our future, the meaning of our salvation. Once we understand it, we understand who we are, where we are going and what we shall one day become. There is more that might be said, but surely not less. In Jesus Christ, fully God and fully man, we have been redeemed, and the Chalcedonian Definition gives us the guidance we need to know just what that really means.

Scripture Meditation

The Word became flesh and made his dwelling among us.
—JOHN 1:14

Thought for the Day

May we redefine our humanity by Christ's divinity, humble and selfless in loving.

Prayer

My dear Lord and Savior ... in your divine glory and your human humility you are totally "Other," so different from the closed-mindedness and high-handedness of humans. You are the wholly "Other," the only true God, so unlike man-made gods.... Lord transform our hearts.... Lord make us humble.
—BERNARD HARING

JUNE 10: FAITH, HOPE, AND LOVE AS THE GRAMMAR
OF THE CHRISTIAN LIFE

Maximus the Confessor (580–662) was a Greek theologian in the monastery
of Chrysopolis in Asia Minor who echoed in this letter many of the thoughts
of Augustine's Enchyridion, *a simple handbook of faith which the layman*
Laurentius had asked Augustine to write for him in 421.

aith is the foundation of everything that comes after it—I mean hope and love—and firmly establishes what is true. Hope is the strength of the extremes—I mean faith and love—for it appears as faithful by itself and loved by both, and teaches through itself to make it to the end of the course. Love is the fulfillment of these, wholly embraced as the final last desire, and furnishes them to rest from their movement.

For love gives faith the reality of what it believes and hope gives the presence of what it hopes for, and the enjoyment of what is present. Love alone, properly speaking, proves that the human person is in the image of the Creator, by making his self-determination submit to reason, not bending reason under it, and persuading the inclination to follow nature and not in any way to be at variance with the *logos* of nature.

In this way we are all, as it were, one nature, so that we are able to have one inclination and one will with God and with one another. Not having any discord with God or with one another is made possible by the law of grace through which our inclination to follow the law of nature is renewed, so that we choose what is ultimate. For it is impossible for those who do not cleave first to God through concord, to be able to agree with others in their inclination.

For since the deceitful devil at the beginning contrived by guile to attack humankind through his self-love, deceiving him through pleasure, he has separated us in our inclinations from God and from one another, and turned us away from rectitude. He has fractured nature at the level of our mode of existence, fragmenting it into a multitude of opinions and imaginations. He has set up the means through which each vice may be discovered, and with time established a law to which all our powers are devoted, introducing into everything a wicked support for the continuance of vice—namely, irreconcilable inclinations. By this he has prevailed on humankind to turn from the natural movement he once had, and to move his longing from what is permitted to what is forbidden.

Thus humankind has brought into being from itself the three greatest, primordial evils, and (to speak simply) the begetters of all vice: ignorance, self-love and tyranny. These are interdependent and are established through one another. For out of ignorance concerning God there arises self-love. And out of this comes tyranny towards one's kin: of this there is no doubt. For it is by the misuse of our own powers— reason, desire and intuition—these evils are established. For reason, instead of being ignorant, ought to be moved through knowledge to seek solely after God; and desire, pure of the passion of self-love, ought to be driven by yearning for God alone; and the power of intuition, freed from tyranny, ought to struggle to live for God alone.

Scripture Meditation

Now I know in part; then I shall know fully, even as I am known. And now these three remain: faith, hope and love. But the greatest of these is love.

—1 CORINTHIANS 13:12–13

Thought for the Day

The grammar of faith is personal in its formation, not merely rational in its communication.

Prayer

Lord, give us hearts never to forget Thy love … therefore Thou whose name and essence is love, enkindle our hearts, enlighten our understanding, sanctify our wills, and fill all the thoughts of our hearts, for Jesus Christ's sake. Amen.

—JOHANN ARNDT

JUNE 11: MEDITATING ON THE SCRIPTURES WITH THE CHURCH FATHERS

Edward Bouverie Pusey (1800–1882), Anglican theologian and a leader of the
Oxford Movement, wrote to a theological student
(letter xxxix, date unknown).

I suppose one can take it for granted that anyone who comes to ask
for a course in theological study is, at least, well acquainted with the letter of Holy Scripture, such as might be acquired through the Divine
Lessons and the frequent reading of Holy Scripture in church.... This
presumed, the object would be to deepen the knowledge of Holy
Scripture, of the substance of the Faith, and of practical wisdom, with
some of knowledge of the History of the Church.

In this we should begin with the Gospels as the center, and in this, I
suppose, what persons chiefly need would be a deeper meaning of the
whole, and of the several words as drawn out by the Fathers, rather than
mere verbal criticism. It would then probably be best to begin to study
the Gospels ... each Gospel with one Father who had commented on it:
St. Matthew with St. Chrysostom and St. Hilary; St. Luke with St.
Ambrose; St. John with St. Augustine and St. Chrysostom.

This study would not only bring out the context and connection and
meanings of Holy Scripture, which people are not in the habit of thinking of, but would incidentally bring a person to become acquainted
with a good deal of exposition of other parts of Holy Scripture. It is like
reading the Holy Scripture with a new sense. St. Ambrose especially
brings one acquainted with a great deal of Holy Scripture. Besides, in
the study of the Gospels, much might be learnt by way of meditating on
them....

The reading of the Fathers themselves has the advantage of their
being a whole, and that the mode of practical teaching, in connection
with the exposition of Holy Scripture, is so learnt.

After, or with this, might be taken the Exposition of the Psalms by St.
Augustine, both as teaching the spiritual meaning of the Psalms ... and
of their meaning as to our Lord and His members, and for the great
value of its moral teaching.... As for the teaching of St. Paul, no work
perhaps gives such a general view of the scope and connection of the

Epistles as St. Chrysostom. St. Augustine again, beautifully unfolds St. John's Epistles.

Scripture Meditation

We have heard with our ears, O God; our fathers have told us what you did in their days, in days long ago.
—PSALM 44:1

Thought for the Day

Bustle hurts the mind and soul and benefits nothing. Set yourself especially to cultivate the presence of God, that is, as you are walking about, acting and thinking of God.
—E. B. PUSEY

Prayer

O God, fill me wholly with Thyself that all self may be absorbed in Thee.
—E. B. PUSEY

JUNE 12: TEMPTATIONS OF THEOLOGICAL SCHOLARSHIP

John Newton, best known for his hymn "Amazing Grace" and for his devotional collection of letters, Cardiphonia *or* Utterances of the Heart *(1781), wrote to a student in divinity, date unknown, from which the following excerpts were taken.*

ear Sir,

Though I am no enemy to the acquisition of useful knowledge, I have seen many instances of young men damaged by what they expected to reap advantage. They went into the academy humble, peaceable, spiritual, and alive in their faith. They came out conceited, dogmatic, censorious, full of the false maims of the world.... This is not to criticize the institution, but as the frequent effect of notions too hastily picked up, when they were not sanctified by grace, nor balanced by a right proportion of data gained with spiritual experience. So I am glad to know you remain dissatisfied with what other people cannot give you, nor books, in order to be fully equipped for Christian ministry, and become "a workman that needs not be ashamed," and indeed be able to rightly divide the word of truth.

[Newton then asks how much we should expect the Holy Spirit to help us prepare and preach our sermons.] ... Perhaps this is a speculative issue, because we cannot distinguish between what we prepare diligently as being our thoughts, from the needful influence of the Holy Spirit. For even if we have a capacity and ability such gifts are also His to bestow on us. But that is no excuse for laziness, to not do our utmost also! For true diligence is actually expressive of the abiding sense of God's love, our awareness of the eternal worth of precious souls, and indeed the importance of eternity....

Moreover, the chief means for gaining wisdom are the Holy Scriptures and prayer. The former is the fountain, the latter the bucket to extract those living waters.... These are not just spiritual exercises we may perform but a disposition of mind, for the one most devoted to prayer and to the Word, will be the one who stands above others. For it is done in humble dependence upon the Lord....

For more advice ... converse much with experienced Christians and exercised souls.... The sum of my advice is this: Examine your heart and views. Can you appeal to Him who knows all things concerning the sincerity of your aim that you devote yourself to the work of the ministry not for worldly regards but with a humble desire to promote the Redeemer's Kingdom.... If you depend upon books, or men, or upon your own faculties and attainments, you will be in danger of falling continually. But if you stay yourself upon the Lord, he will not only make good your expectations, but in time will give you a becoming confidence in his goodness, and free you from your present anxiety.

Scripture Meditation

He [the righteous man] is like a tree planted by streams of water, which yields its fruit in season.
—PSALM 1:3

Thought for the Day

A comfortable attitude for public service depends much upon the spirituality of our walk before God and man.
—JOHN NEWTON

Prayer

Lord ... furnish us all with light and powers
To walk in Wisdom's ways;
So shall the benefit be ours,
And Thou shalt have the praise.
—JOHN NEWTON

JUNE 13: COUNSEL FOR A STUDENT OF THEOLOGY

Dr. Bruce Hindmarsh (b. 1962), associate professor of spiritual theology,
Regent College, Vancouver, Canada, wrote to a student on December 18, 2003.
His letter is counsel also for all of us who have just been
reading the previous section of these letters!

*D*ear David,

You are not the first person to find that the study of theology often brings with it some unique and unexpected spiritual challenges. You begin a course in theological education because you want to know God better, or you want to be able to better live and serve as a Christian. And at first it all feels like an enormous privilege. But then the problems begin: spiritual indigestion, anxiety about academic success, disappointed idealism, or even cynicism. And so on. Is this the sort of thing you mean, when you say that you do not feel as close to God as you thought you would, given that you are dedicating time to formal theological education?

I remember when I was engaged in graduate work in theology and how inspired I was by reading Jean LeClerc's remarkable book, *Love of Learning and the Desire for God.* LeClerc talked about the difference between scholastic theology, which began with reading (*lectio*) and then proceeded to questions (*quaestio*), and debatable theses (*disputatio*). Sounds familiar? It should, since this is the model for most of our formal education today.

The goal of this sort of learning was *scientia*, or abstract knowledge. Thus far, I was tracking with LeClerc, because I had never really known any other sort of learning. But then he wrote about monastic theology which likewise began with the ABCs of reading the text (*lectio*), but proceeded to mull over it reverently (*meditatio*) and to pray (*oratio*), and finally to gaze lovingly with the eyes of the heart upon God himself (*contemplatio*). The goal of this learning was not science but love, compunction, and desire for heaven.

Anyway, there I was at about twenty-seven years old, wishing I could study theology like a monk. I was fired with desire to study in a way that would purely be a pursuit of love for God and that would want nothing less than to enjoy his beauty, goodness, and truth. But—but!—there I was, with my very real anxieties about getting good grades, pleasing my professors, and very down-to-earth life with dishes to wash in the kitchen, and bills to pay. The cleavage between the ideals and my real life was painful.

When I pursued further doctorate studies at Oxford, this all became even more painful. I remember sitting in my study with my books after another sleepless night, hearing our baby crying in the other room. (Bethany was a newborn, then, Sam and Matthew were not yet born.

How time flies.) Full of anxiety about whether I could do what was required of me academically, confused in all sorts of ways in a new culture, I was trying to read Richard Baxter's *The Saints' Everlasting Rest* in the way LeClerc describes. It was not a fruitless exercise, but somehow it wasn't as pure and tranquil as I imagined when I first read LeClerc!

Scripture Meditation

Above all else, guard your heart, for it is the wellspring of life.
—PROVERBS 4:23

Thought for the Day

Familiarity with our Christian faith without constant personal response can become deadening indeed!

Prayer

Behold, Lord, an empty vessel that needs to be filled. My Lord, fill it. I am weak in the faith; strengthen me. I am cold in love; warm me, and make me fervent that my love may go out to my neighbor. I do not have a strong and firm faith; at times I doubt and I am unable to trust you altogether. O Lord, help me.
—MARTIN LUTHER

JUNE 14: LIVING WITH "DOUBLE KNOWLEDGE" IN THE THEOLOGICAL ACADEMY

Dr. Hindmarsh continued his letter on his personal experience of "studying theology."

$\mathcal{D}$ear David,

I realize now that God had to "take me into the wilderness" in a sense, and allow me to face squarely the distance between my ideals and the truth about myself. Nobody had told me that a good half of what you are in for with genuine theological education (if you take the task seriously) is the task of gaining sober self-knowledge. Later I did find out that the early Fathers of the Church all emphasized on the "double knowledge," as expressed by Augustine, "Let me know you, O God. Let me know myself."

I wonder if this is where you find yourself just now? Feeling some of the bitterness of soul that comes not so much with finding your colleagues and professors fall short of your ideals, but finding that *you* yourself are not really the Christian that you need to be, to be equal to the task of learning about God—indeed of knowing him personally. David, you are in good company!—not "good" perhaps but a large audience.

The danger is that in this situation you can go one of two ways. You can become technical about your studies perhaps slightly cynical about doing theology, developing heart-calluses, so to speak. Or you can learn to live *with* this broken-heartedness over your own weaknesses and your sin, by developing a deeper dependence upon God.

As a dear friend wrote to me when I was in crisis in Oxford over these things, and I had spiraled down into depression, "The theological education you're getting might not be the one you were planning on, but it might be the one that is most necessary."

So may I make a few practical suggestions that come from learning some of this, the hard way? The academy is still just the academy, and it is simply impossible to *read everything* that is required of a full-time theology student in the meditative way monks read before the age of printing. Does that make most of your reading inauthentic? Not necessarily. I think that LeClerc's reading is s-l-o-w reading, and indeed, re-reading, where you allow time for inward reflection, further self-challenge, and further self-understanding to grow, to allow time for your life to catch up with the text.

You should probably focus on, say, one book a term to read this way, day by day. (Actually, this is the way I read Baxter while in Oxford—I "lived" with the book for the better part of a year.) For your other theological books that you cannot read this way, think of your reading as "getting acquainted" with the text—like sight-reading a piece of music, or doing a first read-through of a script for a play. You will come back to practice the music or the play, and ultimately you wish to make it yours, and "perform" it, but there is nothing wrong with first having a "first reading." It all has to do with your motives. If you are plundering Anselm with the sole goal of aggrandizing your ego, proving something to the world about how smart you are with your mastery of "the ontological argument," then that is the equivalent of spiritual rape. But if you consider your first reading of Anselm as "getting acquainted with each other," then that has a certain modesty about it, hasn't it?

Anyway, this is where I am right now in trying to live reciprocally between seeking to know God and also knowing more about myself at the same time. I hope then that you will find you can use the experience of spiritual barrenness in the midst of studying theology. Let's talk more about this when we get together.

Yours,

Bruce

Scripture Meditation

I have set the LORD *always before me. Because he is at my right hand, I will not be shaken.*

—PSALM 16:8

Thought for the Day

Let me know Thee, O Lord. Let me know myself, that is all.

—ST. AUGUSTINE

Prayer

Thee may I set at my right hand
Whose eyes my inmost substance see,
And labour on at Thy command,
And offer all my works to Thee.

—CHARLES WESLEY

JUNE 15: WHY ARE THERE SO MANY DISENCHANTED CHRISTIANS TODAY?

Mary Manson, mother, homemaker, and part-time lecturer wrote on
December 23, 2003, about her own struggles to experience
the Christian faith more convincingly.

I recall being at a Bible study recently. We were a motley crew of mostly second generation evangelical Christians, all of whom seemed to be experiencing a sort of disenchantment with the Christianity we'd inherited. Many had stopped going to church.

"I don't know," one fellow said. "When I was twenty I had all the answers. My beliefs were so clean and neat. But when I turned forty, the books with the answers in them seemed to fall off the shelf and try as I might—I just can't get them back up there again."

A few heads nodded in understanding. Life wasn't divided so clearly into Christian and non-Christian, good and evil, right and wrong, as he'd initially believed. The jargon he'd been raised with had a hollow tone. I was reminded of another fellow for whom Christianity was an easy commitment until he meandered into the secular world during university and found really good, kind, generous, just, thoughtful people there too.

At another Bible study, a year or so earlier, a woman commented in a moment of exasperation, "I like the Psalms because they're so … unchristian!"

At yet another Bible study I overheard someone marvel in surprise "you mean you actually read and understand the Bible?"

What is it, I wonder, that has outdated Christianity for Christians approaching mid-life? Why does God seem insufficient, the Bible incomprehensible and irrelevant, and church services so impersonal? Why are we left empty and lonely?

I suspect there are many contributors. The social climate 55 years ago was perhaps brighter and more optimistic than ever before in the Post-War years, and it was into that climate of prosperity and progress that many middle-aged folk today were born. The future was ours for the taking. Mostly we've not encountered the harshness of life or death. Such a sense of self-sufficiency does not breed intimacy with God. It fosters narcissism and ego-fulfillment, resulting in the unhappiness for which we rather perversely end up blaming God.

Also, "the Church has not kept step with the Spirit" someone once said, and sadly, I think this is true. We have fallen behind on almost every front and many churches have become vacant physically and emotionally. Even churches working hard to become relevant often focus on bigger and better programs instead of relational maturity, grace, and wisdom. Other churches entrench themselves deeper into an "us versus them" intolerance of "the world" and live with a black and white split. Either way, our emotional life which is also "in Christ," our deep longing to be heard, understood, valued, liberated, and loved is neglected. We have no place to weep and mourn, cry with outrage, confess and forgive, or jump with joy.

As well, people today are more educated, have access to vast knowledge, have broad experiences combined with the brain numbing speed and persistence of media assault in a secular culture. We have lots of options and we choose the one that best meets our needs—a functional response. Many Christians I know are searching for the "church" that "meets their needs" rather than committing to a local congregation and living out Christ's mandates for loving one another and working out our salvation, even with all of our blunders and flaws. Our unwillingness to resolutely commit to growth is not surprising given the ease with which we abandon our families in this culture.

I suppose it is this combination of our insistence on seeking our own personal fulfillment in an affluent culture and the churches' failure to respond to the questions we are asking, which has led to a pervasive barrenness in the souls of the middle generation.

Scripture Meditation

I long to redeem them but … [t]hey do not cry out to me from their hearts but wail upon their beds. They gather together for grain and new wine but turn away from me.
—HOSEA 7:13–14

Thought for the Day

As the postmodern culture becomes less conventional, Christians are being challenged to personalize their faith more intimately.

Prayer

God of all heaven and earth, we come before you with weary minds and impoverished emotions. We seek your goodness and desire your redemption. Give us the fortitude to cry out to you from our hearts. Instill your wisdom in us. Nourish us. Urge us towards growth. Create in us the longing to authentically love one another. Restore us to yourself. Amen.

—MARY MANSON

JUNE 16: CLEVERNESS DOES NOT ENGENDER GODLINESS:
A LETTER FROM THE UNDERSIDE OF LIFE

Written to the editor by a senior pastor, February 11, 2004.

$\mathcal{D}$ear Dr. Houston,

I resigned from the denomination today. It is almost a year since I resigned from my congregation. The first resignation was a noble thing. There was a big mess and I believed that if I left, the church would suffer the least harm. My second resignation was in disgrace. After leaving the church, I had an adulterous affair.

The transition wasn't quite so blunt as that. The anger and disillusionment that set in after my first resignation couldn't easily be overcome. All my attempts to straighten things out had failed. Those in "authority" in my life manipulated me and called it a misunderstanding. Close friends betrayed me. It wore me down. Still, it was nothing compared to what I did later to my wife and two children. I couldn't straighten myself out either.

In 27 years of marriage I had never thought about adultery as anything but a fantasy. I lived with clear thinking and a strong will that insulated me. We talk about the value of a "broken will" in my tradition. I think that's nonsense now. Moral lives are rooted in iron wills that are well applied. Joseph knew enough to flee. Jacob hung on even when his hip was dislocated. He, like the rest of us, walked with a limp the rest of his life. I suppose I relate better now to the feebler saints. Moses' will vanished for forty years and Elijah's got swallowed up in disillusionment and depression. David goes crazy. Peter goes back fishing and Thomas locks himself in a room where he thinks even God can't get through the door. Their hearts had all failed them. Mine too.

Almost everyone knows what I "should" do now, since it has come out that I have done what I "shouldn't" have. The problem is that after a lifetime of doing what I should, I can't. Paul's words in the seventh chapter of Romans mean something now. I can't do what I know I should and I can't stop myself from doing what I know I shouldn't. Intellect is not enough for godliness. Paul knew that.

Right in the middle of one of the greatest theological treatises in the Bible, Paul is having a moral crisis! Anyone who has been there emotionally recognizes it. Intellectual theology isn't going to save him. He's been writing the book and that hasn't been enough! His will isn't going to save him, it's not strong enough. Doing the right thing doesn't give life, life gives us the ability to do what is right. The Spirit gives life, but not always how or when we want it.

When I prayed for help to stop, I didn't get it. When I prayed for God to kill me before I failed completely, he stopped short of that. Now I know why we are to pray that God will not lead us into temptation.

I have lived as a successful pastor and leader for more than twenty-five years. A large church, dramatic growth, a gifted life, etc., etc. Like Kierkegaard said of Hegel, I had built a magnificent castle, but I was living in the doghouse beside it. My life started withering about seven years ago. The organizational demands that growth prompted sucked life from me and distorted my personality. I was like the voyageurs whose legendary loads eventually built up so much muscle that their internal organs were crushed. They all died young, but the company prospered.

The organization will always tend to look after its own agenda over the needs of individuals. That's the dynamic of organizations. Issues like alignment, strategic planning, and resource allotment fill our daily planners. I know. I did it. But from the underside of the pile the picture looks different.

I don't need someone to tell me what to do. I need someone to walk with me. I need people that will help find ways to fill my heart, not simply go through the motions. I need friends for whom my life is more important than the accomplishments of the church, friends who will stick with me even if I don't make the right choice.

I am still in deep water. I don't know where I will end up. I told my wife, my children, and a few close friends. Word about things like this spreads fast. A high profile makes for tasty gossip. The denominational discipline committee leaked the news before they had even met with me. There's not much to lose now, and that may be a good place for the heart to start.

Scripture Meditation

Do not be overrighteous, neither be overwise—why destroy yourself?
—ECCLESIASTES 7:16

Thought for the Day

When we are at "rock bottom," Christ is the Rock at the bottom.

Prayer

God in heaven, you know how I'm made; you've written my days in your book. May my faith survive this sifting. May my hope not die with my own goodness. Restore my soul, in your time, in your way, for your name's sake. Amen.

JUNE 17: NEW WAYS OF TRANSLATING THE CHRISTIAN FAITH

Dr. Dave A. Diewert (b. 1955), trained as a linguist and teacher of biblical languages, now has a ministry among the poor in the east end of Vancouver, British Columbia. He also wrote about a previous letter of resignation, on the same date, February 11, 2004.

*D*ear Jim,

I thought I would write you about my decision to resign from my position at the college. I have greatly appreciated your encouragement and wisdom in matters of life and spirit, and I'm sure you will understand the internal wrestling I experienced.

I suppose the primary reason for bowing out of the academy was the growing realization that the striking gulf that exists between being a professional interpreter of Scripture and embodying the text in the rhythms and patterns of life was not simply due to personal weakness, though there is no doubt some of that, but was systemic to the academy and its practices. My task as a biblical exegete is to research the text, analyze its setting, form, rhetorical structure, and theological import; then write up my findings and publish them in a journal or a book for a few others to read. In doing so I will enhance my status, earn a reputation, and perhaps be invited to speak at various conferences. This is the momentum of the academic life and practice. But what if following this course leads me farther and farther away from actually conforming my life to the call of the text before me?

In my own case, I was preparing Philippians 2 for a Greek class, and was suddenly struck by the fact that molding my life to the shape of the text, with Jesus as the model of self-relinquishment of status and privilege for the sake of the other, is antithetical to the movement of the academic world. In a cold sweat, I realized that I could be academically acclaimed for exegetical skill and at the same time fail to live obediently to the word that addresses me.

It's not that I couldn't do more as a professor to live in accordance to the vision of this or any other text; it's that the academy's primary concerns seem at odds with the life of faithfulness and discipleship to the

Crucified One. It makes me shudder to think that one could be considered an expert on the Sermon on the Mount without ever living out the way of radical self-giving in love for the other, especially the hostile other. It is also true that to live out this radical care for the other might easily cost a person their academic career. Being estranged from the text as a voice of radical reorientation (conversion) while becoming an expert in textual analysis was profoundly disturbing. For the sake of my soul, I left my job.

On another level, the academic institution was a place that did not provide the space for creative and imaginative teaching and learning that was soul-transforming. Through the necessity to conform to accreditation standards, the practices and procedures were becoming more and more tightly defined, and left little room for courageous imagination of alternative practices. In my official letter of resignation I wrote: *There has certainly been a degree of frustration for me at the college where I teach; but perhaps that is because my interests and imagination cannot be sufficiently nourished within an institutional structure where economic stability, administrative efficiency, and public image seem to be of considerable importance. My own journey of faith is leading me into other realms, places characterized by uncertainty, risk, and increased vulnerability. So I have decided to step away from the demanding rhythms and concerns of the academy in order to make room for a way of being that more creatively and radically instantiates the foolish self-giving grace of God in Jesus.*

I felt that I needed to get off the beaten path, so to speak; to move along the ways of the powerless and the outcasts, and learn there what the call to self-giving love might mean.

Scripture Meditation

Your attitude should be the same as that of Christ Jesus: Who, being in very nature God, ... made himself nothing.
—Philippians 2:5–7

Thought for the Day

Translatability is vital for Christian life, but the translation of ancient texts is far easier than allowing personally "the Word to become flesh."

Prayer

Lord, grant me the courage to relinquish status and privilege, to continuously step out of the sphere of my own strength, to embody the practice of self-giving love for the "other." May your "Word become flesh" in my life, not just more words.

JUNE 18: HAVING A NEW LANGUAGE FOR GOD

Blaise Pascal (1623–1662), French mathematician and inventor of the first calculating machine, was converted to Christianity by reading the seventeenth chapter of John's gospel. He wrote on November 5, 1656, to Mademoiselle de Roannez, about knowing within the heart the Living God. In his Pensees, *he wrote: "The heart has its reason that reason does not know."*

A new way of speaking usually introduces a new heart. Within his gospel Jesus gave us a way of recognizing those who have faith. They will speak a new language. What happens is that a renewal of mind and desires brings about a renewal of language. Renewal is needed constantly, therefore, in order to please God, as the old way of our former life only brought his displeasure. However new earthly things may be at first, they always become old eventually.

Whereas this new spirit renews itself the longer it lasts. The old body dies away, says the apostle Paul, but the new person is renewed day by day, and will only be perfectly new in eternity. There we shall sing without ceasing the new song of which David speaks in the Psalms. This is the song which springs forth from this new spirit of love.

For it is certain the graces which God grants us in this life are a pledge of the glory which he is preparing for us in the world to come. So when I contemplate on the End as the climax of his work, I can anticipate it by "the first-fruits" evidenced in the lives of devout Christians. So I am full of awe for those whom he has called and chosen. I already envisage them—having forsaken everything for his sake—then sitting on his throne, judging the world together with Jesus Christ. For this is the promise he has made.

But when I think of how some people can fall, and be counted instead, among the unfortunate company who will be judged ... I find this insufferable.... Then I have recourse once more to the mercy of God, asking him not to abandon his weak creatures. "For blessed is the one who fears the Lord."

Scripture Meditation

The fear of the Lord teaches a man wisdom, and humility comes before honor.
—PROVERBS 15:33

Thought for the Day

The language of the heart is to fear and trust the Lord.

Prayer

Fear the LORD, you his saints, for those who fear him lack nothing.
—PSALM 34:9

JUNE 19: CHRISTIAN RELATIONS WITH OTHER FAITHS

Archbishop William Temple (1881–1944), philosopher and archbishop of Canterbury, replied to a correspondent on April 26, 1944, about relations Christianity may have with other religions.

*I*t is not possible in correspondence to deal with anything like all the questions you raise, but I will do my best to answer those, which I gather from your letter concern you most and are capable of an answer in something less than a treatise.

(1) It is never right for the adherent of any religion to sneer at the adherents of other religions. That is a failure in charity and is always wrong, but of course if one believes for whatever reasons that a certain religion is true, it is inevitable that one should think that other religions fail in truth just so far as they are different or opposed.

Thus, for example, Christianity lays great stress on the value of individual persons and declares that they are destined for eternal life. Hinduism and Buddhism, especially the latter, deny this high value to individual persons and Buddhism in most of its forms denies their hope of eternal life. That is a point on which if one is right the others must be wrong.

There are many other points where from the Christian's standpoint the other religions are not so much wrong as defective. St. John says that *Our Lord is the light that lighteth every man*. In other words, the grasp of truth reached by any man and by any religion is, as it were, a ray of that light which shone fully in Him; and this is, I think, the true Christian relationship to the non-Christian religions. If so, it is our duty to offer the full light to those who as we think have only a partial light. But we are inviting them to share something; we have no business to try to *impose* anything on them.

(2) The Bible is to be read as a record of the progressive stages by which men were brought up to a sufficient understanding of God to enable some of them to appreciate Our Lord when He came. He is always to be taken as the standard of all revelation, and anything in the Bible or elsewhere that conflicts with what we find in Him, is to be regarded as due to the Human medium through which the Divine Revelation came, and not to the Divine Revelation itself.

You seem to assume that our Lord himself was a complete pacifist. I am sure that is not true. If it was, how did there come to be two swords in the little company of His disciples right at the end of His ministry? He himself said that if He were concerned with an earthly kingdom His servants would be fighting. He seems to me plainly to recognize that it would be right to fight for an earthly kingdom or civilization, but it cannot be right to fight for spiritual truth itself because that wins its way only so far as it is freely accepted, and to try to uphold it by force is in fact to betray it.

There are a few answers, and as many as I can send in a letter. I do not expect you to accept them or to agree with me, but they will at any rate show you how my mind works on these questions.

Scripture Meditation

Since the creation of the world God's invisible qualities—his eternal power and divine nature—have been clearly seen, being understood from what has been made, so that men are without excuse.
—ROMANS 1:20

Thought for the Day

Since God is love, we can only communicate the truth in love.

Prayer

Almighty and Everlasting God, whose will it is to restore all things to thy beloved Son, the King of Kings and Lord of Lords: Mercifully grant that the peoples of the earth, divided and enslaved by sin, may be freed and brought together under his most gracious rule; who liveth and reigneth with thee and the Holy Spirit, one God, now and for ever. Amen.
—COLLECT FOR SUNDAY PROPER 29, *THE BOOK OF COMMON PRAYER*

JUNE 20: THE WORLD CONGRESS OF FAITHS

Lord Samuel, a prominent member of the House of Lords, asked William Temple if he was willing to participate in a world congress of faiths. The archbishop responded on November 26, 1942.

*D*ear Lord Samuel,

Your letter makes a very strong appeal, and I need not say that if you, and such colleagues as have joined you in signing it persist after reading this letter, in asking me to arrange a time for them to come, I will do my best to find one, though it will have to be rather a long way ahead because of the immense amount of pressure on time.

I have had many invitations to become associated with the World Congress of Faiths, and I have always felt obliged to decline because I do not see how it is possible for the activities of that movement to avoid the suggestion that, while one religion may be more true than another, they are all varieties of some one thing which does not find its full expression in any of them. To me it seems that if the Christian Gospel is true at all, it must be the consummation of all religions. Its adherents may fail in appreciating that with sufficient fullness to present it as having this quality. But, unless it has it, it simply is not true. Consequently, while most eager to join with adherents of other Faiths in promoting a human welfare on lines that all can agree to follow, I have never felt able to join myself in the effort to "establish fellowship between all who follow a religion of Spirit," and I cannot imagine that any amount of discussion would alter my conviction in this respect.

Christianity is, I am persuaded, a profoundly intolerant religion, not of course in the sense that it justifies persecution, for its Lord seeks only willing adherents, but in the sense of drawing a very sharp line between those who attempt to follow its way and those who only regard this as one among a number of good ways.

It seemed to me that it might be wasting the time of busy people if I suggested that you should come to see me before you had heard these views of mine. I hope I am not impervious to argument, but I cannot conceive anything inducing me to become associated in any way at all with the World Congress of Faiths.

Scripture Meditation

The LORD will be king over the whole earth. On that day there will be one Lord, and his name the only name.
— ZECHARIAH 14:9

Thought for the Day

It is a human perspective to argue for many faiths or paths to God. It is the Sovereign God to proclaim there is no other Name, nor any other god, but God.

Prayer

Our Father in heaven, hallowed be your name.
—MATTHEW 6:9

JUNE 21: CAN WE HAVE CHRISTIAN VALUES WITHOUT CHRISTIANITY?

Archbishop Temple responded to an air force officer, Lt. H. A. G. Smith,
serving in the war with the central Mediterranean forces, on March 6, 1944.

ear Mr. Smith,

Your most intriguing letter reached me five minutes ago, and as this is a lucid interval and there won't be another for some time, I will try to answer it at once. But strictly speaking it can't be done. There are *no* "principles of Christianity as divorced from any reference to God." Christianity springs from the gospel, which is the proclamation of "good news" about God and His Kingdom or Sovereignty; and all it has to say about the conduct of human life is consequential to that.

It knows quite well what the state of man apart from God is, and it offers emancipation. We have to find out what is the form taken at any time by man's consciousness of need. In our day it is chiefly called "frustration," and "futility." Both of these are part of what St. Paul calls "sin." For "frustration" see Romans 7:7 — end, and for "futility" Romans 8:18 —

end, especially 18–23; and remember that St. Paul is not responsible for the division of his letters into chapters; those two passages are parts of one argument.

But there is a Christian way of living and it is possible for non-theists to appreciate it and try to follow it. They will fail, but it is a good thing to try. The summary of this is, of course, "you shall love your neighbor as yourself"—which means that, when any one else's interest is involved, we let it count with us for as much as our own.

Also, because we believe God is Father of all men and made us for fellowship with Himself, and therein also with one another, Christianity gives us as the direction of true progress the development of personality in fellowship, or of persons in community. If we apply that to education, housing, the organization of industry, etc., it takes us a long way. The difficulty is to do justice to both elements at once; individualists stress personality, collectivists, fellowship. Christianity says the two go together.

Does all this help?

Yours sincerely,

William Cantaur

Scripture Meditation

"*Good teacher, … what must I do to inherit eternal life?*" … "*One thing you lack,*" [Jesus] said. "*Go, sell everything you have and give to the poor, and you will have treasure in heaven. Then come, follow me.*"

—MARK 10:17, 21

Thought for the Day

The Christian life is not a hobby, nor a convention; it is a commitment, a total surrender of self.

Prayer

Lord, what is man to thee,
That thou shouldst minde a rotten tree?

—GEORGE HERBERT, "OBEDIENCE" FROM *THE TEMPLE*

LATER CHRISTENDOM

JUNE 22: MORE THAN A MORAL TEACHER

*Archbishop William Temple again replied on November 10, 1943, to a
churchgoer who wanted the Christian religion to be simplified to
"the teaching and example of Jesus only."*

ear Dr. — —,

I am very glad you should have written freely, and I am of course
aware that there are many who hold something like your position. It
would take too long to set out the reasons why I cannot share it, but I
think my fundamental point would be that Christianity begins with the
church and its missionary work, the quality of which we can estimate
from the Book of the Acts and the Epistles. All the Pauline Epistles were
written before any of the Gospels; the Gospels were written within the
Church, as the first witnesses of Our Lord's life and teaching began to
die off, in order to keep alive the memory of what they had taught.

The net result is an impression that the Apostolic preaching was fundamentally preaching of the Cross and resurrection. And then there was
composed first a collection of Our Lord's sayings which would be left by
the missionary preacher among those who had accepted the fundamental
Gospel, as indicating the manner of life that was required of followers of
Christ. But the Gospel itself was there in the background as the foundation.

Our Lord is not presented in the New Testament as first and foremost
a moral teacher; He is presented as the figure in whom the power of God
broke in upon history. That is the chief significance of the doctrine of the
virgin birth, whatever you may say about the historical fact. This point of
view completely dominates St. Mark's Gospel, which is the earliest of
those we have, though later in composition than the Book of the Sayings,
which is incorporated in Matthew and Luke.

There is no suggestion anywhere in the New Testament that
Christianity is primarily a system of moral teaching, which we are capable of following in our own strength, and I think the effect of doing what
you suggest would be in fact to blunt the cutting edge of the Christian
faith until it was incapable of making any impression at all. Nothing of

course can be too much to say about the supreme importance of Our Lord's teaching, and yet it is also true that what He was and is remains more important than what He taught.

Scripture Meditation

Jesus answered, "I am the way and the truth and the life."
—JOHN 14:6

Thought for the Day

Does the Truth possess us, or do we try to control it?

Prayer

O Lord Jesus Christ, You did not come into the world to be served, but surely also not to be admired or in that sense worshipped. You are the Way and it is followers only You demand to have.
—SØREN KIERKEGAARD

JUNE 23: CHRISTIANITY IS NOT A RELIGIOUS SYSTEM,
BUT THE REMEDY FOR SIN

Charles Simeon (1759–1836), friend of William Wilberforce and an Anglican rector in Cambridge, was mentor to more ministers and missionaries within the Church of England in his time than any other prominent church leader. He wrote to a missionary on August 16, 1822.

*M*y very dear Friend,

Never did I take up my pen to write to you with such pleasure as at this moment. (Your letter is come to hand, dated December 5, 1821. This does that which I both desired and expected; and in that very particular which I was most desirous to see.) It shows me, what I was most anxious to hear, that you are growing in self-knowledge; and it therefore opens to me a fit opportunity of declaring to you, what have been my fears respecting you from the beginning. You have always appeared to me to be sincere. But your views of Christianity seemed to be essentially defective. You have always appeared to admire Christianity *as a system*; but you never seemed to have just views of Christianity *as a remedy;* you never seemed to possess self-knowledge, deep contrition, much less anything of a tender self-loathing and self-abhorrence.

This always made me jealous over you with a godly jealousy; and never till this moment have I had my fears for your ultimate state removed. I beheld in you somewhat of a childlike simplicity; and I well know *that if it be associated with contrition,* it is a virtue of the most sublime quality; but if contrition be wanting, the disposition which assumes that form differs but little from childishness.

But you now begin to feel the burden of sin: You now begin, though still in a very small degree, to have your mind open to the corruptions of the heart, and to your need of a *dying* Savior to atone for you by His blood, and a *living* Savior to renew you by the influences of His Spirit. Seek, my dear friend, to grow in this knowledge; for it is this that will endear the Savior to you, and make you steadfast in your walk with God. This is the foundation, which must be dug deep, if you would ever build high, and the ballast which alone will enable you to carry sail.

You may conceive the brazen serpent, which Moses erected in the wilderness, to have been exquisitely formed, and you may suppose persons to have greatly admired the workmanship, and the contrivance of erecting it upon a pole for the benefit of all who should behold it; but the meanest person in the whole camp, who had but the most indistinct view of it, if he beheld it with a sense of his own dying condition, and with an experience of its efficacy to heal his wounds, would have an incomparably better view of it than the virtuoso, however much he might admire it.

This hint will show you what in my judgment you *were*, and what I hope you *will* be. Christianity is a *personal* matter, not to be commended merely to others, but to your opponents by your arguments, you will never do any essential good, and much less will you reap any saving benefit to your own soul, till you can say, "What mine eyes have seen, mine ears have heard, and mine hands have handled of the word of life, that same declare I unto you."

… In your future letters open your mind fully to me; and expect always both fidelity and love from your very affectionate friend,

C. Simeon

Scripture Meditation

We proclaim to you what we have seen and heard, so that you also may have fellowship with us. And our fellowship is with the Father and with his Son, Jesus Christ.

— I JOHN 1:3

Thought for the Day

The blood of Christ is expressive of his absolute self-giving, so that our life can endlessly become personal in his love.

Prayer

Visit then this soul of mine,
Pierce the gloom of sin and grief!
Fill me, Radiancy Divine,
Scatter all my unbelief!

— CHARLES WESLEY

JUNE 24: A PURITAN'S SUFFERING OF CONSCIENCE FOR THE KINGDOM

Roger Williams (1604–83), founder of the colony of Rhode Island, left the Anglican Church as a "Seeker," in advocacy of the separation of church and state. In 1652 he wrote to the widow of his early patron, a Mrs. Sadleir, whose husband had financed his education while he lived in England.

I have been formerly, and since I landed [i.e., in New England], occasioned to take up the two-edged sword of God's Spirit, the word of God, and to appear in public in some contests against the ministers of Old and New England, as touching the true ministry of Christ and the soul's freedom of the people. Since I landed I have published two or three things, … with which I will not trouble your meditations; only I crave the boldness to send you a plain and peaceable discourse of my own personal experiences [i.e., *The Bloudy Tenent of Persecution for Cause of Conscience*].… I humbly pray you to cast a serious eye on the Holy Scriptures, on which the examinations are grounded.

I could have dressed forth the matter like some sermons which, formerly, I used to pen. But the Father of lights hath long since shown me the vanity and soul-deceit of such points and flourishes. I desire to know nothing, to profess nothing, but the Son of God, the King of souls and consciences; and I desire to be more thankful for a reproof for ought I affirm than for applause and commendation. I have been oft glad in the wilderness of America, to have been reproved for going in a wrong path, and to be directed by a naked Indian boy in my travels. How much more should we rejoice in the wounds of such as we hope love us in Christ Jesus, than in the deceitful kisses of soul-deceiving and soul-killing friends.

My much honored friend, that man of honor, and wisdom, and piety, your dear father, was often pleased to call me his son; and truly it was as bitter as death to me when Bishop Laud pursued me out of this land, and my conscience was persuaded against the national church and ceremonies, and bishops, beyond the conscience of your dear Father. I say it was as bitter as death to me, when I rode Windsor way, to take ship at Bristow, and saw Stoke House, where the blessed man was; and I then durst not acquaint him with my conscience, and my flight. But how many thousand times since have I had honorable and precious remembrance of his person, and the life, the writings, the speeches, and the examples of that glorious light. Any I may truly say, that beside my natural inclination to study and activity, his example, instruction, and encouragement, have spurred me on to a more than ordinary, industrious, and patient course in my whole course hitherto.

What I have done and suffered—and I hope for the truth of God according to my conscience—in Old and New England, I should be a fool in relating.

Scripture Meditation

By following them [the prophecies of Scripture] you may fight the good fight, holding on to faith and a good conscience.
—I TIMOTHY 1:18–19

Thought for the Day

Gratitude for mentors in one's past life enriches oneself.

Prayer

Sing to God, sing praise to his name, … [a] father to the fatherless.
—PSALM 68:4–5

JUNE 25: HAVING A DIFFERENT CONSCIENCE FOR ANOTHER
INTERPRETATION OF THE KINGDOM

Mrs. Anne Sadleir replied indignantly, as a royalist Anglican defender of Charles I, to Roger Williams's previous letter.

ir,

I thank God my blessed parents bred me up in the old and best religion, and it is my glory that I am a member of the Church of England, as it was when all the reformed churches gave her the right hand. When I cast mine eye upon the frontispiece of your book, and saw it entitled, "The Bloudy Tenent," I durst not adventure to look into it, for fear that it should bring into my memory the much blood that has of late been shed [i.e., in the English Civil War], and which I would fain forget; therefore I do, with thanks, return it. I cannot call to mind any blood shed for conscience:—some few that went about to make a rent in our once well-governed church were punished, but none suffered death.

But this I know, that since it has been left to every man's conscience to fancy what religion he list, there has more Christian blood been shed than was in the ten persecutions. And some of that blood, will, I fear, cry till the day of judgment. But you know what the Scripture says, that when there was no king in Israel, every man did that which was right in his own eyes—but what became of that, the sacred story will tell you....

I must let you know, as I did before (Psalm 79), that the Prophet David there complains that the heathen has defiled the holy temple and made Jerusalem a heap of stones. And our blessed Savior, when he whipped the buyers and sellers out of the temple, told them that they had made his Father's house a den of thieves. Those were but material temples, and commanded by God to be built, and his name there to be worshipped.

The living temples are those that the same prophet in the psalm before mentioned (verse the 2nd and 3rd), "The dead bodies of thy servants have they given to the fowls of the air, and the flesh of thy saints to the beasts of the land. Their blood have they shed like water." And these were the living temples whose loss the prophet so much laments; and had he lived in these times, he would have doubled these lamentations. For the foul and false aspirations you have cast upon that king, of ever-blessed memory, Charles, the martyr, I protest. I trembled when I read them, and none but such a villain as yourself would have wrote them....

I cannot conclude without putting you in mind how dear a lover and great an admirer my father was of the liturgy of the church of England, and would often say, no reform church had the like. He was constant to it, both in his life and at his death. I mean to walk in his steps; and, truly, when I consider who were the composers of it, and how they sealed the truth of it with their blood, I cannot but wonder why it should now of late be thus condemned. By what I have now writ, you know how I stand affected. I will walk as directly to heaven as I can, in which place, if you will turn from being a rebel, and fear God and obey the king, there is hope I may meet you there; howsoever, trouble me no more with your letters, for they are very troublesome to her that wishes you in the place from whence you came.

Scripture Meditation

Do not hold against us the sins of the fathers.
—PSALM 79:8

Thought for the Day

Tragically, in the name of the Christian religion, civil war and other forms of violence have bloodied the annals of church history.

Prayer

O God, the nations have invaded your inheritance; they have defiled your holy temple, they have reduced Jerusalem to rubble.
—PSALM 79:1

JUNE 26: THE MORAL AMBIGUITIES OF "CHRISTIAN" NEW ENGLAND

In the spring of 1670, a boundary dispute between Connecticut and Rhode Island forced Roger Williams to write this letter to Major Mason, a magistrate of Connecticut, on June 22.

*F*irst, we are witnessing here a depraved appetite after the great vanities, dreams and shadows of this vanishing life.... As if men were in as great necessity and danger for want of great portions of land, as poor, hungry, thirsty seamen have for food after a sick and stormy, long and starving passage. This is one of the gods of New England, which the living and most high Eternal will destroy and famish.... [H]ere, all over this colony a great number of weak and distressed souls, scattered, are flying hither from Old and New England, the Most High and Only Wise hath, in his infinite wisdom, provided this country and this corner as a shelter for the poor and persecuted, according to their several persuasions....

Sir, I lament that such designs should be carried on at such a time, while we are stripped and whipped, and [being robbed of our land] ... with the Mohawks and Mohegans against us, of which I know and have daily information.

If any please to say, is there no medicine for this malady? Must the nakedness of New England, like some notorious strumpet, be prostituted to the blaspheming eyes of all nations? Must we be put to plead before his Majesty, and consequently the Lord Bishops, our common enemies, &c.

I answer, the Father of mercies and God of all consolations hath graciously discovered to me, as I believe, a remedy, which, if taken will quiet all minds, yours and ours, will keep yours and ours in quiet possession and enjoyment of their lands, which you all have so dearly bought and purchased in this barbarous country, and so long possessed amongst these wild savages; will preserve you both in the liberties and honors of your charters and governments without the least impeachment of yielding one to another; with a strong curb also to those wild barbarians and all the barbarians of this country, without troubling of compromisers and arbitrators between you; without any delay, or long and chargeable and grievous address to our King's Majesty, whose gentle and serene soul must needs be afflicted to be troubled again with us.

Scripture Meditation

Is there no balm in Gilead? Is there no physician there? Why then is there no healing for the wound of my people?
—JEREMIAH 8:22

Thought for the Day

How frequently does the success of numbers or of property destroy the spiritual ideals of the original pioneers of faith!

Prayer

Strengthen us so that the evil and misfortune of the world may not lead us into impatience, anger, revenge, or other wrongs.

—MARTIN LUTHER

JUNE 27: A CONTEMPORARY VIEW OF THE KINGDOM OF GOD

Dr. Tom Hatina, associate professor of New Testament Studies, Trinity University, Langley, British Columbia, wrote to an American inquirer on June 20, 2002, explaining why the United States is still "Messianic."

Last week, while waiting at a checkout in a grocery story, I glanced over at the magazine and tabloid rack and was immediately taken by the front cover of *Time* (July 1, 2002), which had a large white cross rising out of a fire and inside the cross the caption read, "The Bible & the Apocalypse: Why More People Are Reading and Talking About the End of the World."

I had to purchase this issue. As a religious studies professor, I was not at all surprised by the rampant apocalypticism in American Evangelicalism, especially after September 11. I was not surprised by the results of a *Time*/CNN poll finding that 59 percent of Americans believed that the prophecies in Revelation will come true. I was not surprised at the large number of American Christians who read their Bibles in light of the newspaper. And I was certainly not surprised by the astronomical profits that are being generated by opportunists who feed on and fuel the frenzy. What I was surprised about is the virtual silence on Jesus' teaching about the kingdom of God, which was central to his ministry. I had expected at least a few kingdom sayings to be harmonized with Revelation and a handful of passages in Pauline letters (see 1 Thessalonians 4:13–18), the canons within the canon.

Without rehashing the numerous theological and philosophical problems associated with popular apocalypticism, with which I am sure you are well familiar, I would like to share some observations on the kingdom of God as it is presented in the Gospel of Mark, most likely our earliest Gospel. When I ask my freshmen students to define the kingdom of God, most simply say that it refers to heaven, the kingdom which all Christians will share when they die. Most are surprised to learn that Jesus' understanding was quite different. There is very little indication in Mark that Jesus' mission and message was primarily oriented toward an imminent apocalyptic end. Rather, it was primarily oriented to the here and now, namely the political, social, and religious life of Israel within which Jesus found his identity.

In this context, "kingdom of God" has to do with the coming of God in strength and, in my understanding, has a range of meanings affecting our relational life. Jesus ushers in the kingdom with the challenge to live life under the lordship of God, teaching about the "kingdom of God" with a strong sense of social justice and compassion, grounded in the love of God and neighbor. The kingdom is a new community, even a household or family, which one can enter. In the context of Jesus' healings and exorcisms, it represents the coming of God to do battle against evil. For Mark, the kingdom of God was understood in light of the kingdom of Satan.

These are not only among the most central ideas in Mark's Gospel, but the other New Testament writings as well. Why then all this apocalyptic fervor today? I think it has a lot to do with our American culture, always preoccupied with individualism, a thirst for sensationalism, marked by depression, many emotional addictions, an insatiable consumerism, all of this coupled with a strong underlying sense that God is on our side. No wonder many Christians in our culture miss the central teaching of Jesus.

Scripture Meditation

At that time if anyone says to you, "Look, here is the Christ!" or "Look, there he is!" do not believe it. For false Christs and false prophets will appear and perform signs and miracles to deceive the elect—if that were possible. So be on your guard.

—MARK 13:21–23

Thought for the Day

Does the "hype" of the mass media today intensify the cultural possessiveness of our Western way of life?

Prayer

Hear my prayer, O LORD; let my cry for help come to you. Do not hide your face from me when I am in distress.

—PSALM 102:1–2

JUNE 28: THE OFFENSE OF DISTRUSTING GOD

Alexandrina of Ricci (1522–90), of Florentine nobility, entered the Third Dominican Order at age thirteen and took the name Catherine of Ricci. She entered intensely into the sufferings of her Lord. She wrote this letter to Valdimovina, her spiritual advisor, on October 2, 1561.

I would remind you, my dear Father, that when the man who owned ten thousand talents asked his Master to forgive his debt, he did not beg the favor for nine thousand only, but for the whole sum. If this debtor had not acted afresh with hardness and cruelty he would have had nothing to fear about the past debt, as it had been fully and freely remitted; and his Lord would have been actually offended if the servant had not believed simply in the pardon granted to him.... Hence I conclude that, although it be a great error to count presumptuously on oneself, we nevertheless greatly offend the mercy and goodness of God by distrust.

We know that he is very generous: that he became man and suffered a painful passion and death to deliver us from all anxiety as to our salvation; and that by these acts he has opened heaven to us, provided we do not ourselves turn in the opposite direction. In the latter case there can be no uncertainty, as most assuredly he who does not act according to the law of Jesus cannot reach heaven, any more than a man who takes the road to Pistoja, when he wants to go to Florence, can expect to arrive at Florence!

... So one may find in the right way to heaven many hindrances that are serious obstacles; but for these there is the remedy given by Jesus: namely, to walk by the light that will lead us safely, and that light is holy faith. If we will only walk with our eyes fixed on this, we shall see before us a road, clear, level, beautiful, and very pleasant to walk upon; shaded too, by the green leaves of hope, planted with the flowers of holy longings, and abounding in the fruits of good works. By following this road, we shall go straight to our true home. Hence, whoever yields to fear or dread on this way insults his Lord and Master, or that Master's representative who acts as his guarantee.

... What use is it then, dear Father, to be afraid? Of what use, I repeat, except to make us lose time on the way, and walk with but little fervor towards Jerusalem? So let us drive away fear, and put in its stead holy hope: but a hope without presumption, and founded on the goodness of God, not on our own merits.

Scripture Meditation

Trust in the Lord with all your heart and lean not on your own understanding.

—PROVERBS 3:5

Thought for the Day

But to have not nought is ours,
not to confess that we have nought.
I stood amaz'd at this, much troubled,
till a friend expressed,
that all things are more ours by being his.

— GEORGE HERBERT, "THE HOLDFAST"

Prayer

God, have mercy on me, a sinner.

— LUKE 18:13

JUNE 29: IN THE LIGHT OF THE CROSS HOW CAN
CHRISTIANS REMAIN AVARICIOUS?

---

*Philip Neri (1515–95), founder of the Congregation of the Oratory in Italy
and a leader of the Counter-Reformation, was noted for his personal
spirituality. He wrote this letter to his niece, a nun.*

The mole is a blind animal living always underground; it eats earth, burrows in earth, and is never satiated with earth. Such is the avaricious man or woman.... And what a revolting thing is avarice! A human has received so much from God—giving us, besides our being, ... his own Son. The sweet Christ, the Incarnate Word, gave himself unreservedly to us, even to the harsh, shameful death of the Cross. Then he gave himself to us in a Sacrament, ... and humbling himself to become man for us. On the Cross he was stripped of his garments, his precious blood shed, and his soul separated from his body.

All created things express open systems, liberal, and showing forth the goodness of their Creator. So the sun pours forth light, fire gives out heat, every tree stretches forth its arms and reaches to us its fruit. Yes, the water, the air, and all nature, declare the bounty of the Creator.

And we, who are yet his living images, how do we not represent him? — with base distortion, denying him in our works, however much we confess him with our mouths. Now, if greed is so ugly in anyone, what is it in "a religious" who has made a vow of poverty, to abandon everything for the love of God! So we must, at whatever cost, get rid of this foul pestilence of avarice. Nor shall we feel the pain ... if in exchange of this sordid garb, our soul is clothed with a regal and imperial garment. Not only then, do we need to despise gold, silver and pleasure — so prized by a blind, deluded world, but even the very life we love so much.

We do so, both for the honor of God and the salvation of our neighbor, having our hearts ever ready to make this sacrifice, in the strength of divine grace.

Scripture Meditation

A heart at peace gives life to the body, but envy rots the bones.
—PROVERBS 14:30

Thought for the Day

Like pride, envy makes one a prisoner of the self.

Prayer

O thou, whose I am by creation, preservation, redemption, no longer my own, but his who lived, died and rose again, once more I resign this body and soul, mean and worthless as they are, to the blessed disposal of thy holy will. Amen.
—HENRY MARTYN

June 30: A Christian Interpretation of Money

Dr. Craig M. Gay (b. 1955), a sociologist and professor of interdisciplinary studies at Regent College, Vancouver, Canada, wrote to his young son on the occasion of the opening of Andrew's first bank account.

*D*ear Andrew,

I wish I could say I had money all figured out, but I don't. Still, I think money is one of those things that a Christian needs to take seriously, though not too seriously. For after all, money is only a metaphor. That is, it "stands in" for other things, and it's a lot easier to carry around in our pockets than sheep or barrels of oil.

As a tool, it is powerful. Yet tools—especially useful ones—have a way of acting back on their users, often in surprising and unintended ways. "To a man with a hammer," someone once said, "everything looks like a nail." This is true also with money. Having it, everything can begin to look like something to be bought or sold. I suppose that's why so many people today only seem to live to get more and more money as the sole purpose of life. But money is only the means to an end. It shouldn't ever be allowed to become its own purpose. It's only a thing, after all; it isn't alive. It can be used in the service of life, but it can't itself breathe life.

People, making an idol of money, will become cold and metallic. Seeing the world only through the lens of money, we see a dead world. Maybe this is why Jesus after warning us not to store up treasures on earth, goes on to say that the eye is the lamp of the body, and that if our eyes are bad we will be full of darkness. Rather we should use our eyes to look for life, and its personal relationships, and not simply at things to be bought and possessed. A good servant; money is a bad master.

Remember then, money can't buy us true relationships. Indeed, a wealthy person may wonder sometimes who are real friends. So Jesus said: "Watch out! Be on your guard against all kinds of greed; a man's life does not consist in the abundance of his possessions." You may not have to work for money—who knows?—though I think it is a good thing to have to work anyway. We all need to have some occupation, not simply to make money, or even for the sake of work, but also among other things, to exercise patience, perseverance, discipline, etc., which we can learn from work. Such qualities root us more firmly in righteous relationships that do sustain our personal life....

It's a good idea to learn to save, for only the fool is quickly parted from his money. After all, you don't know when your neighbor may need it, as well as yourself. While borrowing money is a risky thing to do with friends, don't be miserly either, striving rather to be lighthearted and generous. I learnt this from my Dad ... that generosity is an antidote to the poisonous enchantment that money can impose on us. God gives everything freely, and in the Kingdom of God nothing is for sale, for everything is freely given.

Unfortunately we don't live there yet, in its fullest sense, so be cautious; don't talk too much about money, and be discreet in your generosity. Remember too, that Jesus said how hard it is for the rich to enter the Kingdom of God, not because they are rich, but because riches can give us the illusion we don't need God so much as the poor.

So my Son, ask God to give you wisdom in the use of your money, trust God to give you ever deepening faith in Him rather than in the money to buy things, and indeed commit your way to love Him above all else.

I love you,

Dad

Scripture Meditation

Why spend money on what is not bread, and your labor on what does not satisfy? Listen, listen to me, and eat what is good, and your soul will delight in the richest of fare.

—Isaiah 55:2

Thought for the Day

In this new world (the Kingdom of God) we are entering, nothing is for sale ... everything is free, and where giving is the normal way to act.

—Jacques Ellul

Prayer

Gracious God, I lift my son Andrew to you, and all other children to walk with you, to be given your Spirit of wisdom concerning possessions, stewardship, and their disposal, in concern for others in need. Amen.

—CRAIG M. GAY

SEASONS OF EVIL AND VIOLENCE

While evil and violence are also permanent features of our human existence, the following letters illustrate specific periods and events when they have been experienced dramatically.

THE EVILS OF WAR, GENOCIDE, AND ECO-CATASTROPHE

JULY 1: WHAT OF THE SPIRITUALITY OF CHRISTIAN PUBLISHING TODAY?

Donald H. Simpson (b. 1943) works as a book editor and is cofounder and president of Helmers & Howard Publishers. He has also worked as circulation director for a Christian periodical and communications director for a missionary organization. He wrote this letter to the editor on February 19, 2004.

While I was launching a new publishing venture in the mid-1980s, one of my wisest mentors was our mutual friend and Regent College professor of theology, the late Klaus Bockmuehl. In addition to many other pursuits, Klaus studied the influence of literature on movements of renewal. He noted that, "Almost always renewal movements were initiated through books and/or they made intensive use of books as the medium of their dissemination and success." His heroes were people like John Wesley, who not only preached widely but made a practice of sending a new tract, pamphlet, or printed sermon to the printer almost every week.

Toward the end of his life, Klaus expressed dismay at the commercializing trends he perceived in contemporary Christian magazine and book publishing in North America. What worried him were things like the increasingly secular ownership of the larger houses, escalating author advances, competition for "big name" authors, the rise of agents and lawyers in the industry, and the shrinking shelf space given to books in lieu of gift items in Christian book stores. Klaus felt that the burgeoning Christian publishing trade was losing its heart for the "harassed and helpless" crowds that aroused Jesus' compassion. He summed up the situation in the industry this way: "They do not weep for the multitudes of Nineveh."

I was stunned by his assessment. At the time, I had been experiencing first hand the hard realities of attempting to establish a viable publishing enterprise. I felt daily the need to compete and make a profit in order to remain in business. But Klaus reminded me of a greater urgency: the tragedy of human life all around me. It was a piercing thought, given poignant articulation through the words of Nahum: "Nineveh is in ruins—who will weep for her?"

The striking nature of Klaus's comment caused me to ask: Is there a particular spiritual emphasis that would bring the deeper concerns of Christ's kingdom into the business of Christian publishing? In time, I found a clue in another setting that's just as public, with even more potential for abuse: the world of politics. A helpful guide became Glenn Tinder's *The Political Meaning of Christianity*. Dr. Tinder describes the situation of postmodern Ninevites: "Everyone can see that the loss of confidence in historical progress, the main key to the meaning of history for the modern age, constitutes a spiritual crisis in the lives of multitudes of ordinary people, giving them the impression of a universe without purpose and order."[1]

In response to this spiritual crisis, Tinder urges what he calls a "prophetic stance." In essence, this is the cultivation of an attitude of waiting on God in hope—and watching for God's leadership in history. This waiting entails solitude and inaction. We observe, reflect, pray, and listen. "Waiting … is not the contrary of action but a preface and approach to action; hence, it belongs to the work of social transformation."[2]

Waiting is counterintuitive for publishers. Does it mean to stop the presses for a while? That might be what it means. Certainly, it means to acknowledge on some level the powerlessness of our publishing operations, to admit to ourselves its utter lack of efficacy—or, to use Jacques Ellul's word, its *inutility*—apart from the power of God.

What will we hear when we wait on God in solitude? Perhaps we will hear something long forgotten—the sound of the Man of Sorrows, weeping for the multitudes of Nineveh. May those of us in Christian publishing be granted the faith to join him.

Yours with best wishes,

Don

Scripture Meditation

Nineveh is in ruins—who will mourn for her?
—NAHAM 3:7

Thought for the Day

Is the world of Christian publishing itself a spiritual battlefield?

Prayer

You hear, O God, the cry of all men without confusing their mixed voices and without distinguishing one from another ... to play favorites.... You hear also the most miserable, the most abandoned, and the most solitary man—in the desert, in the multitude.

—SØREN KIERKEGAARD

JULY 2: THE SIN OF SLAVERY

John Wesley wrote his last letter to William Wilberforce on February 22, 1791, before his death on March 2. Wesley's housekeeper had been reading to him about Gustavus Vassa, a Negro born in 1745 who was kidnapped and sold as a slave in Barbados, sent to England in 1757, baptized in 1759, and had many adventures in the navy. In the reading, Wesley was impressed deeply by the statement that no black man's testimony in the West Indies was admitted legally. So he wrote Wilberforce, a few days before the abolition debate in the House of Commons. The motion was defeated by 163 votes to 88, and only in 1807 was it passed.

*D*ear Sir,

Unless the divine power has raised you up to be as "Athanasius against the world," I see not how you can go through your glorious enterprise in opposing that execrable villainy, which is the scandal of religion, of England, and of human nature. Unless God has raised you up for this very thing, you will be worn out by the opposition of men and devils. But if God be for you, who can be against you? Are all of them together stronger than God? O be not weary of well doing! Go on, in the name of God and in the power of his might, till even American slavery (the vilest that ever saw the sun) shall vanish away before it.

Reading a tract this morning written by a poor African, I was particularly struck by that circumstance, that a man who has a black skin, being wronged or outraged by a white man, can have no redress; it being a *law* in all our Colonies that the *oath* of a black against a white goes for nothing. What villainy is this!

That he who has guided you from youth up may continue to strengthen you in this and all things is the prayer of, dear Sir,

Your affectionate servant.

Scripture Meditation

You might have him back for good—no longer as a slave, but better than a slave, as a dear brother. He is very dear to me.
—PHILEMON vv. 15–16

Thought for the Day

If the inhumanity to enslave is still with us, how do we give freedom to others?

Prayer

With your respect for human freedom, does not your love extend to all creatures?
—ARCHBISHOP HELDER CAMARA

JULY 3: CONFESSIONS OF A TERRORIST

Reverend Tom Tarrants is president of the C. S. Lewis Institute in Washington,
DC, and an ordained Presbyterian minister. But previously in his life he had
been profoundly misled about religion. In a letter to the editor
on July 12, 2002, he wrote of his former life.

*D*ear Jim:

When we last spoke, you asked how I was brainwashed by becoming a member of the Ku Klux Klan in Mississippi, and then actually became a terrorist. I'm sure part of the answer lies in coming of age in the deep South during the Civil Rights era and coming into contact with racist and anti-Semitic people who influenced me in the wrong direction. But there was more to it than that.

Deeply rooted patterns of sin in my family and in me also played a large role. My parents had a difficult marriage and there was a good deal of conflict and instability in our home, especially during my teen years. I blamed my father for most of the family problems and became increasingly angry and rebellious. I was also self-centered, insecure, friendless, purposeless, and thrived on excitement. I was without hope and without God even though raised in the church.

The desegregation of my high school was a catalytic event that provided an outlet for my anger and rebellion. It also attracted racist/anti-Semitic friends. Blinded by hatred, I quickly and uncritically accepted their ideology, which gave me a sense of purpose and importance in life. This ideology distorted reality, fueled rage, and grew into an idolatry that warranted any sacrifice and justified any excess.

Ultimately, it was the distorted needs and desires of my darkened heart, which led me into error, deception, and all the evil that tragically followed in its wake. And in the end, it very nearly destroyed me. For as you know, it led to being gunned down, left bleeding to death, and only saved by a passing ambulance that heard the gunshots and rescued me in time.

So it was in solitary confinement, with nothing to pass the time of day but a Bible, that I read the Gospels with fresh eyes, and became convicted of the love of Jesus. Then I was given the joy of leading the

F.B.I. agent who had infiltrated our gang to also give his heart to Jesus. That was the beginning of a new way of living for me.

Grace and Peace,

Tom

Scripture Meditation

By the grace of God I am what I am, and his grace to me was not without effect.

—1 Corinthians 15:10

Thought for the Day

Let our compassionate attentiveness to others help to reduce the number of alienated terrorists in our dangerous world.

Prayer

I pray that you, being rooted and established in love, may have power, together with all the saints, to grasp how wide and long and high and deep is the love of Christ.

—Ephesians 3:17–18

JULY 4: CONVICTION OF SIN IS DIFFERENT FROM BEING GUILTY OF "SINS"

William Romaine wrote to his sister in response to her letter describing a sense of the conviction of sin. He himself had become a Christian in 1748.

$\mathcal{D}$ear Sister,

Your letter gave me greater joy than I can express. I hope all will soon be well with your soul. You may examine yourself by these following rules, and I hope God will give his blessing to them.

First, look back and see from whence your conviction of sin arose. The Scripture says, true conviction must come from the Holy Spirit; and when he is come, says Christ, he will convict the world of sin. It is his business, and his office; and when he acts in it, conviction has these properties different from the conviction of natural conscience. It respects not so much acts of sin, as the sin of our nature; that entire pollution, and depravity of the faculties of soul and body, which render us by nature children of wrath. Again, it is deep; it goes to the bottom of the heart, and lays open all the lurking places of sin. Farther, it is lasting, it continues its hatred and opposition to all sin, until it be not only seen in the heart, but also driven out of it.

Secondly, if after examining your conviction by these rules, you find it right, and peace and joy begin to arise in your conscience; if it be the peace and joy of the Holy Spirit, it will make you continue to hate sin, and everything sinful. It will leave you more in love with God than it found you. You will love prayer more, and will have a freedom and liberty in it, which you had not before. You will love God's word more, and will understand more of it, being enabled, by his grace, to find instruction in it, suitable to all your spiritual wants. My meaning in all this is, if the convictions have brought you to Jesus Christ, you will know it by its fruits. You will find yourself grow in grace, and more in earnest about the salvation of your soul.

Thirdly, examine your growth in grace by this rule. We remember the sin which did so easily beset us; look at that; see whether you hate it entirely, and whether you have entirely got the mastery over it. God has promised that you shall have grace to help in time of need. Apply to God for the fulfilling of this promise; and be more concerned about this grace, which you always want in time of need than about sensible comforts; because in the one you may be deceived, but in the other you cannot. My dear sister, you have chosen the better part. The kingdom of heaven is worth millions of worlds. May God enable you to seek, until you attain it.

My prayers attend you. Remember me my sister …

Adieu, William Romaine

Scripture Meditation

Confess your sins to each other and pray for each other so that you may be healed.

—JAMES 5:16

Thought for the Day

Sensitivity to sins will bring us closer to our need of God's grace.

Prayer

Almighty God, Father of our Lord Jesus Christ, Maker of all things, Judge of all men: We acknowledge and bewail our manifold sins and wickedness, which we from time to time most grievously have committed, by thought, word, and deed.

—THE CONFESSION

JULY 5: THE PRIMORDIAL MYSTERY OF EVIL

Richard Averbeck, professor of Old Testament at Trinity Evangelical Divinity School, Deerfield, Illinois, is a sumerologist, a specialist in Mesopotamia's oldest civilization of Sumer, where the myth of the sea monster seems to have originated. He wrote this letter to the editor on August 15, 2002.

$\mathcal{D}$ear Jim,

The most persistent and perplexing problem we face in our understanding of God's program of creation and redemption, and in our own life experience in this world, is the problem of evil. This is so whether it be our own evil, that of others around us, or the overall environment or situation in which we live and breathe. There are many bad things that happen in this world. The world is a mess, and so are we. How can this be if our creator and redeemer is the completely holy and all powerful God of scripture? The following does not solve the problem of evil, but, for me at least, puts it in perspective for our lives day-by-day, moment-by-moment.

First, Isaiah 27:1 tells us that in a day yet future the Lord will settle the problem of evil. On that day, he "will punish with his sword, his fierce, great and powerful sword, *Leviathan the gliding serpent*, Leviathan the *coiling serpent;* he will slay *the monster of the sea.*" There is a long literary tradition of this evil twisted sea serpent sometimes called "Leviathan" in the world of the ancient Israelites. I cannot review that here. The point is that all people of all times have had to deal with evil and the great evil one. Furthermore, even though this will not end until the final apocalypse (see Revelation 12–20), it will in fact, end, and there will be a new day in which we will be free from the pain and sorrow of this battle (Revelation 21–22).

Second, God has not left it all until the end of times either. Even now he engages in battle against this evil monster and those who belong to him. Furthermore, those who belong to God are in it with God. Like the Psalmist we need to call upon him now as the eternal, all powerful God who in the past has "split open the sea" by his power, "broke the heads of the monster in the waters," and in fact, "crushed the heads of Leviathan" (Psalm 74:13–14).

Third, the whole thing actually started in the garden when, through crafty deception, the "serpent of old" (see Genesis 3 with Revelation 12:9 and 20:2–3, 7–10) corrupted the man and woman, the crowning creatures of God's creation (Genesis 1:26–28). This was a direct attack on God, his word, and his program, to which the Lord responded: "And I will put enmity between you and the woman, and between your offspring and hers; he will *crush your head* (see Psalm 74 above), and you will strike his heel" (Genesis 3:15).

So the battle began, and we are the territory under dispute. The battle is over us, nothing or no one else! That is why the victory is in Jesus' death, burial, and resurrection on our behalf. Satan "fell" in the garden just as we did in Adam and Eve. Therefore, we are the subject of, and stand right in the middle of, a cosmic fray of immense proportions. No wonder we need armor (Ephesians 6).

Scripture Meditation

If you think you are standing firm, be careful that you don't fall! No temptation has seized you except what is common to man. And God is faithful; he will not let you be tempted beyond what you can bear. But when you are tempted, he will also provide a way out so that you can stand up under it.

—1 CORINTHIANS 10:12–13

Thought for the Day

The problem of evil is bigger than we are, but our God is bigger than all evil.

Prayer

Immanuel, may God truly be with us! We need you every hour in every way, for we are vulnerable to attack in all that we think, do, and say.

—RICHARD AVERBECK

JULY 6: THE FATHER OF MERCY'S WRATH

The American iconoclastic writer of the late 1800s, Mark Twain, voiced a common and popular objection to the violence narrated in the Old Testament. Probably this is the most negative letter in the collection, but it was chosen to express what a growing number of secularists mistakenly believe today. For they have tragically never experienced the love of God, so they project their violent anger upon him as the source of so much evil without having any experience of him personally.

*H*uman history in all ages is red with blood, and bitter with hate, and stained with cruelties; but not since biblical times have these features been without a limit of some kind. Even the Church, which is credited with having spilt more innocent blood, since the beginning of its supremacy, than all the political wars put together, has observed a limit—a sort of limit. But you notice that when the Lord God of Heaven and Earth, adored Father of Man, goes to war, there is no limit. He is totally without mercy—he, who is called the Fountain of Mercy, he slays, slays, slays! All the men, all the beasts, all the boys, all the babies; also all the women and all the girls, except those that have not been deflowered.

He makes no distinction between innocent and guilty. The babies were innocent, the beasts were innocent, many of the men, many of the women, many of the boys, many of the girls were innocent, yet they had to suffer with the guilty.... The heaviest punishment of all was meted out to persons who could not by any possibility have deserved so horrible a fate.... There is nothing in either savage or civilized history that is more utterly complete, more remorselessly sweeping than the Father of Mercy's campaign among the Midianites.

Scripture Meditation

The LORD saw how great man's wickedness on the earth had become, and that every inclination of the thoughts of his heart was only evil all the time.
—GENESIS 6:5

Thought for the Day

Projecting evil upon God only demonstrates how evil are our own thoughts.

Prayer

Almighty God, give us wisdom to perceive thee, intellect to understand thee, diligence to seek thee, patience to wait on thee, eyes to behold thee ... through the power of the Spirit of our Lord Jesus Christ.

—St. Benedict

July 7: The Father of Mercy's Wrath—Confusion

Dr. V. Philip Long (b. 1951) is professor of Old Testament studies at Regent College, Vancouver, Canada. This was his response to Mark Twain's letter, requested by the editor.

Dear Jim,

Mark Twain (whose real name was Samuel Clemens) certainly knew how to write, didn't he? As one who teaches the Old Testament, I am tempted to want to correct many errors of fact and perception (large and small), but on one issue he is absolutely correct, and it will perhaps serve best if we make that our focus. The issue is this: while some would like to contrast the "wrathful" God of the Old Testament with the "gentle" Jesus of the New, the biblical evidence will not allow this. Clemens is of course wrong to describe Jesus as "a thousand billion times crueler, ... incomparably more atrocious," etc., but he at least grasps the fact that Jesus made no bones about a dreadful judgment awaiting those who go to their graves spurning his loving overtures.

The problem of the "severity" of the Father of Mercy cannot be swept aside by appealing to the Son. What are we, then, to make of this severity as exemplified, for instance, in the order to destroy the Canaanites (Clemens mentions also the destruction of the Midianites, in Numbers 31, but seems to conflate bits and pieces from other places)?

No person of normal human sensibilities can read verses like Joshua 6:21—"They devoted the city to the Lord and destroyed with the sword every living thing in it—men and women, young and old, cattle, sheep and donkeys"—and not recoil. Were we able to rationalize these practices as the misguided actions of a primitive people, the problem might be somewhat eased, but the Bible makes it quite plain that the destruction of the Canaanites was commanded by God himself: "in the cities of the nations the Lord your God is giving you as an inheritance, do not leave alive anything that breathes. Completely destroy them ... as the Lord your God has commanded you" (Deut. 20:16–17).

There is much more that can be said in defense of God's actions here (relating to sin, judgment, and protection of his people), and I shall offer some further reflections in a second letter, but for now I would simply say that at one level the God of the Bible confounds me. He is not exactly as I would make him, nor as any other human would make him. Perhaps, in a strange sort of way, this bears testimony to the fact that it is the True God, and no man-made deity, that we encounter in Scripture.

Scripture Meditation

"For my thoughts are not your thoughts, neither are your ways my ways," declares the LORD.

—ISAIAH 55:8

Thought for the Day

If God is truly infinite and unsearchable, should we be surprised that his actions sometimes confound us? Might our recoiling at the severity of his judgments suggest that we recoil too little at the seriousness of sin?

Prayer

God of mercy and of justice, teach me what it means to let you be yourself. Forgive me for my desire to control you by reducing you to attitudes and actions that are comfortable and comprehensible to me. Transform my thinking through your Word and enlarge my ability to trust you, even when I don't understand.

—V. PHILIP LONG

JULY 8: THE FATHER OF MERCY'S WRATH—GOD'S JUDGMENT

Dr. V. Philip Long continued to explain further
the wrath of God in the Old Testament.

In my previous letter I wrote that the God of the Bible confounds me, as he apparently did Samuel Clemens. He also comforts me, however, and so I don't share Clemens' contempt—only a bit of his confusion. A few things can be said, however, that help to clear up some (if not all) of the confusion arising from the Father of Mercy's apparent severity in ordering the destruction of the Canaanites.

First, the order was *not indiscriminate;* this we can see from the instructions given in Deuteronomy 20:10–15 with respect to cities "at a distance." With cities outside the land of promise, the Israelites were allowed to make a treaty of peace.

Secondly, the order was *not senseless;* its purpose was both to *punish* the Canaanites, whose sin had "reached its full measure" (Gen. 15:16), and to *protect* God's people from being drawn into idolatry and apostasy (see Deut. 7:1–6).

Thirdly—and this is extremely important—God's command that the Canaanites of Joshua's day be destroyed *does not establish a pattern of warfare applicable today!* We are dealing with instances of "Yahweh's War" in which God chose to bring judgment upon a people that vehemently opposed him. The issue was *not* ethnicity or even nationality, but intractable opposition to God. It is worth noting that even among the Canaanites there were some who chose to side with the true God, and they were spared (for instance, Rahab in Joshua 2 and the Gibeonites in Joshua 9).

Perhaps most helpful in my own coming to terms with God's treatment of the Canaanites has been Meredith Kline's discussion of "intrusion ethics." We live in the Age of Common Grace in which God's final judgment is delayed and we are commanded to love our enemies. But the Consummation, the Final Judgment, is coming when God's wrath will be poured out upon unrepentant sinners who have finally and irrevocably rejected Christ. Kline's view is that from time to time in human history God has *intruded* the *ethics* of the

Consummation into the Age of Common Grace (that is, given a fore-taste of final judgment in the here and now—think, for instance, of Ananias and Sapphira in Acts 5:1–11). To do so is God's prerogative, not ours, and thus it would be utterly wrong to cite such intrusions as warrant for our taking violent action today. Our struggle, at present, is *not* against flesh and blood but against spiritual forces of wickedness (Eph. 6:2).

Scripture Meditation

Those eighteen who died when the tower in Siloam fell on them— do you think they were more guilty than all the others living in Jerusalem? I tell you, no! But unless you repent, you too will all perish.

—Luke 13:4–5

Thought for the Day

In the fallen world in which we live, bad things like public, criminal actions and natural disasters happen for all kinds of reasons. How do we respond when bad things happen to us or around us?

Prayer

O God of such grace, grant that my life may be characterized by repentance and gratitude, even when your ways are beyond my full comprehension.

—V. Philip Long

JULY 9: HITLER AND RETRIBUTION

*As the Archbishop of Canterbury during World War II, Dr. William Temple
was frequently challenged about his views on the crimes of Adolf Hitler and
of the Nazis. In this letter he replied to a questioner on July 2, 1942.*

*D*ear Mr. _____,

The question how far one can separate a criminal from his crime
depends, I think, upon the purpose for which one might attempt to do
so. If what one is dealing with is the question of just retribution then
the criminal must be identified with his crime, and so far as earthly
punishment is concerned, no subsequent repentance could be accepted
as a ground for remission of penalty because the purpose of the penalty
is threefold. It is partly to bring home to the criminal the nature of his
act and lead to a change of outlook, and no doubt, if he has repented
that has already happened. But it is also to express the repudiation of
the crime on the part of the community and to deter others from
behaving in a similar way, and these two grounds for the retribution
remain. But if you are thinking not of earthly punishment but of true
and ultimate welfare then it is possible to distinguish and both to desire
and, if the opportunity exists, work for the repentance and reformation
of the criminal.

There is no way we can work for this in the case of Hitler except by
defeating him and if this were secured, retribution, in my judgment,
ought to follow. But it ought to be a judicial act quite deliberately and
calmly carried out as free as possible from violent passions; and with
the hope and prayer that through his defeat, and the punishment which
the civilized world inflicts upon him, he may be led to a new way of
thinking about life and the claims of other people and other nations.

I should have supposed that the Church in all its official utterances
made it as clear as possible that it regards this war as a fight for good
against evil. I never personally say "crusade" because I regard the historical crusades as such a deplorable episode in the history of Christendom
and I do not want to be associated with them. But a fight for good against
evil broadly speaking, I think it is. I have said so repeatedly in the clear-
est language I know; so has my predecessor; so did all the bishops when

assembled together last summer, in a statement which they then published. But of course the main concern for the Church must be with the quality of the people carrying on the fight. Therefore one cannot say only that it is a fight of good against evil but also that we have to make ourselves more fit to serve the good cause, and this quite as much as the other—in my judgment more than the other—is a Church's primary business.

Scripture Meditation

To fear the LORD is to hate evil.

—PROVERBS 8:13

Thought for the Day

Without the fear of the Lord, we cannot discern what is evil.

Prayer

The LORD ... will rule in the midst of your enemies.

—PSALM 110:2

JULY 10: CHRISTIANS AND PACIFISM

---

*Another wartime issue addressed by Archbishop Temple is whether Christians
should always be pacifists. On this question he responded
to a friend, Derek Fane, on January 14, 1944.*

*D*ear Derek,

... It seems to me that there are people who are called to what I described as the "special witness" of pacifism just as there are some who have been called to the special witness of voluntary poverty. St. Francis never said that everybody ought to abandon all their worldly goods; he said that he was sure *he* ought, and he wanted them to consider whether they ought; but he fully recognized that there were some who ought to retain them and use them in the service of God and man.

There is nothing wicked about having worldly goods, but they do constitute a temptation and a distraction. Similarly with the use of force in the maintenance of law and the prevention of oppression; but it has great power to pervert the minds of those who use it and obscure from the supremacy of love as the only principle fit for the supreme place in the direction of life; and I think that there are some called to renounce the use of force in order to give witness to that fundamentally important truth in complete freedom from such distraction or temptation.

So that if any man says to me "I am sure that my service to Christ can only be fulfilled if I refuse to fight," I accept it from him at once; if he goes on to say this is true also of every other Christian, though no doubt he cannot be required so to act until his own conscience is awakened to it, then I have to resist, because I believe that this is a theological error. And, as you will see, the position that I am stating is completely covered by the clause in the article which you think, from your point of view, erroneous.

Scripture Meditation

There is a future for the man of peace.
—PSALM 37:37

Thought for the Day

Our own conscience cannot be the judge of another's.

Prayer

Lord, make me an instrument of your peace.
—ST. FRANCIS OF ASSISI

JULY 11: COLD WAR, WARM HEART (PART 1)

In the late 1970s and 1980s, informal conferences between Dutch and Russian
experts in economics, industry, agriculture, and military affairs took place
regularly in The Netherlands and Moscow. Their goal was to help to defreeze the
bilateral relations between Russia and the West that had been frozen during the
former Cold War period. Ernst H. van Eeghan, head of the oldest trading
company in The Netherlands, initiated the efforts, which were relatively
successful. Here he wrote to some friends of an unexpected result of the meetings.

Soviet delegations (coming to our home in Heemstede, near Amsterdam) were always accompanied by the same high ranking KGB officer, a plain-clothes major general. Let me refer to him as Radomir. [The late Baroness van Eeghan often talked privately about her Christian faith to this KGB officer, who himself had a Christian mother]....

During one of these, Radomir told me his wife was suffering from a very serious liver disease. When I saw her, I was shocked. He asked me for advice and I told him ... of a Belgium medication that had been developed, capable of curing certain liver diseases completely. I suggested I would try to get hold of this medication for him. With great difficulty, I managed to get the medication pills and sent them to him. During my following visit, he told me that his wife had been entirely cured, and in fact, she looked as well as when I first met her.

Three years later, I suddenly had a visit from two well-known members of the American Congress. They showed me correspondence between 114 members of Congress and the Russian government concerning the Ukrainian Baptist family Khailo, of which the father and one son had been locked away in a psychiatric institution for more than seven years. Two other sons had been sentenced to eighteen and twenty years of imprisonment. The correspondence had led to nothing, and they now asked me to make an effort through my contacts. With little hope for success, I promised to do my best, and I traveled to Moscow to visit Radomir. I asked him to do his best to set free all members of the Khailo family that had been deprived of their freedom and to allow the whole family to emigrate to the United States.

Radomir turned out to be fully aware of the Khailo case, but throwing his arms in the air, he pleaded, "Not Khailo!" When I insisted and told him that I was not willing to go into any discussion, he said after a short silence, "You will get them, but only if you reserve for me a place in heaven!" I responded that I considered this an unfair condition. There was no doubt that he did not owe his KGB rank to his kindly blue eyes. It had taken more than that! Nevertheless, I was prepared to intercede in his favor, knowing that God is a loving, merciful, and forgiving God. I promised I would do my best should the occasion present itself.

Scripture Meditation

Queen Esther answered, "If I have found favor with you, O king ... spare my people—this is my request.... For how can I bear to see disaster fall on my people? How can I bear to see the destruction of my family?"
—ESTHER 7:3; 8:6

Thought for the Day

Through many extraordinary means and circumstances, God may place us in a position of favor to intercede for others. Are we always ready to seize the opportune time?

Prayer

Praise be to the name of God for ever and ever; wisdom and power are his.
—DANIEL 2:20

JULY 12: COLD WAR, WARM HEART (PART 2)

*Ernst van Eeghan continued his letter, expressing his own Christian courage,
which he never interpreted to be more than simply acting
as a compassionate human being.*

The following day, I learned that effectively all imprisoned members of the Khailo family had been liberated; that they had returned to their village of Krasnaloetsj (in the Ukraine), but that they did not wish to emigrate to the United States. I didn't trust the message, and took off on a trying journey to visit them [suffering from war wounds, and now over seventy years of age]. My suspicion proved to be justified because they did want to emigrate.

Back in Moscow, after much discussion, permission came for them to travel to the Netherlands, but not to the United States. Since there was no mention as to what should happen after their arrival in Holland, I felt free to accept this condition.

The Khailo family consisted of seventeen members, including in-laws. But once the news had spread in the village that the Khailos were allowed to emigrate, the remaining daughters (not the greatest beauties!) quickly married, causing the family to grow to twenty-three members. One son, who had been in a psychiatric institution for seven years, had suffered severe brain damage and speech impediments from the drugs and injections administered to him; upon the family's arrival at the Schiphol airport, the American immigration officer who was supposed to grant transit visas to the whole family refused to give him a visa. At that point, the whole family refused to continue their journey. Thus, from one minute to the next, I found myself in charge of twenty-three Ukrainians in need of instant help!

Within an hour, the solutions came through the amazing cooperation of Mr. Hendrick Koekkoek, who owned a trailer camp in the Dutch province of Friesland. The inhabitants of the village immediately conjured up a tent-shop, providing all sorts of convenience articles. The Khailos could find what they needed there without having to pay. A Ukrainian kitchen was even specially installed for them. The Netherlands government confined itself to letting me know that they could be of no help to the Khailo family, not even financially.

After six months, the Deputy Secretary of Foreign Affairs of the United States issued a waiver allowing the Khailo family, by the greatest exception, to enter the country. I was slightly disappointed that all this should take a full half year's doing, since, after all, it had been 114 members of Congress who had asked me to intervene in the first place!

During my next visit to the U.S., some members of Congress offered me a lunch at Capitol Hill, and the deputy Secretary of Foreign Affairs invited me for dinner in the Benjamin Franklin Room of his ministry. I also received an honorary medal.

I concluded for myself that the whole episode had been an *act of God,* in which I had played only a minor part. Things like this can't be organized.

Scripture Meditation

Mordecai recorded these events ... as the time when ... their sorrow was turned into joy and their mourning into a day of celebration.
—ESTHER 9:20, 22

Thought for the Day

When the Lord declares his salvation through human agencies, how ready and willing are we to be his agents?

Prayer

Sing to the LORD a new song, for he has done marvelous things.
—PSALM 98:1

JULY 13: KARL BARTH ON FIGHTING FOR RIGHTEOUSNESS

Karl Barth, the twentieth century's leading theologian, was invited to address the Christian churches in Great Britain on the subject of war during WWII. This is an extract of the first of two letters written in December 1939.

*D*ear Christian Brethren in Great Britain,

Let me begin with an assertion in which I think most of you will find yourselves substantially in agreement with me: we Christians, in all lands, find ourselves, as far as this war is concerned, in a situation strikingly different from anything that we experienced twenty-five years ago. That is to say different in so far as we do not just accept this war as a necessary evil, but that we approve it as a righteous war, which God does not simply allow, but which He commands us to wage.

And we hold this to be so in spite of the fact that it is not less terrible, and indeed may be much more terrible than the last war!—in spite of the fact that we believe we have studied the Holy Scriptures since the last war not more superficially but more thoroughly!—in spite of the fact that we think that since the last war we have given deeper consideration to the Christian obligations to the world!—in spite of the fact that since the last war our expectation of the coming of the Kingdom of God and its peace has grown not more feeble but more fervent!

In spite of all this, we cannot resist the necessity of giving a different answer to what is today a different question.... We must not overlook the fact that this war is being fought for a cause which is worthy to be defended by all the means in our power—even by war; and further, that this cause could no longer be defended by any other means than by war.... On the contrary, this new war was finally declared only after many years of continued hesitation and evasion, in order to check a movement which was alleged to be an attempt to put right the mistakes which had been made in previous years, but which was actually—and still is—a threat ten times worse than all those mistakes put together.

This threat (I need not mention Mussolini, who has proved himself to be a mere lackey) was the attempt of Adolf Hitler to force his "New

Order" on Central Europe today, on the whole of Europe tomorrow, and on the whole of the world the day after tomorrow.... It was perhaps through blindness to the true nature and power of this enterprise, perhaps in the weakness which came from a bad conscience about the past, perhaps because they realized they had neglected their duty to arm themselves for war in order to save peace, that the victors of 1918, negotiated with Adolf Hitler.

Scripture Meditation

I myself am convinced, my brothers, that you yourselves are full of goodness, complete in knowledge and competent to instruct one another.

—ROMANS 15:14

Thought for the Day

True boldness comes from experiencing the grace of God.

Prayer

Now to him who is able to establish you by my gospel ... to the only wise God be glory forever through Jesus Christ! Amen.

—ROMANS 16:25, 27

JULY 14: KARL BARTH ON GOD'S SOVEREIGNTY

Karl Barth continued his previous first letter with more theological reflections.

*T*he world in which we live is the place where Jesus Christ rose from the dead, and the present age is the time of God's long-suffering until the day when the same Jesus Christ shall come again in his glory. It is on the world in which we live, in all the transience of its present existence, with the sins which we commit and the misery they bring, and with the shadow of death cast over it—it is on this world in its entirety that God has set his mark, in that he has exalted the name of Jesus above every name, "that at the name of Jesus every knee should bow, in heaven and on earth and under the earth" (Phil. 2:10). Since this is true, the world in which we live is not some sinister wilderness where fate or chance holds sway, or where all sorts of "principalities and powers" run riot unrestrained and rage about unchecked. Since this is true, the world has not been given up to the devil or to man, that they may make of it some vast "Insanity Fair" according to the whimsical impulses of some individual or collective spirits of mischief.

There is no doubt that such "principalities and powers," and indeed such mischievous spirits *do* exist, as the Scriptures say and as we are realizing once again today. But at the same time it is written, and we can and must hold on to it even today: that although at present the glory of the Kingdom of God is held out to us only as a hope, yet the Kingly Rule of Christ extends not merely over the Church as the congregation of the faith but, regardless of whether men believe or not, over the whole of the universe in all its heights and depths; and it also confronts and overrules with sovereign dignity the principalities and powers and evil spirits of this world.

It is indeed true that the whole creation groans with us, because, as the place where Jesus suffered and died, it has been made subject to vanity. But it is also true that this same creation is already consecrated through the resurrection of Jesus Christ, in expectation of his coming again and of "a new heaven and a new earth." For just as Christ, according to the teaching of the whole of the New Testament, has already borne away sin and destroyed death, so also has he already (according to Col. 2:15) completely disarmed those "principalities and powers," and made a spectacle of them in his own triumph, in order finally to tread them down under his feet on the day of his coming again (1 Cor. 15:15).

It is only as shadows without real substance and power that they can still beset us. We Christians, of all men, have no right whatsoever to fear and respect them or to resign ourselves to the fact that they are spreading throughout the world as though they know neither bounds nor lord. We should be slighting the resurrection of Jesus Christ and denying his reign on the right hand of the Father, if we forgot that the world in which we live is already consecrated, and if we did not, for Christ's sake, come to grips spiritedly and resolutely with these evil spirits; and at the same time we should have no more peace in the Church, in our worship of God, in our preaching and hearing of his Word, in our own personal faith, love and hope; we should find in these things no more comfort and strength; we should have to stand ashamed before God and his angels and all his creatures.

Scripture Meditation

Having disarmed the powers and authorities, he [Christ] made a public spectacle of them, triumphing over them by the cross.
—COLOSSIANS 2:15

Thought for the Day

Christians should be fearless before tyranny in the light of the Cross of Christ.

Prayer

You alone are the LORD. You made the heavens ... and all their starry host, the earth and all that is on it, the seas and all that is in them. You give life to everything, and the multitudes of heaven worship you.
—NEHEMIAH 9:6

JULY 15: KARL BARTH ON CHURCH AND STATE

Karl Barth helped to compose the Barmen Declaration in 1934, opposing state interference with Christian doctrine, such as the logic of the Nazis that a state fuehrer should be reflected in "fuehrer bishops." So in his letter to the British churches, Barth discussed the separate roles of church and state.

*A*ccording to the New Testament ... God has instituted for us Christians not only *the Church*, to build us up in faith, love and hope, but also *the political hierarchy, the State* (for us, and also for the rest of the world), to testify to the Kingly Rule of Christ. Paul called the State in the most solemn way a "Minister of God" (Rom. 13:4, 6). He exhorted the Christians most emphatically to fit themselves into its framework and to pray for its good estate "that we may lead a quiet and peaceable life in all godliness and holiness" (1 Tim. 2:2).

The State which thus counterbalances the Church, and to which Christians are thus bound, is obviously a purely earthly institution. It cannot and must not be regarded as a second Church, much less as a beginning of the Kingdom of God (to which the Church itself can only look forward). When the State speaks, we must not expect to hear a confession of Christian Faith, nor when the State acts must we expect to see a demonstration or an example of brotherly love. If we expect too much of the State, we shall fail to appreciate the little that there is to be found. The State embraces the life of all men in as much as the life of all is actually and objectively under the sway of Jesus Christ, even in its unredeemed, and therefore dangerous, natural condition, even apart from the faith, love and hope of the Christian.

The State is therefore the sign of that consecration which the world has received through the resurrection of Jesus Christ: it is the sign of the patience with which God bears with, protects and upholds the world until the day when he shall make all things new. Therefore the State is a constant reminder that the self-will of men, the imaginations and confusions arising from their self-conceit, the lusts which they may satisfy as they desire, are not without limits, and that these demons have indeed a master. For, according to Romans 13:1–7 and 1 Peter 2:13–17, the task of the State is this: to discriminate between right and wrong in the lives of all men and to set certain bounds for their conduct. The State must keep constant watch on these bounds, and constantly defend them, first of all *on behalf of* everybody, since the life of all requires such bounds, and then, if necessary, *against* anybody who may be so arrogant as to seek to go round or to break through them. The State was instituted by God to do this, and, as it does this, it is the "Minister of God" in its own sphere and in its own way, just as much as the Church itself. The State bears the sword in order to fulfill this very function.

Scripture Meditation

Everyone must submit himself to the governing authorities, for there is no authority except that which God has established.
—ROMANS 13:1

Thought for the Day

The Christian's responsibility should include participation in governance and statecraft.

Prayer

[Pray] for kings and all those in authority, that we may live peaceful and quiet lives in all godliness and holiness.
—1 TIMOTHY 2:2

In the latter section of his second letter to the British churches,
Karl Barth affirmed what he himself had experienced in his own
theological journey. Human abstractions of reality are a poor
substitute for the person of Jesus Christ.

Our readiness for the future is complete only when we submit to the demands of the present, and when we accept the assurance, which even in the present is not denied to us. Should we not lay hold of the strong confidence that, if this war is waged well so that it achieves its aim, it will definitely be followed ... by a new piece of work, which must then be begun—in this case, the work of building the peace when the time comes, even though at the moment we cannot visualize its character? If we base our arguments on Natural Law rather than on Jesus Christ, then I do not know how we shall be able to lay hold of that confidence. If men either openly or secretly consider Natural Law to be the revelation which governs their attitude, then they cannot help escaping from the present and taking refuge in some self-made shape of things to come. Those who do not seek to escape from the present, because they were guided into it by Jesus Christ, need no such refuge.

And here is one other practical consequence. If Jesus Christ is indeed the reason for our present decision, then it will be made manifest in the humility and sincerity of the faith in which we do what we have decided.

First, in *humility*. It is evident that the continued existence in the world of some form of political order (however imperfect and however needful of reformation it may appear) is not due to human worth, but rather to the working of God's grace and patience; and it is only by his grace and patience that we have the honor of co-operation in its protection and defense....

And, secondly, in *sincerity*. Faith is sincere when ... it is directed wholly towards God.... It is certainly right and necessary to assemble and to put in action all our forces in order to master the tasks which today are pressing on us. But it will not do to rely on ourselves, or our aircraft, or our tanks, or our "inexhaustible resources," or our shrewdness and our morale. It will not do to deny that the devil has even more self-confidence, and that he is probably even richer in all these material and spiritual possessions than we are. Only one thing will do, namely, to put our whole confidence in God alone, so that in this exclusive confidence we may do any and everything which it is in our power to do. This one thing alone will do, because only when we have put our whole confidence in God shall we face, with wide open—not pessimistic but undeceived—eyes, the difficulties and obstructions which we have to overcome, and meet them accordingly.... Only faith in Jesus Christ can be such humble and sincere faith.

Scripture Meditation

The authorities that exist have been established by God.
—ROMANS 13:1

Thought for the Day

It is only the legitimacy of God's righteous character that is truly authoritative; otherwise power without legitimacy is tyranny.

Prayer

God, the blessed and only Ruler, the King of kings and Lord of lords, who alone is immortal and who lives in unapproachable light, whom no one has seen or can see. To him be honor and might forever. Amen.
—1 TIMOTHY 6:15–16

JULY 17: JOURNEYING INTO CHRIST: FAREWELL OF A CONVERTED JAPANESE WAR CRIMINAL

Hideo Ishizaki, a Japanese war criminal who converted to Christianity in prison, wrote this farewell letter to a missionary, Irene Webster-Smith, on February 11, 1949, shortly before being executed.

Dear Teacher Smith,

I thank you very much for your guidance to lead me to Christ, especially me who is a stranger to you. Today I am going back to the Eternal Life under the feet of God by his grace. It is a joy which exceeds all. Brothers Nishizawa and Shibano have gone back to him, and now Brother Mizuguchi and I follow. I am so grateful to God that I can go to him in such peace and as a child of God. I owe it to your guidance and to Jesus Christ, and to my reading of the Bible. Under any circumstance the Almighty God saves those who are lost and who are troubled.

I was afraid that I had to go on this journey alone with Brother Mizuguchi, but fortunately a Protestant chaplain Captain, O. W. Schoech, visited us this morning with a Bible and a hymnal. He read from the second chapter of Luke, from verse 25 to verse 35 together with us and encouraged us. We prayed that he will receive us as his servants by his grace. I told Captain Schoech that we wanted to sing some hymns which we had in our minds before we start on this journey. He thought it was fine, and asked us to give the hymnal to him when we are through with it. I consented to do so, and we picked Nos. 507, 274, 306, 441, and 563. We sang these hymns this morning from the bottom of our hearts and tears rain down. How happy we are! To go back to him, saved by his gracious hand! The chaplain visited us again in the afternoon to give us words of cheer; though I could not fully understand his English, I was consoled and encouraged. He told us he would accompany us to the last moment. I cannot thank too strongly for the great love of Christ.

I hear you are taking a trip. I pray that you would work harder for Jesus Christ, and also take great care of your body. May the mercy of Jesus Christ abide with you. Amen.

—Hideo Ishizaki

Scripture Meditation

The Lord has done this for me ... he has shown his favor and
taken away my disgrace among the people.

—LUKE 2:25

Thought for the Day

Truly Jesus Christ is able to save to the uttermost, those who come unto
him by faith.

Prayer

Jesus, remember me when you come into your kingdom.

—LUKE 23:42

SEASONS OF PERSECUTION
AND JUDGMENT

*A*s God's Kingdom intersects and penetrates into the affairs of humankind, so the exposure of evil and violence becomes more obvious. This then leads us to see the two-edged sword of judgment, both of the world and of the Church, as generating the genre of the Letters to the Seven Churches in the book of Revelation, as well as to our national churches today.

PERSECUTION

JULY 18: FAREWELL: FACING THE ETERNAL JUDGE

*This is the first of two excerpts written by Fränz Jägerstatter, beheaded after
a Nazi military trial on August 9, 1943, in his farewell letter
to his family the day before his execution.*

*A*ll my dear ones,

The hour comes ever closer when I will be giving my soul back to
God, the Master. I would have liked to say so many things to you in
farewell so that it is hard not to be able to take leave of you any more. I
would have liked too, to spare you the pain and sorrow that you must
bear because of me. But you know we must love God even more than
family, and we must lose everything dear and worthwhile on earth rather
than commit even the slightest offense against God. And if, for your
sake, I had not shrunk back from offending God, how can we know what
sufferings God might have sent us on my account? It must surely have
been hard for our dear Savior to bring such pain upon his dear mother
through his death: what, then, are our sorrows compared with what these
two innocent hearts had to suffer—and all on account of us sinners?

And what kind of a leave-taking must it be for those who only halfway
believe in an eternal life and, consequently, no longer have much hope of
a reunion? If I did not have faith in God's mercy, that he would forgive
me all my sins, I could scarcely have endured life in a lonely prison with
such calm. Moreover, though people charge me with a crime and have
condemned me to death as a criminal, I take comfort in the knowledge
that not everything which this world may consider a crime, is a crime in
the eyes of God. And I have hope that I need not fear the eternal Judge
because of this crime.

Still this sentence of death should serve as a warning. For the Lord
God will not deal much differently with us if we think we do not have to
obey everything he commands us through his Church to believe and to
do. Except that the eternal Judge will not only condemn us to mortal
death but to everlasting death as well. For this reason, I have nothing
pressing upon my heart more urgently than to make the firm decision to

keep all the commandments and to avoid every sin. You must love God, your Lord, and your neighbor as yourself. On these two commandments rests the whole law. Keep these and we can look forward to an early reunion in heaven. For this reason, too, we must not think evil of others who act differently than I. It is much better to pray for everyone than to pass judgment upon them, for God desires that all become blessed.

Scripture Meditation

Will not the Judge of all the earth do right?
—GENESIS 18:25

Thought for the Day

Our circumstances can shape our actions, but still God is sovereign.

Prayer

O Father of all, to whom every life is precious, look in pity and in healing power on all who still suffer as the result of war.
—LESLIE D. WEATHERHEAD

JULY 19: FAREWELL: THE COST OF TRUTH

Fränz Jägerstatter continued his farewell letter.

Many actually believe quite simply that things have to be the way they are. If this should happen to mean that they are obliged to commit injustice, then they believe that others are responsible. The oath would not be a lie for someone who believes he can go along and is willing to do so. But if I know in advance that I cannot accept and obey everything I would promise under that oath, then I would be guilty of a lie. For this reason I am convinced that it is still best that I speak the truth, even if it costs me my life. For you will not find it written in any of the commandments of God or of the Church that a man is obliged under pain of sin to take an oath committing him to obey whatever might be commanded of him by his secular ruler. Therefore, you should not be heavy of heart if others see my decision as a sin, as some already have.

In the same way, if someone argues from the standpoint of the family, do not be troubled, for it is not permitted to lie even for the sake of the family. If I had ten children, the greatest demand upon me would still be the one I must make of myself.

Educate the children to be pious Catholics as long as it is possible. (Now, of course, one cannot expect them to understand much.) I can say from my own experience how painful life is when we live like halfway Christians, that is more like vegetating than living.

If a man were to possess all the wisdom of the world and call half the earth his own, he still could not and would not be as happy as one of those men who can still call virtually nothing in this world their own except their Catholic faith. I would not exchange my lonely cell—which is not at all bad ... it will pass away, but God's word remains for all eternity. I can assure you that if you pray a single sincere "Our Father" for our children, you will have given them a greater gift than if you had provided them with the most lavish dowry a landholder ever dreamed of giving his daughter. Many people would laugh at these words, but they are true just the same.

Now, my dear children, when Mother reads this letter to you, your father will already be dead. He would have loved to come to you again, but the Heavenly Father willed it otherwise. Be good and obedient children and pray for me so that we may soon be reunited in heaven.

Dear wife, forgive me everything by which I have grieved or offended you. For my part, I have forgiven everything. Ask all those in Radegund whom I have ever injured or offended to forgive me too.

Scripture Meditation

He ... who speaks truth from his heart ... will never be shaken.
—PSALM 15:2, 5

Thought for the Day

The person of truth expresses eternal realities.

Prayer

Into your hands, I commend my loved ones.... I commend to you
my body and soul. O God, your holy name be praised.

—DIETRICH BONHOEFFER

JULY 20: GOD'S LOVE TRANSCENDS ALL PRISON BARS

Madame Guyon, friend of Archbishop François Fenelon, had a faithful
maid who spent eight years in the prison of Vincennes for her faith.
After her fourth year there, the maid wrote to Fenelon.

My dear Brother,

I don't know if I shall have the consolation of ever seeing you again. I wish it more for your sake than mine, since I can receive no consolation other than in God alone.... I have not been able to inform you about Madame Guyon [in the Bastille prison]. I am aware of your concern for me, knowing very well your love for me, and desirous to look after my material well-being. You were very concerned about my welfare, but it was God who has placed me where I am now, for it is his love which forced me away, and would have me separated from all that would tie me to this earth. If your house had been made of precious stones, and I might have been waited upon like a Queen, yet I should have forsaken it all, to follow my God who called me, not to pleasures and gratifications, but gave me a strong and lively impression of the Cross. For the

Cross has had a much greater attraction and power over my heart than all the things of this world.

Yet if I had been able to tell you all this beforehand, my dear brother, would you not have thought me as a fool.... But now I can open my heart freely to you; for I am in no fear of anybody's putting an obstacle in the way of my own sufferings. I am writing this in the prison of Vincennes, where I have been for the last four years, and know not if I shall ever be released, so I accept I may never have any consolation except further suffering.

Having by chance got hold of a piece of paper, I am writing with a stick instead of a pen, and with soot instead of ink to encourage you— taking much risk in doing so—but you have a hundred times more worries and concerns than I have! ... For a prison can only confine the body, not the union of souls. This I have long since experienced, for I am in solitary confinement, yet where I am more strongly united to her [Madame Guyon] in God than I have ever been in her presence. Don't be surprised about this, dear Brother, for she showed me the grace to love my God, whom I now love, whom I shall ever love, and whom I continually love ... drawing me away from the love of myself.... Do you wonder then why I should love her, when she so loves her God, with a boundless love, living and effective love. And this love has the power to unite our hearts in such a way that I am unable to express it, but believe it to be the beginning of the union which we shall have in heaven, where the love of God will unite us all to him.

Scripture Meditation

Who shall separate us from the love of Christ? Shall trouble or hardship or persecution?
—Romans 8:35

Thought for the Day

Suffering for Christ's sake can give us a transcendent spirit, which rises above all our afflictions.

Prayer

O my God, Jesus Christ, make me worthy that I may know thy most high mystery, wrought by thy most ardent love—the mystery of thy Incarnation.

—ANGELA OF FOLIGNO

JULY 21: THE CHRISTIAN CHALLENGE TO THE ROMAN WORLD

Pliny the Elder, Roman governor of Bithynia in Asia Minor, wrote to Emperor Trajan seeking legal advice about how to deal with the Christians at the beginning of the second century AD.

Meanwhile the method I have observed towards those who have been denounced to me as Christians, is this: I interrogated them whether they were Christians; if they confessed I repeated the question twice again, adding a threat of capital punishment; if they still persevered, I ordered them to be executed. For I was persuaded that whatever the nature of their creed, a contumacious and inflexible obstinacy certainly deserved chastisement....

These accusations began to spread, from the mere fact that the matter was being investigated. Several forms of the mischief came to light. A placard was posted up without any signature, accusing a number of people by name. Those who denied that they were Christians, or had ever been so, who repeated after me an invocation to the gods, and offered religious rites with wine and frankincense to your statue (which I had ordered to be brought for the purpose, together with those of the gods), and finally cursed the name of Christ (none of which, it is said, those who are really Christians can be forced into performing), I thought proper to discharge....

I judged it … necessary to extract the real truth, with the assistance of torture, from two female slaves, called deaconesses. But I could discover nothing but depraved and excessive superstition.

I therefore thought it proper to adjourn all further proceedings in this affair, to consult you. For the matter is well worth referring to you, especially considering the numbers endangered: persons of all ranks and ages, and of both sexes, are and will be involved in the prosecution. For this contagious superstition is not confined to the cities only, but has spread through the villages and the countryside. Nevertheless it seems still possible to check and cure it. The temples, at last, which were once almost deserted, begin now to be frequented, and the sacred solemnities, after a long intermission, are again revived; while there is a general demand for sacrificial animals—which for some time past have met with but few purchasers. From hence it is easy to imagine, what numbers might be reclaimed from this error if the door is left open to repentance.

Scripture Meditation

As I walked around and looked carefully at your objects of worship, I even found an altar with this inscription: "TO AN UNKNOWN GOD."
—ACTS 17:23

Thought for the Day

To confront the world is to confront idolatry, for human beings are incurably worshippers.

Prayer

May the Lord direct your hearts into God's love.
—2 THESSALONIANS 3:5

JULY 22: BEING THE CHRIST-BEARER TO OTHERS

When Ignatius of Antioch was martyred about AD 100, he left behind seven letters to various communities he had visited on his way from Antioch to Rome. Outside of the New Testament, they are among the earliest Christian letters. Ignatius's baptismal name Theophorus means "a child borne of God" or "God-bearer." In this most personal of his letters, he wrote to the Christians in Rome on August 24, year unknown. It became known as "the marytr's manual" and was very inspiring to the early Church.

Ignatius, Theophorus to the Church, on whom the majesty of the Most High Father and Jesus Christ, his only Son, has shown mercy ... since I prayed to God that I might see your faces, the faces of his friends. He has granted me my request, more even than I could ask. For bound as I am in Christ Jesus, I hope to embrace you, if indeed it is his will that I should be deemed worthy to finish the course.

A good beginning has been made only let me finish it also, by God's grace, and claim my portion unhindered ... leaving me alone to do so [by martyrdom]. For I don't want you to court the approval of men, but to please God alone ... so grant me to be offered as a sacrifice to God now, while the altar is being prepared.... Then as a choir united in love, you may sing to the Father of our Lord Jesus Christ, because God has granted the Bishop of Syria worthy to be summoned ... from the sunrise to the sunset. For it is good to sink below the horizon of this world into God, in order to rise again in him....

I am writing to all the churches, and I declare to all that I am willing to die for God's sake, so long as you do not hinder me from doing so, out of your own misguided kindness. Let the wild beasts have me, for through them my way to God lies open. I am God's wheat, and I am ground by the teeth of wild beasts so that I may be found as pure bread of Christ. Rather let the wild animals become my tomb, leaving nothing at all of my body. Thus when I sleep in death I shall burden no one, becoming instead truly a disciple of Jesus Christ, even when the world can see nothing of my body.

... Remember the Syrian Church, which in my absence is shepherded by God himself. Jesus Christ alone will watch over it now, and with your love ... I am writing this to you from Smyrna by the kind services of the Ephesians—may they be blessed as they deserve! ... Farewell: be strengthened unto the end in the patient endurance of Jesus Christ.

Scripture Meditation

You will receive power when the Holy Spirit comes on you; and you will be my witnesses ... to the ends of the earth.
—ACTS 1:8

Thought for the Day

Those about to be martyred frequently experienced God's indwelling Spirit to help them to face death with transcendent joy.

Prayer

My Jesus, let me contemplate your death that I may learn to die. How can I fail to be faithful to you, when I contemplate the death your faithfulness proved?
—R. M. BENSON

LETTERS FROM THE BOOK OF REVELATION

John the apostle who resided in Ephesus is the attributed author of
Revelation. This is the first of eight letters written by John to
the universal Church in Revelation 1:4–20.

To the seven churches in the province of Asia:

Grace and peace to you from him who is, and who was, and who is to come, and from the seven spirits before his throne, and from Jesus Christ, who is the faithful witness, the firstborn from the dead, and the ruler of the kings of the earth.

To him who loves us and has freed us from our sins by his blood, and has made us to be a kingdom and priests to serve his God and Father — to him be glory and power for ever and ever! Amen.

Look, he is coming with the clouds, and every eye will see him, even those who pierced him; and all the peoples of the earth will mourn because of him. So shall it be! Amen.

"I am the Alpha and the Omega," says the Lord God, "who is, and who was, and who is to come, the Almighty."

I, John, your brother and companion in the suffering and kingdom and patient endurance that are ours in Jesus, was on the island of Patmos because of the word of God and the testimony of Jesus. On the Lord's Day I was in the Spirit, and I heard behind me a loud voice like a trumpet, which said: "Write on a scroll what you see and send it to the seven churches: to Ephesus, Smyrna, Pergamum, Thyatira, Sardis, Philadelphia and Laodicea."

I turned around to see the voice that was speaking to me. And when I turned I saw seven golden lampstands, and among the lampstands was someone "like a son of man," dressed in a robe reaching down to his feet and with a golden sash around his chest. His head and hair were white like wool, as white as snow, and his eyes were like blazing fire. His feet were like bronze glowing in a furnace, and his voice was like the sound of rushing waters. In his right hand he held seven stars, and out of his mouth came a sharp double-edged sword. His face was like the sun shining in all its brilliance.

When I saw him, I fell at his feet as though dead. Then he placed his right hand on me and said: "Do not be afraid. I am the First and the Last. I am the Living One; I was dead, and behold I am alive for ever and ever! And I hold the keys of death and Hades.

"Write, therefore, what you have seen, what is now and what will take place later. The mystery of the seven stars that you saw in my right hand and of the seven golden lampstands is this: The seven stars are the angels of the seven churches, and the seven lampstands are the seven churches."

Scripture Meditation

Do not be afraid. I am the First and the Last. I am the Living One; I was dead, and behold I am alive for ever and ever!
—REVELATION 1:17–18

Thought for the Day

Our creation was as worshippers, and our destiny is eternal worship.

Prayer

To him who loves us and has freed us from our sins by his blood, and has made us to be a kingdom and priests to serve his God and Father—to him be glory and power for ever and ever! Amen.
—REVELATION 1:5–6

JULY 24: THE SEVEN CHURCHES:
WHY THE BOOK OF REVELATION DRAWS US

Reverend Darrell W. Johnson (b. 1958), associate professor of Pastoral
Theology and Preaching at Regent College, Vancouver, Canada, wrote on
June 29, 2002, in response to the question, "Why are you so excited
about the book of Revelation?"

he answer lies in one of the letter's fundamental convictions. It is a
letter … in fact, the longest letter in the New Testament! In my view, the
best letter! And one of its fundamental convictions is, "things are not as
they seem." Or, to be more precise, "things are not only as they seem."
The title of the letter is "The Apocalypse of Jesus Christ." Unfortunately,
in our time the word apocalypse means, "oh no, something awful is about
to happen." Thus we speak of natural disasters and horrible events like
the collapse of the New York City World Trade Towers as having "apocalyptic proportions."

But the word did not have that sense in the first century. It was a perfectly good word, meaning, simply, "unveiling," or "disclosure," or
"breaking through from hiddenness." The apostle Paul uses the word in
his letter to the Romans. He claims the Gospel of God concerning his
Son Jesus Christ is power of God unto salvation, for in it the righteousness of God breaks through (1:16–17). For Paul, the Gospel is
"apocalyptic," a "breaking through from hiddenness," a "disclosure of
what could not be deduced." In the first century "apocalypse" was used
of "lifting a cover" and of "pulling back of a curtain."

And that is why the letter draws me. There is more to reality than
meets the unaided senses. There is more to this present moment, there is
more to the flow of history, than meets our unaided intellect and emotions. And it is the purpose, the pastoral purpose, of the letter to "open
up" that more. In particular, the letter seeks to set the present moment
(with all its ambiguity) in the light of the unseen realities of the future.
And, more primarily, the letter seeks to set the present moment (with all
its ambiguity) in light of the unseen realities of the present. "Things are
not as they seem." There is more, so much more. And through its rich
symbolism and vivid imagery, the letter "opens up" that more. The letter

115

gives us an alternative reading of the present. The letter gives us a new set of glasses through which to look out at life around us, enabling us to react to our circumstances differently. Oh to see as John sees!

Scripture Meditation

"No eye has seen, no ear has heard, no mind has conceived what God has prepared for those who love him."

—I Corinthians 2:9

Thought for the Day

Man's perceptions are not bounded by organs of perception; he perceives more than sense (tho' so acute) can discover.

—William Blake

Prayer

To you, O Lord, I lift up my soul.... My eyes are ever on the Lord.

—Psalm 25:1, 15

July 25: The Seven Churches: Things Not as They Seem

Darrell Johnson continued his observations on the book of Revelation as a letter.

We are not surprised, therefore, to discover that the whole letter is built around the verb "open." 4:1—"I looked, and, behold, a door was opened in heaven." 11:19—"And the temple of God was opened in heaven." 15:5—"the temple of the tabernacle of the testimony in heaven was opened." And 19:11—"And I saw heaven opened." All in fulfillment of the promise Jesus made to the first disciples, "Truly, truly, I say to you, you shall see the heavens opened" (John 1:51).

Nor should we be surprised that the most frequent exhortation of the letter, and therefore John's major pastoral burden, is "look!" It is all over the letter. "Behold," or "lo," is the imperative form of the verb "to see." Unfortunately, a number of modern translations miss this, and render John's words "there before me was." No, no, no. John is calling us to action: "Look." The word carries the nuance of "wow, who would have expected that!" Here are some examples. 1:7—"Look, He is coming with the clouds of heaven." 1:18—"I was dead, and look, I am alive forevermore." 4:1—"Look, a door standing open in heaven." 4:2—"Look, a throne was standing in heaven … and One sitting on the throne." There is a Supreme Headquarters. And it is not up for grabs! 5:5—"Look, the Lion … has triumphed. He is able to open the scroll.… I saw in the very center of the throne a Lamb, as if slain." What, the Lion wins by being a Lamb? Things are not as they seem. 21:3—"Look, the tabernacle of God is among men." 21:5—"Look, I am making all things new." 22:7—"Look, I am coming quickly."

The second most frequent exhortation of the letter is "do not be afraid." We live the second by living the first. It is as we "look" at what is "open" that we overcome our fears and we are able to live as faithful disciples of the Lamb.

Things are not as they seem. I thank God for the vision he has given you over the years. I pray that as you read and pray with John God will give you even clearer vision in these turbulent days. Pray that he also may do the same for me.

Scripture Meditation

Then I looked, and there before me was the Lamb, standing on Mount Zion.

—REVELATION 14:1

Thought for the Day

God's radical Kingdom inaugurated in Christ requires new eyes to see.

Prayer

Be Thou my vision, O Lord of my heart;
naught be all else to me, save that Thou art!
—ANONYMOUS, ANCIENT IRISH HYMN

JULY 26: THE SEVEN CHURCHES: EPHESUS

The book of Revelation begins with seven pastoral letters to Jewish
Christian churches in and around Ephesus (Rev. 2:1—3:22). John, the
prisoner on Patmos, is the writer, and he makes clear that the letters are
messages to the congregations from the Holy Spirit. The church at
Ephesus is the first letter, addressed to the overseer
of the church in Revelation 2:1-7.

To the angel of the church in Ephesus write:

These are the words of him who holds the seven stars in his right hand and walks among the seven golden lampstands: I know your deeds, your hard work and your perseverance. I know that you cannot tolerate wicked men, that you have tested those who claim to be apostles but are not, and have found them false. You have persevered and have endured hardships for my name, and have not grown weary.

Yet I hold this against you: You have forsaken your first love. Remember the height from which you have fallen! Repent and do the things you did at first. If you do not repent, I will come to you and remove your lampstand from its place. But you have this in your favor: You hate the practices of the Nicolaitans, which I also hate.

He who has an ear, let him hear what the Spirit says to the churches. To him who overcomes, I will give the right to eat from the tree of life, which is in the paradise of God.

Scripture Meditation

Yet I hold this against you: You have forsaken your first love.
—REVELATION 2:4

Thought for the Day

Are you still as excited about your faith in Christ as when you first became a Christian?

Prayer

Jesus, I must trust thee, pondering thy ways, full of love and mercy, all thy earthly days.
—MARY JANE WALKER

JULY 27: THE SEVEN CHURCHES: THE "FIRST LOVE"

Reverend Earl F. Palmer is senior pastor of the University Presbyterian Church in Seattle, Washington. He responded in a meditation about the challenge of the previous letter.

*T*he Christians in Ephesus are honored for their courageous stand against false teachers and teaching. But something is wrong. There is a cold wind that dominates this church and perhaps its fight against error has contributed to the coldness. The text of Revelation 2 puts the crises in a stark and brief sentence, which is made the more dramatic in the way that the Greek language, unlike English, usually places the key verb of a sentence at the end of the sentence. Listen to the way the Ephesians heard this word from the Lord: "But against you I have this; the love at first yours, you have left behind."

How could a people or a person leave behind the love which first met them, and which they experienced at the very beginning of their journey with Jesus Christ? Is this letter pointing back to the love these Christians first experienced *from* God, when they discovered forgiveness and the healing of the dread consequences of sin when God found them? Or is the letter pointing to the love that these Christians expressed in their living because of the sheer grace of Christ at work in them? What new illness has overtaken them so that they now live as if they have moved beyond this first love? Has their fascination with the battle for the truth become the mark of their Christian identity?

Perhaps these Christians have convinced themselves that they know enough about the love theme, and they feel that they have matured beyond it. Perhaps for them Christian maturity has been defined in "truth language" to such an extent that the "event love" language of the gospel is downgraded in their minds.

We cannot be sure of the motives of the Ephesians who receive this first of the seven letters. But the message of the Book of Revelation with the exhortation of the Holy Spirit is unmistakable and clear both to the Ephesians and to us twenty centuries later.

The first love is so profound in itself that they or we can never outgrow it or move beyond it. God's love is the "event love" of Jesus Christ who finds a man named Zacchaeus and spends the night in his home; it is the love that touches children in a blessing; it is Jesus Christ at the cross of Mt. Calvary who takes upon himself the full tragedy and lostness of human sin and death itself. So that Jesus in that event disarmed sin and death and the power of the devil. We will never grow beyond this love; it is the first love that must stay and live its power through our daily lives throughout our lives.

The good news of Revelation is the invitation that calls us to come home to the beginning place, to the love we first discovered and that first discovered us.

Scripture Meditation

The love at first yours, you have left behind.
—REVELATION 2:4 (PARAPHRASE)

Thought for the Day

A Christian "career" or a Christian "professional reputation" can take us away from experiencing God's love, which is the basis of them all!

Prayer

I know, O Lord, and acknowledge with all humility that I am wholly unworthy of your love. But I am fully certain you are the worthiest object of my devotion. I am not good enough to serve you, but you have the right to the best service I can ever give you.
—ST. AUGUSTINE

JULY 28: THE SEVEN CHURCHES: SMYRNA

Each of the letters to the seven historical churches—Ephesus, Smyrna, Pergamum, Thyatira, Sardis, Philadelphia, and Laodicea—found in the second and third chapters of Revelation is addressed "To the angel of the church." This has been interpreted either as each church's heavenly or earthly messenger or its moral character and spirit. This series of contemporary responses from representatives of differing geographical contexts focuses on the latter interpretation. The church at Smyrna is the second letter, addressed to the overseer of the church in Revelation 2:8–11.

To the angel of the church in Smyrna write:

These are the words of him who is the First and the Last, who died and came to life again. I know your afflictions and your poverty—yet you are rich! I know the slander of those who say they are Jews and are not, but are a synagogue of Satan. Do not be afraid of what you are about to suffer. I tell you, the devil will put some of you in prison to test you, and you will suffer persecution for ten days. Be faithful, even to the point of death, and I will give you the crown of life.

He who has an ear, let him hear what the Spirit says to the churches. He who overcomes will not be hurt at all by the second death.

Scripture Meditation

Do not be afraid of what you are about to suffer.

—REVELATION 2:10

Thought for the Day

To live in Smyrna as a Christian is to be reminded of the hostile environment that shaped the godliness of Polycarp, and all who follow his example.

Prayer

May I be received this day in thy presence, a sacrifice rich and acceptable.... For this, and for all else besides, I praise you, I bless you, I glorify you; through our eternal priest in heaven, your beloved Son, Jesus Christ, by whom and with whom be glory to you and the Holy Ghost, now and for all ages to come. Amen.

—POLYCARP (AT HIS MARTYRDOM)

July 29: The Seven Churches: Comments on Symrna

*Allen Goddard (b. 1963) is in a mentoring ministry to
students in Pietermaritzberg, Republic of South Africa.
On September 21, 2002, he wrote the following.*

In the past, Africa perhaps has represented more of the poverty and persecution of Smyrna than it does today. For today, our continent basks in the limelight of newly won international recognition. Our media makers are speaking of an African Renaissance at the dawn of the Third Millennium; in one sense times have not been better for Africa.

And yet as I write, tens of millions of our children are without enough protein to save them until Christmas. Scores of our nations face social and economic collapse in the wake of the HIV and AIDS pandemic. The military legacies of our despots, Amin, Botha, Abacha, Mobutu Sese Seko, and Mugabe, pose a constant threat to our fragile peace. And rampant greed makes violent crime, widespread corruption, and unthinkable forms of abuse against women and children a daily reality in thousands of African cities.

Is then the African Church in the 21st Century merely a carbon copy of the moral and social two-facedness that our continent is guilty of today? Is the African Church colorful, bright, and promising on the outside, yet wretched with the stench of moral and social putrefaction on the inside? Is to save face and to preserve self-image rather than genuine sacrifice the benchmark of our "faith"? In regard to church growth in the last half-century, the numbers are very impressive. But did Rwanda's 70 percent Christian population stand in the way of genocide? Were Dutch Reformed Afrikaaners affronted by Apartheid? Are Nigeria's Christian millions stemming corruption?

What is "the salt and light" of African Christianity? African churches sing and shout. Africa's preachers mimic the hands-in-pockets antics of America's million dollar televangelists. African Christians boast they have left behind the "pagan world" of their traditions. But how much of this amounts to lives transformed by the Gospel?

As the Church of Jesus Christ in Africa, have we experienced the love of God, the grace of Christ, and the comfort of the Holy Spirit? Have we fully known the Creator's self-expression and joy in aspects of every African language and tradition? What have we remembered of our discarded folklore, our disregarded proverbs, and our maligned African wisdom? What has become of the best African sagas and tales? Have we ended up exchanging real African life stories transformed by the Father's unconditional love for a brand of Christianity which guarantees material prosperity or a narcotic solution to pain, or a politically correct vision of human development?

Jesus longs for Africans to waken to his call. Let us rouse ourselves from the moral drowsiness of a secularized, politically packaged, globalized, mechanized, or merchandised faith. A borrowed or "bright lights" Christianity is in reality darkness and death. There are but a few African saints whose lives and writings can point us to truly experience the concreteness and depth of Christ's love for Africa. Let us search out these bothers and sisters to help us discover afresh what it means that Africa matters to the Triune God of grace. And above all, let us pray to the Holy Spirit of comfort and truth to guide and empower us to choose life.

Scripture Meditation

I know your afflictions and your poverty—yet you are rich!
—REVELATION 2:9

Thought for the Day

Africa has become the home of all sorts of junk. Do we in the same way in the West gullibly embrace all forms of strange doctrines?
—FEMI ADELEYE

Prayer

Heavenly Father, forgive us for any way we may have caused our weaker brothers or sisters to stumble or fall. Strengthen us all to be your "overcomers" like the church at Smyrna.
—ALLEN GODDARD

JULY 30: THE SEVEN CHURCHES: PERGAMUM

The church at Pergamum is the third letter, addressed
to the overseer of the church in Revelation 2:12–17.

To the angel of the church in Pergamum write:

These are the words of him who has the sharp, double-edged sword. I know where you live—where Satan has his throne. Yet you remain true to my name. You did not renounce your faith in me, even in the days of Antipas, my faithful witness, who was put to death in your city—where Satan lives.

Nevertheless, I have a few things against you: You have people there who hold to the teaching of Balaam, who taught Balak to entice the Israelites to sin by eating food sacrificed to idols and by committing sexual immorality. Likewise you also have those who hold to the teaching of the Nicolaitans. Repent therefore! Otherwise, I will soon come to you and will fight against them with the sword of my mouth.

He who has an ear, let him hear what the Spirit says to the churches. To him who overcomes, I will give some of the hidden manna. I will also give him a white stone with a new name written on it, known only to him who receives it.

Scripture Meditation

I know where you live—where Satan has his throne. Yet you remain true to my name.

—REVELATION 2:13

Thought for the Day

Even in our efforts to live faithfully to God, we still fall short in testimony.

Prayer

*Grant, O Lord, that I may in future judge myself by this destruc-
tion, which you have wrought on my behalf, so that you may not
condemn me to that utter destruction which you will make of my
present life, and of the world.*

—BLAISE PASCAL

JULY 31: THE SEVEN CHURCHES: FIGHTING SATAN

---

*Reverend Peter Dugalescu, formerly a Baptist pastor of Timisoara in western
Romania, was an elected member of the National Assembly. In this personal
letter of August 19, 2002, Rev. Dugalescu reflected on the comfort given by
the letter to Pergamum during the events of the revolution in Romania,
to which he contributed significantly.*

Like those in the church of Pergamum who had been "true to
Christ's name," and some martyred for their faithful witness—most
Romanian Christians—after almost fifty years of atheist and Communist
dictatorship, had abandoned all hope of political change. The stronghold
of atheist ideology had taken over the minds of Romanians, in a brutal
and ruthless way. As in my case, every generation of children was systematically taught from kindergarten that God did not exist.

The supreme goal of Communism everywhere in the world was to
remove the idea that God ruled from the minds of people. Yet in an iron-
ical and paradoxical way, in Romania, like in Poland, the Church played
an important role in destroying the Communism.

Ever since August 1989, the pastor of the Hungarian Reformed
Church in Timisoara had started to speak openly in his sermons against
Communism and the village demolition program. His messages were

broadcast on Hungarian and Dutch Television. Therefore, the authorities decided to move Laszlo Tokes and his family back to his native village in Transylvania, under house arrest. Since he was not prepared to leave voluntarily, the rumor got around that the Police and the Secret Service were about to seize him and transport his family there.

On that morning before ten o'clock, I was there in front of the Reformed church in Timotei Cipariu Street with my son, Cristi, and a number of Baptist believers from Betel and the other churches. There we met a number of brothers from the Elim Pentecostal Church, as well as other people we did not know. A large number of Reformed believers were posted at the entrance and in the corridor to defend their pastor. The authorities arrived armed, and arrested him.

Nevertheless, the presence of the group in the street meant that the police hesitated to proceed immediately with their intention of evicting the pastor's family by force. They were waiting for us to leave first. But the crowd in the street kept on growing. I remember the Communist mayor, M.I., addressing us: "Romanians, go home, please! Why are you wasting your time here? If the Hungarians wish to stay, it's their business; it's their church. They're chauvinists, anyway. But you Romanians, go home!"

Many voices immediately answered him: "We're not leaving, we're not leaving!" It now seemed that the eviction of the pastor and his family had been postponed, but many of those present remained there throughout the night. Before nightfall, one of the young men from our church, Danut Gavra, who was then 24 years old, asked my permission to go to the Orthodox church nearby in Sinaia square to buy candles. Danut had come to help as a volunteer almost every single day during the two and a half years that it had taken to construct our new church building. He returned in ten minutes with a large packet of them, lit the first candle, then the people in the street lit the other candles, and began to sing, pray, and hold hands together. It was a fairylike spectacle never normally seen in a Communist country. None of us there realized this was the beginning of the end for Communism in Romania. We did not understand that within that small group of believers, with those hymns, candles and quiet prayers, lay the force that would start the most violent political revolution in Europe. Many people remained in front of the church overnight.

The next morning, December 16, I learned that many other people had joined those who had stayed throughout the night. The group of peaceful fighters was now large and was constantly growing [as the factory workers went on strike, swelling their ranks]. Although I had never met with Pastor Tokes personally before, he had heard about my recent persecutions and about the attempt of the Secret Police to take my life in a car accident. We knew each other in Christ. He sent two of the church elders secretly, to send more young people to the Hungarian Church to protest peacefully outside.

Scripture Meditation

To him who overcomes, I will give some of the hidden manna. I
will also give him a white stone with a new name written on it,
known only to him who receives it.

—REVELATION 2:17

Thought for the Day

We may never see the consequences of our small actions on behalf of God.

Prayer

Ready for all thy perfect will,
My acts of faith and love repeat,
Till death thine endless mercies seal,
And make the sacrifice complete.

—CHARLES WESLEY

AUGUST 1: THE SEVEN CHURCHES: FIGHTING SATAN (CONT.)

Peter Dugalescu proceeded to describe the Romanian revolution in Timisoara.

*O*nly God turned our religious renewal at a critical moment into a political revolution. It was after eight o'clock in the evening, December 16, and as I was coming from a revival service at our church, I could see two fire engines scattering the crowd with water and foam cannons. About 1500 people who had attended the service had left and were heading home. Seeing what was going on, most of them chose to join the demonstrators. Five of our young people were arrested and taken to the Police Headquarters.

On Sunday December 17, the entire population of Timisoara was on the streets. The people took over the City Hall, the County Council, and threw out of the window all the books, magazines, and paintings containing Communist symbols. On the street, they were all set on fire. They took all the flags and cut out the Communist symbol from the middle. All over Timisoara you could see people going around with flags with that hole in the middle—now symbolizing the emptiness of the Romanian souls, which Communist ideology never could fill.

Tanks and the armored cars and hundreds of soldiers were everywhere in town. For the Romanian army was sent to fight against its own people. After five o'clock on Sunday evening, the soldiers opened fire against the population simultaneously in different parts of the city. Two young women from our church were shot in the head. Danut, the young man who brought the candles to the Reformed Church, was also shot in the leg and his girlfriend walking with him was killed.

On December 20, the Army joined the revolutionaries. From the balcony of the Opera House, Timisoara was proclaimed the first free town in Romania. Then on December 21, the Revolution began in the capital, Bucharest.

On the morning of December 22, a priest or pastor was asked to come and address the crowd in Timisoara's Main Square from the balcony of the Opera House. After fifty years of Communism, the Romanian people needed desperately to hear about God. Since nobody volunteered to go up there and speak, I decided to address the crowd with the help of God.

My children did not approve of this at first, fearing for my life. Before some 200,000 people gathered in the Square, I said: "I am Pastor Peter Dugulescu and after fifty years of Communism I want to bring God back to you, to Romania! The Communists wanted to remove God from our families, from our minds, from our lives. They tried to take my life several times. Today I am alive because my God is alive!" In that moment, the crowd started to shout: "God exists! God exists!"

I demanded from the balcony: all Romanians should now have religious and economic freedom; that the Bible and prayer should be introduced in schools; and that Pastor Tokes should be released. About the same time in Bucharest, the dictator [Nicolae] Ceausescu was trying to escape with his life. But he was soon caught and condemned to death. In Timisoara, the crowd in the Opera Square kneeled down and uttered the Lord's Prayer, all in one voice. It felt like Timisoara and the whole [of] Romania was shaking in those moments. And they actually were. Within less than a day, Romania had new leadership.

Scripture Meditation

Our Father ... your kingdom come, your will be done on earth as it is in heaven.
—MATTHEW 6:9–10

Thought for the Day

What changes could the public recitation of the Lord's Prayer have in our secular society if we really prayed it faithfully?

Prayer

Help me this day to do some work of peace for you, perhaps to one I had thought to be my enemy.
—ALAN PATON

AUGUST 2: THE SEVEN CHURCHES: THYATIRA

The church at Thyatira is the fourth letter, addressed
to the overseer of the church in Revelation 2:18–29.

To the angel of the church in Thyatira write:

These are the words of the Son of God, whose eyes are like blazing fire and whose feet are like burnished bronze. I know your deeds, your love and faith, your service and perseverance, and that you are now doing more than you did at first.

Nevertheless, I have this against you: You tolerate that woman Jezebel, who calls herself a prophetess. By her teaching she misleads my servants into sexual immorality and the eating of food sacrificed to idols. I have given her time to repent of her immorality, but she is unwilling. So I will cast her on a bed of suffering, and I will make those who commit adultery with her suffer intensely, unless they repent of her ways. I will strike her children dead. Then all the churches will know that I am he who searches hearts and minds, and I will repay each of you according to your deeds. Now I say to the rest of you in Thyatira, to you who do not hold to her teaching and have not learned Satan's so-called deep secrets (I will not impose any other burden on you): Only hold on to what you have until I come.

To him who overcomes and does my will to the end, I will give authority over the nations—He will rule them with an iron scepter; he will dash them to pieces like pottery—just as I have received authority from my Father. I will also give him the morning star. He who has an ear, let him hear what the Spirit says to the churches.

Scripture Meditation

I know your deeds, your love and faith, your service and perseverance, and that you are now doing more than you did at first.

—REVELATION 2:19

Thought for the Day

Advancing techniques enable us to do far more than in the past, and therefore we need more spiritual discernment about what we "do."

Prayer

This is the most earnest desire of my soul, O Lord, to live in such a lively sense of my entire dependence upon your bounty, and of my unworthiness to enjoy the least of those blessings which you bestow on me ... so that I may never be puffed up with a vain opinion of myself.

—SIMON PATRICK

AUGUST 3: THE SEVEN CHURCHES: A PRAYERFUL RESPONSE ABOUT THE KOREAN CHURCH

Dr. Sang-Bok Kim (b. 1939), from Pyong Yang in North Korea, fled as an orphan refugee at age eleven into South Korea. President of the Evangelical Fellowship of Korea, and of Asia, he has pastored many churches, both in South Korea and in the United States. He responded to the situation in South Korea as analogous to that of Thyatira, in a letter written before the Lord on February 27, 2003.

Dear Lord,

Your commendation of Thyatira reminds me of the Korean church today vigorously pursuing ever-increasing works and service. However, we often see ourselves doing such action without love, faith, and patience. The church comprises 14.8 million out of the total population of 45 million, the largest national percentage in Asia. Over 80,000 pastors serve 40,000 churches, with 166 mission agencies serving 15 countries, with 12,000 missionaries. This is the largest national effort, second only to the United States. Of the eleven largest mega-congregations in the world, ten are in Seoul, which has also the largest seminaries among its two hundred and eighty theological colleges. Some of the largest evangelistic gatherings in the history of the Church have been held in Korea, together with early morning prayer meetings, in churches as well as on mountains. Thousands of home groups have Bible study. From its youth organizations, over two thousand mission candidates are recruited annually.

However, Lord, you see the many individual agendas and self-interest, the moral failure of prominent leaders, and the way we live full of compromises. For we live religiously on Sundays, but like our secular society the rest of the week. We need forgiveness also, O Lord, for our pride in statistical growth, our wealth, our impressive buildings, and our many schisms—at least one hundred different Presbyterian denominations alone! We deplore the patterns of domineering leadership, legalism, inadequate discipleship, low ethical standards, bribery and corruption, and the neglect of social wrongs.

We confess also, O Lord, that we have "Jezebel and her followers" in our midst, with some 600,000 shamanistic practitioners, a cult of fatalism, followers of Moon Sun Myung, and much else that is pagan and secular. We have a culture of idolatry, as in North Korea where the dead president Kim Il Sung is still worshipped as a god.

Yet we thank you, O God, for the remnant of your children, wholly committed to you, who seek to overcome and do your will to the end.

Scripture Meditation

To him that overcomes and does my will to the end, I will give authority over the nations.
—REVELATION 2:26

Thought for the Day

In an age of mass culture, personal faith is more vital than ever.

Prayer

Lord, we want to see the transforming reality of Christian faith in our lives, not mere oral confessions. Amen.

—Sang-Bok Kim

AUGUST 4: THE SEVEN CHURCHES: SARDIS

The church at Sardis is the fifth letter, addressed to the overseer of the church in Revelation 3:1–6.

To the angel of the church in Sardis write:

These are the words of him who holds the seven spirits of God and the seven stars. I know your deeds; you have a reputation of being alive, but you are dead. Wake up! Strengthen what remains and is about to die, for I have not found your deeds complete in the sight of my God. Remember, therefore, what you have received and heard; obey it, and repent. But if you do not wake up, I will come like a thief, and you will not know at what time I will come to you.

Yet you have a few people in Sardis who have not soiled their clothes. They will walk with me, dressed in white, for they are worthy. He who overcomes will, like them, be dressed in white. I will never blot out his name from the book of life, but will acknowledge his name before my Father and his angels. He who has an ear, let him hear what the Spirit says to the churches.

Scripture Meditation

You have a reputation for being alive, but you are dead.

—Revelation 3:1

Thought for the Day

The crowd in untruth is always an indictment of consensus.

Prayer

We call you our Redeemer and Savior because you save us from our empty, trivial existence.

—SØREN KIERKEGAARD

AUGUST 5: THE SEVEN CHURCHES: AN AUSTRALIAN RESPONSE TO SARDIS

The Rev. Dr. Paul Barnett (b. 1935) has been bishop of North Sydney and is now senior fellow in the Institute of Ancient Documents Research Centre, Macquarrie University, New South Wales, Australia. Reverend Dr. Barnett is also a teaching fellow of Moore College, Sydney, Australia. His letter is dated September 25, 2003.

ord Jesus,

Your words came as a sharp rebuke to us.

We Christians in Australia are only a minority but we have a name for being alive. It's true that brave missionaries from "down under" have done great work in Africa and Asia. Many of these churches in the developing world are indebted to our messengers who have gone there.

It's also true that Billy Graham's ministry in Australian cities in 1959 had a huge impact. Work among tertiary students is strong and good. Our seminaries and Bible colleges are blessed with overflowing numbers. We have many fine church leaders and preachers.

And yet …

We are too much like the Sardisians.

We have a name based on how things appear. But the truth is that things are not what they appear. We are too much like our fellow Australians—comfortable and affluent. We know our theology but we are sometimes cold-hearted and lack genuine humanity. Our preoccupation with truth is not matched by a concern to love one another or our fellow Australians. We have a name for being "political" and for being ruthless with one another.

Not surprisingly our fellow Australians don't think much of us. Many have written us off as irrelevant to their lives. In writing us off they have written you off, too.

So, Lord, we will "wake up" as you have said we must. Please help us to overcome our exalted view of ourselves and face the facts!

Scripture Meditation

Wake up! Strengthen what remains and is about to die.
—REVELATION 3:2

Thought for the Day

Our name as "Christians" may not mean very much. Why?

Prayer

Thank you, O Lord, for promising us a fresh start for keeping our names in your book of life.
—PAUL BARNETT

AUGUST 6: THE SEVEN CHURCHES: PHILADELPHIA

The church at Philadelphia is the sixth letter, addressed
to the overseer of the church in Revelation 3:7–13.

To the angel of the church in Philadelphia write:

These are the words of him who is holy and true, who holds the key of David. What he opens no one can shut, and what he shuts no one can open. I know your deeds. See, I have placed before you an open door that no one can shut. I know that you have little strength, yet you have kept my word and have not denied my name. I will make those who are of the synagogue of Satan, who claim to be Jews though they are not, but are liars—I will make them come and fall down at your feet and acknowledge that I have loved you. Since you have kept my command to endure patiently, I will also keep you from the hour of trial that is going to come upon the whole world to test those who live on the earth.

I am coming soon. Hold on to what you have, so that no one will take your crown. Him who overcomes I will make a pillar in the temple of my God. Never again will he leave it. I will write on him the name of my God and the name of the city of my God, the new Jerusalem, which is coming down out of heaven from my God; and I will also write on him my new name. He who has an ear, let him hear what the Spirit says to the churches.

Scripture Meditation

I know that you have little strength, yet you have kept my word
and have not denied my name.

—REVELATION 3:8

Thought for the Day

In God's sight faithfulness is more important than success.

Prayer

Lord, help me never to forget that a desire for great things is generally a delusion of self-love. Whereas faithfulness in little things is daily required, and for these I can constantly seek your abiding help and presence.

—JEAN NICOLAS GROU

AUGUST 7: THE SEVEN CHURCHES: COMMENTS ON PHILADELPHIA

Reverend Dr. J. I. Packer (b. 1927), Board of Governors' professor of systematic theology at Regent College, Vancouver, Canada, is a well-known theologian, church leader, and writer. On September 23, 2002, he responded to the letter to Philadelphia, as if he were a member of that church.

Dear John,

We, the Philadelphian church of Jesus Christ, write to acknowledge with a letter the letter that you sent us on Christ's behalf—a staggering letter indeed; well might one call it Revelation—and we want to thank you, our sometime teacher, for the devoted and obviously demanding service that you rendered as secretary to the Savior, transcribing as you did all that you heard and saw during those fantastic hours of vision. We had it all read out to us in church, just as you directed, and we are trying now to take it to heart. We have held special praise and prayer gatherings to express to Jesus himself our response to his words, and we thought we should write to you as well to tell you what effect his letter has had.

We saw that it came to us as a sort of report card from the Lord who loves us, and died for us, and now lives for us, and is always with us and knows everything about us and searches us through and through, missing nothing. As we heard his rebukes to other churches read out, we braced ourselves for something similar, but to our amazement, his letter mentioned none of our shortcomings and was encouragement all the way.

We found it startling and humbling to be praised for faithful endurance by the Master himself, but soon we realized what he was doing. We motivate our children by praising them for what we ourselves have helped them to do, so that they will want to do it again, and be helped to do it by that very wanting. Knowing, as he says, and as you know too, that we are a small fellowship who do not seem to have much effect on anything or anybody, Jesus, who has helped us to be faithful thus far, is motivating us for the future, and we are taking the point. (After all, as you yourself used to tell us, we are all little children really before the Lord, aren't we?)

We saw that it was our encouragement too that Jesus said he had set before us an open door. We were unsure whether that meant for access to heaven or for reaching out with the gospel, so we have resolved to take it in both senses, so as to be on the safe side.

His promise to make the obstructionists who trouble us so much realize that we are the ones he loves put new heart into us. Keeping them at bay in their arrogance and hostility has been a draining business. And to be told that our little church will be shielded somewhat as this empire-building persecution builds up was a wonderful mercy.

All of us were ecstatic—the word is not too strong—at Jesus' final promises to overcomers, which fired our hearts and our imaginations equally. Whether sheep enjoy being branded we don't know, but the thought of Jesus, who loves us, saved us, and owns us, grasping hold of us to brand us with the Father's name—new Jerusalem's name—and his own new name, whatever that is, so identifying us as his own for ever, and anchoring us as pillars in God's temple, so as to be always as close to him as one can be, left us literally weeping for joy.

As a past pastor to us, we thought you would like to know this. Now may Jesus encourage you there in exile in Patmos, as he has encouraged us here in Philadelphia.

Scripture Meditation

I have loved you.

—REVELATION 3:9

Thought for the Day

What is the Spirit saying through this letter to our church? And to us?

Prayer

O God, who has prepared for those who love thee such good things as pass man's understanding; Pour into our hearts such love towards thee, that we, loving thee in all things, may obtain thy promises, which exceed all we can desire.

—COLLECT FOR THE SIXTH SUNDAY AFTER EASTER, *THE BOOK OF COMMON PRAYER*

AUGUST 8: THE SEVEN CHURCHES: LAODICEA

The church at Laodicea is the seventh letter, addressed to the overseer of the church in Revelation 3:14–22.

To the angel of the church in Laodicea write:

These are the words of the Amen, the faithful and true witness, the ruler of God's creation. I know your deeds, that you are neither cold nor hot. I wish you were either one or the other! So, because you are luke-warm—neither hot nor cold—I am about to spit you out of my mouth. You say, "I am rich; I have acquired wealth and do not need a thing." But you do not realize that you are wretched, pitiful, poor, blind and naked. I counsel you to buy from me gold refined in the fire, so you can become rich; and white clothes to wear, so you can cover your shameful naked-ness; and salve to put on your eyes, so you can see.

Those whom I love I rebuke and discipline. So be earnest, and repent.

Here I am! I stand at the door and knock. If anyone hears my voice and opens the door, I will come in and eat with him, and he with me.

To him who overcomes, I will give the right to sit with me on my throne, just as I overcame and sat down with my Father on his throne. He who has an ear, let him hear what the Spirit says to the churches.

Scripture Meditation

He who has an ear, let him hear what the Spirit says to the churches.
—REVELATION 3:22

Thought for the Day

When we read such an epistle, it is the ruler of all creation who speaks directly to us.

Prayer

Merciful Lord, we beseech thee to cast thy bright beams of light upon thy Church, that being enlightened by the doctrine of thy blessed Apostle and Evangelist Saint John may so walk in the light of thy truth, that it may attain at length to the fullness of everlasting light; through Jesus Christ our Lord. Amen.
—COLLECT FOR ST. JOHN'S DAY, DEC. 27, *THE BOOK OF COMMON PRAYER*

AUGUST 9: THE SEVEN CHURCHES: COMMENTS ON LAODICEA

*Reverend M. Craig Barnes (b. 1956) was the senior pastor of the National
Presbyterian Church, Washington, DC, when he wrote this response
in September 2002. He is now professor of theology
at Pittsburgh Theological Seminary.*

Laodicea was a very impressive town. It was prosperous, educated, and on the cutting edge of technology. It only had one small problem—lousy drinking water.

The town wasn't near a natural supply of fresh water, so the city engineers constructed a stone aqueduct to carry cold water from a town six miles to the south. And from a town in the north, hot water flowed down from the natural hot springs. Like many good engineering ideas, though, this one didn't quite work. By the time the water arrived into town, the cold water had warmed up and the hot water had cooled down. So all the water in Laodicea was lukewarm. That's how the Lord describes the Laodicean's commitment to him.

Imagine discovering someone's commitment to you is lukewarm? It's like taking a big gulp from a cup of coffee that has sat on the desk all day. It leaves such an awful taste in the mouth that Jesus said he was just looking for a good place to throw up.

As with most relationships, things between Jesus and the Laodiceans didn't start bad. Like the water that started out hot up north, the Christians in Laodicea began with hot faith, but along the way things cooled down. Their wealth, commerce, education, technology, and their hard work to build a better life had distracted them from following Jesus.

That is the great danger for the American church today. The problem of living in a secular culture is not that our teachers cannot pray out loud in school, or that we cannot put the Ten Commandments in our courts of law. No, the problem is that our very secular resolve to get things just right distracts us from the true passions of the soul.

The assumption today is that if we just try hard enough, we can get the life of our dreams. This has the effect of constantly preoccupying us with what is wrong. Don't you think this water thing drove the Laodiceans crazy? The editorials of the local paper must have constantly pontificated about this public embarrassment that the city's leaders couldn't fix. It was a great town. It had an incredible opportunity to lead the empire in charity and compassion, but it was too obsessed with making improvements. And the church did nothing to teach the people how to direct their passions toward the important things in life. Things like building the kingdom of Christ. The frightening thing is that Jesus held the church accountable for the attitude of the city.

Scripture Meditation

Because you are lukewarm—neither hot nor cold—I am about to spit you out of my mouth.

—REVELATION 3:16

Thought for the Day

The church isn't called to mimic the culture's idolatry of excellence. It's called to fall in love with Jesus.

Prayer

O God, as your Son was dying to love us, so may our churches know how to lose their lives in acts of passion for him.

—M. CRAIG BARNES

AUGUST 10: THE BOOK OF REVELATION: THE LAMB UPON THE THRONE

Homiletics professor Darrell Johnson wrote a second letter on what he found in the book of Revelation. It was dated August 15, 2002.

*D*ear Jim,

You asked me to further explain why the last book of the Bible, the letter entitled "The Revelation of Jesus Christ," has got such a hold on me. It has to do with the letter's central message. *"Things are not as they seem: the Lamb is on the Throne."* That there is a Throne is good news enough. There is a central headquarters; there is a control center of the universe; there is a seat of authority. And it is occupied! It is not up for grabs! Oh, it so often feels otherwise! It so often feels that headquarters is vacant, that no one is at the control panel. Or worse yet, that there has been a coup, that the powers of chaos and evil have stormed the compound and taken over.

"Look!" says John, "a throne was standing in heaven, and One sitting on the throne" (Rev. 4:2). Shout it from the mountaintops! We need not be afraid: there is a Throne, and Someone is sitting on it. Again, this is good news enough.

But there is more. John sees in the right hand of the One sitting on the Throne a scroll, sealed up with seven seals (5:1). He hears a strong angel proclaiming with a loud voice, "Who is worthy to open the scroll and break its seals?" (5:2). Who indeed? The scroll contains God's plan for history, God's plan for bringing the Kingdom of the heavens to earth, God's plan for rectifying all that is wrong in creation. Who is worthy to reveal the plan and then execute it on the stage of history? John says that the angel found no one—"in heaven or on the earth or under the earth" (5:3)—worthy to open the scroll. And John weeps "greatly" (5:4). So does our world. I can hear it in the music.

Then we come to the dramatic moment of the vision. Whenever I am reading the text out loud it is here that tears begin to well up in my eyes and my voice begins to crack. John says, "One of the elders said to me 'stop weeping: look, the Lion that is from the tribe of Judah ... has overcome so as to open the scroll and its seven seals'" (5:5). Glory! as our Pentecostal friends say. Someone is worthy to grasp the secret of history and put it into effect! The lion has overcome. And here is why the tears begin to flow.

John says then he turned around, presumably to see the Lion. But to his surprise, he sees a Lamb "as if slain" (5:6), or more accurately, "as if slaughtered." "The Lion has overcome ... and I saw a Lamb." The Lion is the image of superior strength and power overcoming by slaughtering its opponents. The Lamb is the image of trusting vulnerability. "The Lion has overcome … and I saw a Lamb, as if slaughtered." The lion overcomes by becoming a Lamb, a little Lamb (*arnion* in Greek), who through servant love even for his enemies, overcomes by being slaughtered by his enemies.

That is the secret of history. That is the message of the scroll. Almighty God brings the Kingdom of the heavens to earth through sacrificial love.

Scripture Meditation

Worthy is the Lamb, who was slain, to receive power and wealth and wisdom and strength and honor and glory and praise!
—REVELATION 5:12

Thought for the Day

God is not as he seems to be, to those who do not know the Lamb that was slain.

Prayer

To him who sits on the throne and to the Lamb be praise and honor and glory and power, for ever and ever.
—REVELATION 5:13

AUGUST 11: THE BOOK OF REVELATION: THE LAMB UPON THE THRONE
(CONT.)

Darrell Johnson continued with a second letter on the book of Revelation.

*A*ll this first began to make sense to me during our time in the Philippines, living through the so-called "People Power Revolution" of 1986. Cory Aquino, the widow of slain Senator Benito Aquino, dared to run for the office of President against the incumbent Ferdinand Marcos. A "simple housewife," as she called herself, with no prior political experience, with no power structure around her, supported only by ordinary un-armed citizens, topples an entrenched dictatorship, supported by a massive military machine (and by the United States). Cory entered into the battle knowing the secret: the Lion does not win by being a Lion. Lion-ness is foolishness and weakness. Oh, it looks like strength and wisdom. But things are not as they seem.

Three and a half years before she challenged Mr. Marcos, the forces of Mr. Marcos killed her husband. Benito had flown back to the Philippines from the United States knowing full well that his life was in danger. But he also knew the secret. As he stepped off the plane, he was shot, falling dead on the airport tarmac. In his coat pocket was the speech he was to deliver to the writing press-corps. Here is the opening line. "The willing sacrifice of an innocent victim is the most powerful response to insolent tyranny God or man has ever dreamed of." In the moment Benito Aquino was murdered, he overcame. The moment the forces of Mr. Marcos murdered Benito, they were defeated.

The Lion gets to the Throne, not by being a Lion, but by being a Lamb, and giving himself in self-emptying love. "In the middle of the throne," says John (5:6). The Lamb *stands* in service, in the very middle of the Throne. Which means he stands in the very middle of the One who *sits* sovereignly on the Throne. At the center of realty, in the very heart of the Holy, Almighty Creator is the Lamb.

That is why the letter has such a hold on me. The Lamb has a hold on me!

I look forward to more encounters in the days to come. God grant us grace to go the way of the Lamb.

Darrell

Scripture Meditation

I wept and I wept because no one was found who was worthy to open the scroll or look inside.

—REVELATION 5:4

Thought for the Day

When I am weak, then I am made strong.

Prayer

You are worthy to take the scroll and to open its seals, because you were slain, and with your blood you purchased men for God from every tribe and language and people and nation.

—REVELATION 5:9

ISSUES BETWEEN CHRISTIANS, JEWS, AND SECULARISTS

AUGUST 12: PREACHING THE GOSPEL—PROCLAIMING THE "END TIMES"

St. Vincent Ferrer (1350–1418) was born in Valencia, Spain, entered the Order of Preachers at age eighteen, and devoted his life to preaching the Word of God within the schismatic Church of his time, inspired to do so by the apocalyptic warnings of the New Testament.

𝒯o our most holy Lord, Benedict XIII, Pope,

Brother Vincent Ferrer, Preacher, a useless servant in regard to both preaching and actions, places himself at the feet of His Holiness.

The Apostle Paul, after fulfilling the mission entrusted to him in preaching the gospel, constrained by revelation, went up to Jerusalem to confer with Peter and the rest. As he himself tells us in the epistle to the Galatians chapter two.... The Apostles also returned from their God-given mission of preaching, in which they had diligently exercised themselves, and "coming together unto Jesus, related to him all the things they had done and taught," as we read in the sixth chapter of the gospel according to Saint Mark.... So this is what I have preached for so long throughout the world, especially in regard to the Antichrist and the end of the world....

Firstly, I preach that the death of Antichrist and the end of the world will occur at the same time.... Secondly, I conclude that the time of the birth of the Antichrist will be hidden from mankind.... Thirdly, that the coming of Antichrist and the end of the world are drawing near.... Fourthly, I conclude that the time of Antichrist and the end of the world will take place in a short space of time, mercifully short and exceedingly quickly.

Our Lord Jesus Christ, foreknowing that this doctrine will be unacceptable to carnal persons and the lovers of this world, said in the Gospel of Saint Luke: "And as it was in the days of Noah, so shall it be also in the days of the Son of Man. They did eat, they drank, they married wives, they were given in marriage, until the day that Noah entered into the ark, and the flood came, and destroyed them all" (17:26–27 KJV).

"It was the same in the days of Lot. People were eating and drinking, buying and selling, planting and building. But the day that Lot left Sodom, fire and sulfur rained down from heaven and destroyed them all. It will be just like this on the day the Son of Man is revealed. On that day no one who is on the roof of his house, with his goods inside, should go down to get them. Likewise, no one in the field should go back for anything. Remember Lot's wife!" (vv. 30–32).

Again in the First Epistle to the Thessalonians, we read: "But concerning the times and seasons, brethren, you have no need that I should write to you. For you yourselves know perfectly that the day of the Lord will come as a thief in the night" (5:1–2).

This, most Holy Father, is what I am preaching concerning the time of Antichrist and the end of the world, subject to the correction and determination of Your Holiness, whom may the Most High preserve.

Scripture Meditation

Blessed is the one who reads the words of this prophecy, and blessed are those who hear it and take to heart what is written in it.

—REVELATION 1:3

Thought for the Day

It is easy to be taken with literal statements and lose sight of the moral significance of those same statements.

Prayer

Amen. Come, Lord Jesus. The grace of the Lord Jesus be with God's people. Amen.

—REVELATION 22:20–21

AUGUST 13: FACING A NEW SENSE OF VULNERABILITY,
PERSONAL AND GLOBAL

---

*Dr. Olav Slaymaker (b. 1939) was professor of geography at the University of
British Columbia and chairman of South-North studies at the Liu Centre
for the Study of Global Issues. He wrote on August 20, 2002.*

*M*uch of the novelty of our situation at the start of the twenty-first
century can be summarized as a new sense of personal insecurity or vulnerability. The events of September 11, 2001, underlined this widespread
fear. There are many different elements, which are compounding this
sense of vulnerability. There is a new consciousness of the fragility of
planet Earth under direct attack by human alteration of its surface; the
size and rate of growth of the Earth's population is without precedent in
human history; the rate of reduction of Earth's biodiversity and of its cultural diversity is unique; there is a pervasive sense of helplessness in face
of economic globalization; the threat of global contagious disease is real;
there is a continuing proliferation of armed conflict leading to massive
human migration and there is an urgent sense of the inadequacy of the
mechanisms of global governance.

None of these tendencies towards a sense of personal insecurity has
been entirely absent in the past and the antidote then, as now, is "The
fear of the Lord," which produces a necessary humility as well as security of heart. But the overwhelming sense is that there has never been a
time when all these elements have been so threatening at one and the
same time, just when society has never been more secularized, that is acting atheistically. So to what extent do we, as members of the Christian
community, take seriously the other requirement to love our neighbor?
To what extent are we known as those who give priority to the poor? Is
there any evidence of the kind of generosity to the poorest of the poor
(namely slaves) that was the hallmark of early nineteenth century
Christians? To what extent are we identified as a generous community?
It might well be that an increase in the budget for Overseas
Development Assistance (now at an all time low since the policy was initiated in 1945) would produce less international tension than the
obsessive chasing of terrorists, as presently practiced and condoned by

the so-called leaders of the Western Christian world. Perhaps we need to ponder afresh over the words of the psalmist.

Scripture Meditation

Blessed is the man who fears the LORD, who finds great delight in his commands.... He will have no fear of bad news; his heart is steadfast, trusting in the Lord. His heart is secure, he will have no fear.... He has scattered abroad his gifts to the poor.
—PSALM 112:1, 7–9

Thought for the Day

Are all these global problems not pointing us to recognize the need of the sovereignty of God at every level of human reality, instead of accepting the intensification of the secular spirit?

Prayer

O Lord my God, fountain of all true and holy love; who has made me, and preserved me, that I might love you ... that humility may be my sanctuary, and your service the joy of my soul, and death itself the entrance of eternal life. Amen.
—JEREMY TAYLOR

AUGUST 14: A CHRISTIAN LIVING IN THE "PROMISED LAND"

*Karen Mulle (b. 1959) is an American nurse who left a successful medical
career to minister to Arab children in Lebanon. From where she is placed,
the political ambitions of "Christian Zionism," of interpreting biblical
prophecy as being fulfilled by the return of the Jews to Palestine to create
the state of Israel, put her own life in jeopardy. She wrote to
several friends on July 28, 2002.*

It wasn't until I was twenty-two or more that I even heard about a modern Palestinian State. A Palestinian Christian attending our church stood up one Sunday and with tears in his eyes asked for prayer for his displaced people. I was struck by the love and longing in his voice. *Where is Palestine?* I wondered. I thought it all belonged to Israel. Wasn't that a country from Old Testament times? Why had I never heard of modern day Palestine before? My ignorance was lamentable, but likely it still reflects the ignorance of many in the U.S.

It wasn't until many years later that I heard the whole story of Palestine and their being driven from their land at the will of newly established Israel, the result of Western sympathy (and guilt?) after World War II.

Today, I live and work in Lebanon. God, our loving Father and Lord, has sent me here to counsel children at a Christian school in Sidon. This school is situated between two Palestinian refugee camps. One camp overflows into my own neighborhood, and I find myself aching for their plight and frustrated that popular American "dispensational" theology actually supports Israel's oppression. I am equally frustrated at the lack of wisdom and insight on the Palestinian side at the futility and inconsistency of the suicide bombings—why must the abused abuse others? I am not ignorant of the grievances on both sides. Innocents have been brutally killed in bombings and fear reigns all over Palestine and Israel.

Are these the last days? Has Israel been promised the land again? Are we as believers supposed to rally around Israel as the winning team and ignore the injustice and sin that is called "holy war" on both sides? By insisting that this is all prophetic fulfillment we too claim a holy war and the crusades rage again. The folly of the Pharisees is repeated.

Will we never learn? Have we forsaken Christ for a return to the law?

For only in Christ are we set free from sin and death. Christ alone is the Promised Land. The Word made Flesh is the Promise made Real. Jews and Arabs alike do not need the land religiously, they need Christ. God's apocalypse in history is not ours to choreograph—it is his to bring about in his time (Acts 1:6–7).

Jesus' first coming was looked for literally and missed (John 7:41–42). He will come again to take his own but will he find faithful witnesses or children preoccupied with political predictions? Graciously he will take all his children in spite of our ongoing foolishness—we have the luxury and grace of knowing Jesus, but what of our Arab and Jewish friends who don't know Christ? Let us be ministers of reconciliation in our actions—seeking to reconcile the lost to Christ, the true Prince of Peace.

A favorite Arab hymn sings out: Peace, Peace to the people of the Lord in every place. Yes, this can occur wherever Jesus dwells within our hearts.

Scripture Meditation

Christ is the end of the law so that there may be righteousness for everyone who believes.

—ROMANS 10:4

Thought for the Day

Even Jewish humanists like Martin Buber could not accept political Zionism. On what grounds can Christians do so now?

Prayer

Righteous Father, though the world does not know you, I know you, and they know that you have sent me. I have made you known to them, and will continue to make you known in order that the love you have for me may be in them and that I myself may be in them.

—JOHN 17:25–26

AUGUST 15: SEEING CHRISTIANITY AS A JEW

The following exchange of letters was between two German soldiers during World War I. Franz Rosenzweig (1886–1929) was a Jew serving as a gunner in Macedonia. His friend Eugen Rosenstock-Huessy (1888–1973), an officer at the Western front and also a Jew, became a Christian at age sixteen. Their exchange has been called "one of the most important religious documents of our age." Both saw that without educated passions, German academic idealism would drag the world irresponsibly into moral chaos. As early as 1910, Rosenstock had anticipated that such irresponsible "intellectual neutrality" would lead to major world disasters, as indeed the Jewish Holocaust proved to be. Rosenzweig wrote the following letter to Rosenstock sometime in September 1916.

*D*ear Eugen,

I grant you frankly everything that you say about the public side of religion, right up to the details of your way of putting it. I have also lived like that since then, and I can say that it is only now that I know what life—with people—means [to live personally, not just nominally as a Jew]. Only don't you grumble about the Enlightenment; it is not its fault that inertia stuffed its discoveries into cushions, instead of industrious people getting to work on them.... You make it difficult for me ... for you once rightly compelled me in Leipzig, in 1913, when you did not seriously believe me, and did not allow anything I said to be my own words, until I myself was horrified [at my own religious complacency]....

But now, here you are ... directly hindering me from treating my Judaism in the first person, in that you call yourself a Jew too. That is to me equally intolerable, emotionally and intellectually. For me, you can be nothing else but a Christian: the emptiest Jew, cut off root and branch, and a Jew only in the legal sense is still an object of concern to me as a Jew, but you are not....

This "individual Jew" does not become a Christian as a Jew, but if he becomes one after heart-searching ... just as it were as a heathen, but as a heathen before the Fall.... For him the preaching of the Cross was not really a stumbling block, for he was never a Jew.... Nor was the Cross really foolishness, since as I am here presenting him—he was never properly a Greek. Thus there is a Christian naïveté in such people, a Johannine desire to take the world for "a world that is by nature Christian."

Scripture Meditation

What advantage, then, is there in being a Jew, or what value is there in circumcision? Much in every way! First of all, they have been entrusted with the very words of God.
—ROMANS 3:1–2

Thought for the Day

Yahweh is as "personal" in the Old Testament as Jesus Christ is in the New Testament. Both demand of us a personal faith!

Prayer

Brothers, my heart's desire and prayer to God for the Israelites is that they may be saved.
—ROMANS 10:1

AUGUST 16: "THE STUBBORNNESS OF THE JEWS"
IS ITSELF A CHRISTIAN DOGMA

Eugen Rosenstock-Huessy replied to his friend, Franz Rosenzweig on October 4, 1916, in a very long epistle, only a small part of which is quoted here, together with a response from Franz.

*D*ear Franz,

You give me every time a veritable breakfast of caviar. I know people, indeed, with whom one can be concerned with truth and find truth, but "truth" in a form corresponding to the present position of scholarship: that is something only the learned can enjoy, and it is therefore a rare treat. Moreover, you overestimate, unfortunately, the Christian in me. I am not Paul of Tarsus—unfortunately not. Before you, my mission comes to a halt. You are the human individual, one whose particular quality I recognize in spite of his being "outside Christianity." I see Judaism just as you prescribe it to the "Church" [as a form of nominalism] and to yourself—as for me, the revelation of God in the world from day to day, far from being a mere abstract, metaphorical conception in the background, becomes more and more a present reality here and now.

The Jews are so much the chosen people, and the Old Testament is so much the book of the law of the Father, just as the New is the book of the love of the children, (Abraham and Christ sacrifice the two poles, on the one hand the Father, on the other the Son), that altogether the Church needs "its Jews" to strengthen its own truth. The stubbornness of the Jews is, so to speak, a Christian dogma. But is it, can it also be, a Jewish one? That is the fence I do not see you taking....

[Franz responded immediately the next day as follows.]

You could have formulated your objection still more strongly; I should like perhaps later to do it for you. But first of all, let's stick to your formulation. Yes, the stubbornness of the Jews is a Christian dogma. So much so that the Church, after she had built up the substantial part of her particular dogma—the part having to do with God and Man—in the first century, during the whole of the second century turned aside to lay down the "second dogma" (the formal part of her dogma, i.e. her historical consciousness of herself). And in its after-effects this process continued through the third and fourth centuries and beyond: and Augustine applied himself personally to it, though the Church had already for some time been moving away from it. That is, it had become a Church of writings or rather of tradition, instead of spirit; in other words, it was becoming exactly the Church that history knows....

Thus, in the firm establishment of the Old Testament in the Canon, and in the building of the Church on this double scripture (Old and New Testament), the stubbornness of the Jews is in fact brought out as the other half of the Christian dogma [along with its formal consciousness of itself in the dogma of the Church—if we may point to the creed as "the dogma of Christianity"]. But could this same idea (that of the stubbornness of the Jews) also be Jewish dogma? Yes, it could be, and in fact it is. But this Jewish consciousness of being rejected has a quite different place in our dogmatic system, and would correspond to a Christian consciousness of being chosen to rule, a consciousness that is in fact present beyond any doubt.

Scripture Meditation

Christ is the end of the law.... "The word is near you; it is in your mouth and in your heart," that is, the word of faith.
—Romans 10:4, 8

Thought for the Day

True faith in God is distorted through philosophical abstraction, whether it be the "hellenization of Judaism" or the contemporary rationalism of Christendom.

Prayer

Fire! The God of Abraham, the God of Isaac, the God of Jacob. Not of the philosophers and intellectuals. Certitude, feeling, joy, peace. The God of Jesus Christ. My God and your God.
—Blaise Pascal

AUGUST 17: NATURE AND REVELATION

To the previous outpouring from his philosophical friend,
Eugen Rosenstock-Huessy defended vigorously the central
importance of Christian faith being personal.

*D*ear Franz …

You have a way of asking me things in such a correct, impersonal way that I stand nonplussed. I have never been asked anything like that before, and so I do not know how to answer … for I don't think systematically, but from need, and I follow my needs one by one. And this temporal character in my thinking is in fact the Alpha and Omega from which I grasp everything afresh. Speech reflects this mode of procedure, even for someone who has been infected by philosophy. For that reason I used to prefer to talk of speech rather than about reason.

The question you put, "Nature and Revelation," I can only understand as "natural understanding" and revelation. Nature and Revelation are not comparable. Natural Understanding, then, knows front and back, left hand, right hand, and helps itself in this enclosure with a net of analogies. It makes comparisons and thus limps from one place to the next in this vast space … [Rosenstock later called this "spatial thinking," filling the void like a mathematician or physicist with abstract theorems].

The resolution not to take one's position in this quarter of space as the center of knowledge, but as conditioned from above—this renunciation of being no longer the hub of the universe—is no longer a matter of the natural human understanding, but is the means within us that makes revelation to, in, and for us possible. [Friedrich David] Schliermacher's "absolute dependence," therefore, ought no longer to be comprehended in an external way as a feeling of fate, but should be understood as an illumination.

However, since thought and speech constitute a continuous mutual relation of giving and receiving, and since both are a universal gift to the human race, for this twofold relation a double process is possible. You can believe in your autonomy. The Kantians [i.e., those who follow Immanuel Kant in his philosophical premises] believe in a senseless exaggeration of the autonomy of thought. The actual fact of seeing, on the contrary, testifies only to the autonomy of the married couple, speech and reason. For the self-confidence of reason and trust in speech are both equally essential to a person who wants to have knowledge.

But all such autonomous knowledge is without standards, supported only by experience, and without any Archimedian fulcrum. I call this "luxuriating" thinking, for it behaves like a weed. It doesn't die down. It comprehends gaily without any idea of there being a "measure of all things," and it is ingenuous about itself. This kind of knowledge lives in all ages…. Its mightiest outbreak is that of 1789 [with the enthronement of the Goddess of Reason, in the French Revolution]. This has led to a complete undermining of Protestant Christianity, which today often threatens to become a mere theism without mediator, without conversion, without that bond from heaven to earth which makes space stable, like a rock of bronze, through the concept of Above.

Scripture Meditation

My message and my preaching were not with wise and persuasive words, but with a demonstration of the Spirit's power, so that your faith might not rest on men's wisdom, but on God's power.
— I CORINTHIANS 2:4–5

Thought for the Day

The "Autonomous Thinker" is closed in from ever being open to the possibility of divine revelation.

Prayer

Open my eyes that I may see wonderful things in your law.
—PSALM 119:18

AUGUST 18: CHRISTIAN REVELATION IS PERSONAL

Eugen Rosenstock-Huessy concluded the previous letter by arguing that the
rationalistic defenses of both Judaism and Protestantism
are equally erroneous ways of thinking.

ear Franz,

The Protestants, even the most radical of biblical critics, believe they can read the New Testament without the Holy Spirit of the Church, and they read it not with the help of the last two thousand years, but against and without it. Thus, the collective mind deals in the same way with time and space. It likes here, too, to forget the standard—that is, the reckoning of time from "the year of our Lord." Just as in space it ends by having nothing above it, so it lives out its subjective life without the myth of the reckoning of time, without the profound saying: "If they were not dead, they would still be living today."

To this end, it has created the vacuum space of concepts with which it fabricates for itself an artistic drop scene for its acrobatics out of petrified and paper linguistic and intellectual properties. If it did not do so, it would have to go raving mad. Because for the natural mind an infinite regression unfolds itself; sensing this and trembling, it clings to its concrete base, the intellectual arena, catching on to its own creation, which of course had been planked down by preceding thinkers, much older subjects, but nonetheless just as much highly subjective. Fear for the destruction of the naive ego, which constitutes its own standards, cheats the natural mind of its mastery over time and space.

Here the Logos doctrine of the Savior comes in. The Logos is redeemed from itself, from the curse of always only being able to correct itself by itself. It enters into relationship with the object of knowledge. "The Word became Flesh"—on that proposition everything indeed depends. While the word of man must always become a concept and thereby stagnant and degenerate, God speaks to us with the "word become flesh," through the Son. And so the Christian revelation is the healing of the Babylonian confusion of tongues, the bursting open of the prison, but also the sign on the new tongues, speech that is now informed with soil. Since then, it has become worthwhile to think again, because thought has a standard outside itself, in the visible foot-steps of God.

Do you now understand why I am so far from finding in Christianity the Judaizing of the pagans? That from which Christ redeems is exactly the boundless naive pride of the Jew himself, which you yourself exhibit. In contrast to the peoples talking the 372 languages of Babel, this pride was and is well founded, and therefore the Jews were separated and cho-sen out of all the peoples of the earth, until the destruction of the Temple. But Christianity redeems the individual from the family, and people through the new unity of all sinners, of all who are weary and heavy laden. That is Christianity, and its "yoke is easy." [Yoke of sonship, not the heavy yoke of Judaism, see Matthew 11:25–30].... Fortunately you do not know what you do. ["Father, forgive them; for they know not what they do" Luke 23:34 KJV.]

Scripture Meditation

The Word became flesh and made his dwelling among us.

—JOHN.1:14

Thought for the Day

Since the focus at Pentecost was upon "the Word made flesh," being filled with the Spirit of God, everyone heard the message in "his own tongue."

Prayer

Almighty God, you desire us not only to call you Father but "Our Father," that we may pray unitedly for all people. Give us frater-nal affection that we may recognize each other as true brothers and sisters, and petition you as our common Father for all mankind as one child pleads with its father for another. Amen.

—MARTIN LUTHER

AUGUST 19: BEING A CHRISTIAN IS BEING FREE FROM ONESELF

Eugen Rosenstock-Huessy wrote further to Franz Rosenzweig on
October 30, 1916, and again on November 2, 1916.

$\mathcal{D}$ear Franz,

I must go on now. It is the question of the un-Jewish life to which the Jew, and the un-Christian life to which the Christian, is condemned. With the Christian, this incurable rift between his actual life, from his frog-like point of view, and "the blessed, illuminative life" for which he longs, is the foundation and the cornerstone of his faith. "Let everyone take up his Cross and follow me." A person becomes a Christian only if he or she doesn't indulge in oneself.... For the human being goes best on two legs. All revelation is something that gives us a standard, and at the same time it is a sensible, perceptible event; and so for the Kantians it is an additional contradiction. The Christian Kingdom is not of this world, nor is it even the kingdom of the Christian priest [of ecclesial institutionalism]. His actual un-Christian life here and now is a stumbling block to him, and he is perhaps put hard to it, even to treat himself as his neighbor.

But when the Jew is un-Jewish, what then? ... Where is there the metaphysics of the seed of Abraham? ... In appearance the Jews wait upon the word of the Lord, but they have grown through and through, so far away from revelation, that they do everything they can to hinder its reality. With all the power of their being they set themselves against their own promises.... This naive way of thinking that one has won inalienable rights in perpetuity against God, which by nature remain for posterity as properties inherited by bequest, is the relic of blind antiquity in Judaism....

In order that Israel may live, the individual Jew depends on his success, on the number of his children. He is a paragraph of the Law. *C'est tout.* [That's all.] You may well believe you have a ship of your own. But you have no idea of the sea or you would not talk like that. You know no shipwreck; you cannot go astray; you see God with constant clarity; and so you need no mediator, who looks at you when you can no longer look out over the edge of the world and are frustrated in failure. You do not know that the world is movement and change. The Christian says there are day and night. You are so moonstruck that you take the sight of night for the only sight there is, and take the minimum of light, the night, for the all-inclusive idea that embraces day and night! "Renounce all hope, before you come to life, you already have renounced it."

Scripture Meditation

"If you were Abraham's children," said Jesus, "then you would do the things Abraham did. As it is, you are determined to kill me, a man who has told you the truth that I heard from God. Abraham did not do such things."

—JOHN 8:39–40

Thought for the Day

Neither a child of Abraham nor a follower of Christ can ever live an autonomous existence.

Prayer

A broken Altar, Lord, thy servant rears, made of a heart and cemented with tears: ... O let thy blessed Sacrifice be mine, and sanctify this Altar to be thine.

—GEORGE HERBERT

AUGUST 20: "SPIRITUALITY" AS DISEMBODIED IDEAS OR PERSONAL LIFE?

Reverend Eugene Peterson (b. 1932), the well-known pastor, writer, and translator of the biblical paraphrase The Message, *wrote a letter to Professor Rosenstock-Huessy on September 5, 2002.*

came upon your writings in my early twenties when my vocation as pastor, teacher, and writer was still in formation. Now, nearly fifty years later as I review what has happened, I realize with gratitude how timely your influence was, and how much it has continued to shape my life.

In my lifetime, more so than yours probably, the term "spirituality" has been much in the air. In many ways that has been a good thing. A lot of people have gotten fed up with a way of life that is mostly ideas on the one hand, or a sack full of projects on the other. They are interested in life, in a living God being fully alive in whatever tasks we perform, and getting whatever truths we believe in to come alive in personal relationships.... And that has been where you have been of so much help with your insistence that speech is the "life-blood of society." The dogged attention that you have given to insisting and showing that speech is living and makes alive, has been invaluable to me, both personally and vocationally.

I decided at one point that I could perhaps serve my generation best by harnessing "spirituality" in biblical leather. In the contemporary word around me the fits and starts towards a living faith (spirituality) skittered this way and that, stimulated by fashion, fad, celebrity, and publicity. I wanted to rescue the desire for God that I discerned in my parishioners and students from the "winds and doctrines" of spiritual consumerism and harness them to the purposes of God revealed in our Scriptures.

And this is where you helped so much. Your impatience with language that merely trafficked in disembodied ideas and your scorn for language that failed to engage personal participation gave me a keener sense for the robustness of biblical story and grammar and how essential vital speech was—not just the employment of words—for health of body, mind, and soul. But my first readings of your books left me reeling: your brilliant exposition of the strategic place of names; your conviction of the priority of the imperative in keeping speech immediate and effective; the dynamic quality that you revealed as inherent in the future tense. All this and so much more.

I have wanted to articulate and give witness to a spirituality that was shaped by Holy Scripture, an organically biblical spirituality, a way of living (a spirituality indeed) that had a biblical pulse and rhythm as well as a biblical meaning. For fifty years now, you have kept me focused. You gave me courage to distance myself from the presumptuous historical criticism that places itself above the Scriptures and showed me how to place myself deliberately under them, submitting to the revelation as given to us in these marvelous writers with their riveting prose, their scintillating poetry, their dancing metaphors and syntax.

Whenever I sensed that the world-weariness of my professional religious associates was rubbing off on me, I'd spend an hour or so in your company and come away energized. Your vigorous refutation of Descartes' *cogito ergo sum* ["I think therefore I am"], has helped its replacement by *respondeo etsi mutabor*, "I respond *although* I will be changed." This has served me well in my work with Scripture and Souls. It has kept me wary of pedantry in the classroom and condescension in the pulpit.

Scripture Meditation

[Jesus] said, "I am the light of the world. Whoever follows me will never walk in darkness, but will have the light of life."
—JOHN 8:12

Thought for the Day

Christian ideas are not enough for the reality of the Christian life.

Prayer

Light up thy Word; the fettered page from killing bondage, free!
Light up our way; lead forth this age in love's large liberty.
O Light of light! Within us dwell, through us thy radiance pour,
that word and life thy truths may tell, and praise thee evermore.
—WASHINGTON GLADDEN

AUGUST 21: WHAT IT MEANS TO BE A CHRISTIAN PERSON

*Dr. Alan Torrance (b. 1956), professor of systematic theology at the University
of St Andrews, Scotland, has specialized on the topic of Christian personhood.
He wrote this letter to the editor on September 27, 2002.*

*D*ear Jim,

Has not our society made us so self-conscious by its pressures to consume? Yet does this narcissistic introspection generate real self-awareness any more successfully than real personal relationships? As a Jew, Paul knew well a core strand in the Bible, which speaks of a very different conception of personal fulfillment. When Moses came down from the mountain having been talking with the Lord, we are told that he was completely oblivious to the fact that his face shone—shone so much indeed that he finally had to put a veil over his face! It was the radiance of one so wrapped up in the other, that introspection was the last thing on his mind! Likewise, the righteous in Matthew 25 don't think of themselves as righteous or merciful in feeding the hungry; they simply care for the poor.

Paul spells this out still further by saying of those who are "in Christ," that it is not they who live but Christ who lives in them. In a telling little self-correction in his letter to the Galatians, Paul expresses this: "Now, however, that you have come to know God, or rather to be known by God" (Gal. 4:9). The righteous doesn't look to its knowing, or believing—it looks to God, to his grace, to his embrace, to his knowing and loving and forgiving of us.

What does this tell us therefore about "the person?" To be "a person" is to be liberated from seeking to be anything. True fulfillment is about being lost in the other—being liberated from being "in-curved into ourselves" to being "out-curved" out of ourselves in the discovery of God's grace and that righteousness which holds us and forgives us.

For Karl Barth, the eye, the ear and the mouth are symbols of our co-humanity. We are persons, that is, co-humans, when we can look the other in the eye, when we hear the other, and when we speak to the other. Most importantly, he adds, it is when we do all this *gladly*. Contemporary culture seems to define humanity differently. The eye becomes a means of detached voyeurism and its primary object is itself—the fascination with self-discovery. The ear listens to one's needs and the mouth becomes the means of satisfying one's appetites, those tastes, those predilections that the ear determines. But we don't do this gladly, we do it desperately … because time is short!

By contrast, Paul's letters could barely illustrate the former more gloriously. "For I could wish that I myself were accursed and cut off from Christ for the sake of my own people." To discover the extent of God's radical altruism, God's self-giving commitment right to the cross, is to be taken to participate in that mission of the divine love. It is also to be taken to participate in all that that loving fulfills for us, on our behalf and in our place. To the extent that we ought to fulfill the obligations of grace, that is, the obligations of the law, God fulfills them for us in Christ. Where we are obliged to worship and pray but cannot, the Spirit intercedes for us and our ascended High Priest offers the worship we cannot offer—in our place and on our behalf.

The essence of personhood is co-humanity. It is nothing less than God's co-humanity with us in Christ. Truly it is that co-personhood which the Son has enjoyed with the Father and the Spirit from all eternity.

Scripture Meditation

I have been crucified with Christ and I no longer live, but Christ lives in me.
—GALATIANS 2:20

Thought for the Day

How keenly sensitive we Christians should be against all forms of narcissism, when God's love is so radically altruistic!

Prayer

Sing about a fruitful vineyard: I, the LORD, watch over it; I water it continually. I guard it day and night so that no one may harm it.
—ISAIAH 27:2–3

AUGUST 22: DEFINING OUR PERSONAL IDENTITY

Susana Kramer de Mesquita Oliveira (b. 1964) is a mother and professor of psychology at the University of Ceara, in northeast Brazil, specializing in issues of human relational behavior. She wrote on September 25, 2003.

*D*ear Pedro,

I received your letter with your questions and doubts, and I have kept it in my heart for a few days.... I would have preferred to talk with you in person, but since that isn't possible, I will start to share with you some of life's principles that I have tried to know more deeply and apply in my own life and relationships.... Your questions probe very deep and I don't know whether you realized it or not, but they all have to do with love; whether it exists at all, what is its nature, how it manifests itself, and why homosexual relationships are so criticized.... In your letter, you also share your homosexual desires and relationships.... Thank you for your trust and respect. Being the scholar that you are, I know that you have kept abreast of all the enormous changes that have taken place in post-modernity. You are aware of the philosophical, sociological and psychological issues involving "the new man." I have also tried to study and read a great deal in order not to be "swallowed" by the notion that "everyone knows what's best for one." Rather, I have tried to contribute as a psychologist, discussing ideas that will make a difference instead of simply "going along with everyone else." ... Therefore, based on what I have studied and understood, I think it is important to make a distinction between some of the concepts that have to do with our social life and our affections, that is, emotions, experiences, desires, relationships and love, in life's relationships in general and also more specifically in the area of homosexuality, which is the area you asked me about.

I understand that these concepts try to harmonize themselves in our identity as persons, giving us a sense of our own story and guiding our relational choices. We begin the search for meaning in our life, drawing from our own emotions and other vital needs (nurture, protection, pleasure and support). All of these things are necessary in our human development, but they are not sufficient to explain who we are and to give us an identity. Thus autism can be described as "the child of social disconnection," whether at a neuro-anatomical level or other social developmental levels. But even an autistic child has an identity more than its handicap. This can also mean that later in adolescence, being attracted physically to someone can be part of an important set of life experiences, but it is not enough to identify us sexually. The same can be said of our many later experiences of life: what we do or don't do (or even what was done to us) is not a sufficient condition to define who we are.

On the other hand, "feeling" and "doing" things leads us to take on very specific positions in our relationships, so that we name or are named by our experiences and then start to explain and attribute meaning to this experience based on a specific form of saying.... In all this process, many things end up being "mis-said," misinterpreted, misunderstood.... For example, just recently a child came up to me and said: "I'm a homosexual." ... I asked him why and from what I could perceive, he had exchanged some attitudes, information and curious gestures with another boy about his genitals.... Of course I told him that that did not mean he "was" a homosexual.

But if our experiences and emotions cannot serve as a trustworthy parameter for us to define our identities, then how will we know who we are? Some psychologies (you know that we cannot refer to one single psychology, don't you?) say that our "desire" is the reference; other psychologies consider our "relations" to be the reference. Am I what I am because that's what I wanted to be, or because that's how my relations defined me? I don't think we have to spend a great deal of time to realize that both our desires and our relations are very vulnerable to the "power of the word," in the same way that our emotions and experiences are. The question seems to be: who names, who defines, who attributes meaning to what I have done or felt, to the relationships I am experiencing, to the wishes that I have felt? Is it me or is it the other?

Pedro, all this seems to me to be very serious, because we become trapped in an existential paradox, simply because we don't even know who gave us our own identity. This includes different places in life's choices: profession, sex and other social status indicators. Maybe that's why a young man, very confused in his vocational choice, said to me one day: "I wish my father had said to me that I was going to be a doctor or anything else. At least then I would have been able to agree or disagree with his choice."

Scripture Meditation

Train a child in the way he should go, and when he is old he will not turn from it.

—PROVERBS 22:6

Thought for the Day

Could it be that infant brains are no longer adequately "connected," because our family values and influences have diminished first?

Prayer

Lord, enrich my emotional capacity to love you and others, so that all my social connections are enriched and enriching of others.

—SUSANA KRAMER DE MESQUITA OLIVEIRA

AUGUST 23: IS LOVE THE KEY TO THE ISSUE OF HOMOSEXUALITY?

Susana Kramer de Mesquita Oliveira continued her letter to Pedro.

Deeply, I believe only love can free us from this existential paradox. For instead of love being the great axis that structures us as persons, and around which emotions, experiences, desires and relationships acquire new meanings, we are part of a transition generation that believes in contrary ideas, such as "being named by a higher institution" (such as science, family, religion etc....), or "being what we want to be, independently of what others may think." So instead of the identity being formed by the capacity to love, it is formed by a contradiction of ideas and thus in a power struggle!

Many assume they can tell us who we are or who we should be—not based on honest and true relationships, but from their own self interest. The resultant identity is thus defined from a reaction to an unwanted authority appearing as a free choice. Actually this is not "freedom" to choose, but the "capacity" to choose, in other words "a power game."

Theoretically, our first experience of love (with our parents) should prepare us for the experiences of "receiving" from the other and "being received" by the other. Later, in a fraternal relationship, we may learn how to "share" with others that which we have received. Ideally then, we should begin to experience love as emotionally complementary, where the "I," the "you" and "the relationship" are discerned in the sense of belonging being complemented by the sense of being unique and different from that to which we are bound in a special way. Based on this interpretation, the other categories (emotions, desires, relationships and experiences) associate themselves in the constitution of our identity. Then love will not just be "an emotional state," nor "a specific action," nor "a desire." Neither is it present in all "the relationships we maintain."

So a relationship may be sustained by something other than by the "ties of love." It may be sustained by "compensatory ties" (when "what I do for you" is more important than "what I am for you") or by "ties of convenience" (when "what I gain when I am with you" has more value for me than "you yourself"). In this sense, love may exist, but "it is not ready to be consumed," so it has to be further developed.... And, in a generation that is reactive and without references, the capacity to love is, to say the least, a great challenge. I believe we need a vital relational honesty to overcome the conditions of existence created by our generation: of love as an emotion, as a reaction to unwanted authority, as something dictated by others, etc.... As you call it, "Homosexual love," belongs to this context.

In the same way that the affections are understood as a relational element that can and should be developed, sexuation [sexuality as power] also follows developmental stages: first as concentrated in ourselves; then at a later stage, as concentrated in someone similar to us. These stages can be interrupted, generating self-eroticism (sex turned in on oneself), or homosexuality (where sexual expression is directed to someone of the same sex). Heterosexuality comes at a subsequent stage, where affections and sexuality are expressed when we can discern ourselves, the other, and the relationship. Thus, the identity as a person, and the sexual identity, both develop from the ability to define oneself as a human being, letting oneself belong to the other, in a loving and complementary relation that includes the erotic dimension.

Finally, you ask me why homosexual relations are so criticized. We can use the two parameters of analysis already mentioned here: of "power" and of "love." If homosexuality is criticized on the basis of a power struggle, then we know that heterosexual*ity* is in power, attributing to itself the right to say what is right. This is an ideological action and it generates a counter-reaction from the ideology of homosexuality. The best we can expect from this clash is a 0 x 0 score, "each knowing abstractly what is best for oneself." Or we can confront ourselves and ask: "what can love accomplish in us all?"

Avoiding sexuation, that is of sexuality as power, we need to eliminate the "ity's," while in the promotion of love we need to develop the ability to love "the different." We can then abandon the power struggle, nurturing love, for all to seek self-transformation. This requires a critical awareness of all the conceptual contradictions and relational ambiguities we are in today. So I hope, Pedro, you will make the best choices that love can bring out in you; not merely as ideas but as strong desires you have received in your heart.

A warm embrace, Susana

Scripture Meditation

Love the LORD your God with all your heart and with all your soul and with all your strength. These commandments that I give you today are to be upon your hearts. Impress them on your children.... Write them on the doorframes of your houses.
—Deuteronomy 6:5–7, 9

Thought for the Day

To truly be a "human being" is to transcend oneself, in love of others.

Prayer

Thou hast given us hearts to love: Give us also the grace to love Thee with all our strength; and, for Thy sake, our neighbour more than oneself.

—ERIC MILNER-WHITE

SEASONS OF BIBLICAL INSTRUCTION AND PERSONAL NURTURE

*T*o interpret the Bible as God's love-letter to his people encourages us to seek and to trust its intimacy. Certainly the New Testament Letters are just that—personal letters of teaching, counsel, and nurture—to instruct, enlighten, and personalize our faith, as we shall now explore with biblical scholars who know these letters well.

THE NEW TESTAMENT CHURCHES

AUGUST 24: THE DANGER OF INTROSPECTION

*Introspection, a contemporary affliction, is indicted in this letter by John of
Avila (1500–1569) in writing to a young lady. He studied law at the University
of Salamanca, then biblical studies at the new Biblical Institute of Alcala,
near Madrid. He intended to become a missionary in Mexico, but ill
health forced him to live a restricted life, devoted to letter writing.
His* Spiritual Letters *were translated into English in 1620.*

ow long will you continue your minute self-examinations? It is like
raking up a dust heap from which nothing can come but rubbish and
unpleasantness. Feel sure of this, that it is not for your own merits, but for
those of Jesus crucified, that you are loved and made whole. Do not give
way to such discouragement about your faults, the results will show you
how displeasing it is to God. It would be far better to be courageous and
strong-hearted. Meditate on the benefits you have received through Jesus
Christ in the past and possess now; reflect on them in such a manner as to
lead you to sorrow for your sins against him and to avoid offending him,
without losing your peace and patience if you happen to fall. As I have
often repeated, God loves you as you are. Be content that his love should
come from his goodness, and not from your merits. What does it matter to
a bride if she is not beautiful, if the bridegroom's affection for her makes
her seem so in his eyes? If you look only on yourself, you will loathe yourself and your many defects will take away all your courage.

What more have you to wish for? In heaven there is One to whom you
appear all fair, for he looks at you through the apertures of the wounds
he received for you: by these he gives you grace, and supplies what is
lacking in you, healing you and making you lovely. Be at peace: you are
indeed the handmaid of the crucified Christ: forget your past misdoings
as if they had never been.... Trust in him; he has given you many reasons
to do so; and when you consider your own defects, consider also the
depths of his mercy which will help you far more than thinking about
your deficiencies.

May God's mercy shelter you beneath his everlasting love, as I desire, and pray, and trust that it may, and for this I bid you hope. Recommend me to the same Lord for the sake of his love.

Scripture Meditation

The LORD is my shepherd, I shall not be in want.... He guides me in paths of righteousness for his name's sake.
—PSALM 23:1, 3

Thought for the Day

The central concern of a Christian is drawing into ever closer intimacy with our Lord.

Prayer

I will fear no evil, for you are with me; your rod and your staff, they comfort me.
—PSALM 23:4

AUGUST 25: WHY ARE NEW TESTAMENT LETTERS NOT EPISTLES?

Dr. Bruce W. Winter, former director of the Institute for Early Christianity in the Graeco-Roman World, Tyndale House, fellow of St Edmund's College, and a member of the Divinity Faculty, University of Cambridge, England, wrote as a supervisor to a doctoral student on January 25, 2003.

*D*ear Lyn,

You are entering in on what is an exciting and daunting path as you begin a PhD on Paul's first letter to the Corinthians. I am writing because some who have trod your path noticed that intellectual process was marked for them by spiritual regression. They emerged all head and little else, having undergone the spiritual equivalent of a biological regression from a frog to a tadpole.

One reason for this pilgrim's regress was their failure to see a fundamental issue concerning the texts they are poring over. By first-century standards 1 Corinthians was not an epistle written in the grand style of rhetoric that had become the fad for such communication in the academy. That style always aimed to demonstrate the intellectual prowess and rhetorical sophistication of the writer. Paul's great concern in penning 1 Corinthians was that all his readers could engage with the mind of our great God and Savior.

In your chosen letter for your thesis topic Paul used the term "brothers" thirty-eight times which you know from your study of Koine Greek encompasses sisters also. The term "brothers and sisters" must have shocked those first-century outsiders who heard fellow Christians addressing each other in terms strictly reserved for siblings. It was a letter written to the family of God, and the way you write to your brothers and sisters is planets away from thesis composition or applying to the university for entry. Have you also ever wondered why Paul, in his letters, only referred to Corinthian Christians by their first names compared with the epistles of his day where all three Roman names were used?

First-century people loved to meet in contexts that adorned the occasion, whether in the theatre when a sophist was performing an oration, the Odeon for the latest play, or the gardens of Peribolos of Apollo for an intellectual discussion. Have you ever wondered why those Christians did not meet in halls as did others, but in homes? The setting re-enforced for them the fact that they were in a family setting. What they were outside in their class-ridden society meant nothing when they stopped into the home to gather for worship.

It would therefore have been wholly incongruous of Paul to write an epistle to such a gathering where the status of the wise, the well-born and powerful meant absolutely nothing. They had come home to God and his family. The family "letter" must be reflected in all your research on it.

Remember that the gifts you have been given are for that family. The Christian people you work with are your siblings. What you are studying is not for the posh, but a letter from God for all the family, and that is true for all the letters in the New Testament.

Scripture Meditation

I always thank God for you because of his grace given you in Christ Jesus. For in him you have been enriched in every way—in all your speaking and in all your knowledge—because our testimony about Christ was confirmed in you.

—I CORINTHIANS 1:4–6

Thought for the Day

Baruch, the scribe and research assistant of Jeremiah, also handled the Word of God, but his motives were skewed. (See Jer. 45:1–5.) Are ours?

Prayer

Lord, I thank you that in Jesus Christ I have been enriched in everything, for there is nothing I have, which I have not received for the benefit of your family.

—BRUCE W. WINTER

AUGUST 26: READING NEW TESTAMENT LETTERS

New Testament scholar Dr. Tom Hatina wrote this letter to the editor from personal concern.

$\mathcal{D}$ear Jim,

While letters have played a significant role in every facet of life throughout the history of Western culture—and increasingly continue to do so with the growing popularity of the Internet—I would like to share with you a few reflections on the reading of early Christian letters. I have often marveled at the significant role that letters have played in Early Christianity. With more than nine thousand extant letters written in antiquity by Christians, including the twenty-one in the NT (not to mention the embedded letters in Acts and Revelation), the sheer number alone is certainly cause for bewilderment. But to say that the early Christians were somehow unique in their use of letters would be an overstatement. Letters were simply the primary means of communication on every social level in antiquity in the Mediterranean region.

What amazes me the most about the letters in the New Testament is not so much the information they communicate, which needless to say is of great interest, but the way in which they are read "spiritually" by devout Christians. Since these letters are believed to be inspired, they have continued to live and be relevant for the Christian life. As a Christian biblical scholar, I have no problem with a meditative reading which emerges from an assumed overall theological aim. A spiritual reading within the context of the Church's teaching and worship tradition has been, and should continue to be, considered a vital exercise.

What is particularly disturbing to me, however, is the individualistic way in which many Christians today read these letters.... I fear that apathy toward any kind of historical examination of the letters, not only exhibits an anti-intellectual gnosticism, but in the process kills the very life of the letters themselves—all of this, of course, transpiring innocently. When the letters are mined for propositional statements that can serve as applicable principles or apologetic proof texts, the genre disappears, the cultural framework as context becomes irrelevant, and the author is completely discredited. The author's argument is not permitted to be fully expressed (as is often the case with the reading of Paul); his creativity is stunted for fear of theological disharmony (as is the case with the reading of James); and his emotional expression is rarely encountered with empathy and even struggle (as is the case with the reading of John the Elder). In short, the letter is transformed into axiom and controlled in such a way that its expression of humanness is killed. What is often forgotten is that these letters were written by persons, about persons, to persons in the context of deep relationships.

Our love for these letters comes with a paradoxical risk: the more we clench these letters, the more we can squeeze the life out of them. If we truly love them, we will abrogate our egoism and let them transform us. I am convinced that these letters can teach us much about ourselves and our new way of life, but they can only do so if we let them.

Scriptural Meditation

You show that you are a letter from Christ, the result of our ministry, written not with ink but with the Spirit of the living God, not on tablets of stone, but on tablets of human hearts.

—2 CORINTHIANS 3:3

Thought for the Day

Just as we should read each letter in its context, so we should pay attention to the uniqueness of each person we meet.

Prayer

Lord, we beseech thee to keep thy household the Church in continual godliness.

—COLLECT, *THE BOOK OF COMMON PRAYER*

AUGUST 27: NEW TESTAMENT LETTERS: FIRST JOHN

---

*Father Vasile Mihoc, an Orthodox priest, is professor of New Testament
studies at the Romanian Orthodox Seminary in Sabiu, Romania. Here he
summarized the first epistle of John. In the next entry he will respond to it.*

The author of this letter is the same person who wrote the Fourth
Gospel. The same style, the same vocabulary, the same themes are in the
two writings. The oldest tradition identifies this author in the person of St.
John the apostle. It is difficult to give a logical outline of St. John's thought
in this letter. But as in the Gospel, there are a number of key words and
phrases, which recur again in similar but subtly altered contexts.

In the *prologue (1:1–4)* the Beloved Disciple shares with his readers,
as one of the eyewitnesses who saw and heard Jesus, his testimony on
"the Word of Life," i.e., the incarnated Son of God.

Part one (1:5—3:10): "God is light" and therefore we must walk in the
light. Walking in light and acting in truth guarantee fellowship with God
and with one another, for the blood of Jesus cleanses us from all sin.
Unlike the false teachers, the true Christians confess their wrongdoing as
sin and are forgiven, having "Jesus Christ the just one" as *paraclete*
(advocate) with the Father (1:8—2:2). But our confession is real only if
we keep his commandments, his word (2:3–6). Living the commandment
of love for one's fellow Christian ("brother") is the true test of walking
in light (2:7–11). The addressees, having their sins forgiven and possessing the true knowledge of God, have conquered the Evil One (2:12–14).
It follows an impassioned denunciation of the world and its attractions:
sensuous lust, enticement for the eyes, and pride of self-centered existence (2:15–17). St. John sees the apocalyptic struggle already going on
and the false teachers as antichrists; they bear the mark of Satan, the liar
par excellence. The believers know the truth by their anointing from the
Holy One (2:18–27). We are children of God; at the appearance of Christ
we will be like him and shall see him as he is (2:28—3:3). The children of
God and the children of the devil are plainly distinct because the former
do not sin and love their brothers (3:4–10).

Part two (3:11—5:12): We must love one another, because God is love.

St. John proclaims now the message as love. Christ is the supreme revelation of God's love. Faith and love are the summary of God's commandments (3:11–24). If the spirit of antichrist denies Christ, the right christological doctrine, in accord with St. John's teaching, is the mark of the authentic prophetic spirit (4:1–6). Abruptly 4:7–21 returns to the theme of love for one another with the proclamation, "God is love" (4:8; cf. 4:16). He supremely manifested his love by sending his Son into the world so that we might have life. God had the initiative: "We love because he first loved us" (4:19). If we love one another, God remains in us. Faith, love, and commandments go together (5:1–5). The Spirit, the water (of baptism), and the blood testify to faith in Christ (5:6–8). The acceptance of the divine testimony leads to belief in God's Son and the possession of life (5:9–12).

In the *conclusion (5:13–21)*, St. John first clarifies the purpose of his letter: that the believers know that they possess eternal life (5:13). Also, that God hears our prayers, and we can intercede for a sinful brother. But the apostle does not ask us to pray for those who commit "deadly sin" (5:16). Some basic ideas of the letter are then introduced by three solemn reiterations of "we know" (5:18–20). Like the fourth Gospel (20:28), 1 John ends with a clear affirmation of the divinity of Christ (5:20).

Scripture Meditation

Our fellowship is with the Father and with his Son, Jesus Christ.
We write this to make our joy complete.
—1 JOHN 1:3–4

Thought for the Day

The greatest message God has revealed to us is that God is love.

Prayer

I praise the Godhead, unity in three persons, for the Father is light,
the Son is light, the Spirit is light. But the light is undivided, shining forth in oneness of nature, yet in the three rays of the persons.
—LENTEN TRIODION

AUGUST 28: NEW TESTAMENT LETTERS: FIRST JOHN, A RESPONSE

Father Vasile Mihoc and his three brothers, all fellow priests in the Romanian
Orthodox Church, recently built five new churches on sites destroyed by
Romania's Communist regime. Their father was one of the founders of "The
Lord's Army," a renewal movement within Romanian Orthodoxy. Here Mihoc
responded to John's epistle by summarizing the message of St. John's first epistle.

*B*eloved Apostle John,

What a wonderful message you have communicated to us. For you are showing us that Christian love is not just a commandment. Actually, it has an ontological basis, for the fellowship of believers is grounded upon the Holy Trinity (1:3). So that, to be born of God, we are God's children and share his nature. For, "God is love" (4:8, 16). The true Christians, the ones who know God, will live and act like him, rightly answering God's love and loving one another and the whole creation.

So when you make the statement, "Love of God" (2:5; 4:9; 5:3) you are meaning both God's love for us, and our love for God. For of course, we should remember love can only be mutual. The only right answer to love is to love, not debate about it! But you also make it clear that only God can initiate love: "He first loved us" (4:19). And God has supremely manifested his love by sending "His only Son into the world, so that we might live through him" (4:9). Christ's sacrifice for us is the supreme revelation of God's love. But you are emphatic also that this revelation cannot remain a simple theoretical affirmation; it demands a practical response, a response of love. What you want is that we Christians should live out God's love. So you put it bluntly: "By this we know love, that he (Christ) laid down his life for us" (3:16a), adding immediately: "we too, then, ought to lay down our lives for our brothers" (3:16b).

Oh yes, you make it so clear that loving one another is the test of our love to God. "If someone says, 'I love God,' but hates his brother, he is a liar" (4:20). We really prove our love to God, our knowledge of him (2:3), and our fellowship with him (4:12, 16) only when we keep his commandments (2:3–5; 5:3), summarized in both the old and yet new commandment of love (2:7–8).

Thank you then, Apostle, for showing us what it really means to be a

Christian! Before we see the light of God we can only live like the blind. But when our mind and heart are becoming open to the revelation of God's love in Christ we feel overcome in horror, that we shall remain forever unworthy of *such* a God. Then we start to measure how far distant we are from our purpose. We even wonder how repentant we are! So we can understand St. Sisoe's plea when the Lord appeared to him as he lay dying, "Give me time to repent, O Christ." Yet we do experience how grace comes to our aid, and then longing for God, we start to perceive the boundless horizons of God's love and of his commandment to love one another.

Scripture Meditation

This is the message you have heard from the beginning: We should love one another.

—I JOHN 3:11

Thought for the Day

Man finds his true self in the Church alone; not in the helplessness of spiritual isolation but in the strength of his communion with his brothers and sisters, and with his Saviour.

—FR. ALEXANDER ELCHANINOV

Prayer

May your whole spirit, soul and body be kept blameless at the coming of our Lord Jesus Christ.

—I THESSALONIANS 5:23

AUGUST 29: NEW TESTAMENT LETTERS: EPHESIANS

Dr. Rikk Watts, associate professor of New Testament Studies at Regent
College in Vancouver, Canada, offered a summary of Ephesians
and then continued the discussion with the next entry.

The articulation of the Gospel, as given in Paul's letter to the Ephesians, is unique in its sweeping lyrical grandeur. Its central theme is that God's divine plan—nothing less than the reconciliation of all things in heaven and earth—has been inaugurated in keeping with his eternal purpose in his Son (1:10).

In a deep mystery, Christ has made peace by eradicating through his own body the wall of division between Jew and Gentile, namely Torah, and so created in himself a new humanity (2:14–18). The nations are now participants with Israel and full heirs of God's promises (3:6). Together this one new people is not only the recipient and mediator of the new creation but is itself part of it.

Having succeeded (where Torah could not) in subjugating the principalities and powers that sought to alienate humanity from God and from one another (cf. 2:2), Christ now reigns at the right hand of the Father (2:20f). He is head over all things for the church, his body, which is the fullness of him who completes everything in every way (1:23), who even now shares in his victorious rule (2:6), and through whom God reveals his wisdom to the powers (3:10).

As such the Ephesians' lives must reflect this new reality, maintaining the unity of the Spirit through peace and love (4:1–6). Enriched by the abundant spoils showered in them by Christ's victory (4:7–12) and speaking the truth in love in mutual submission (5:21) they are together to grow up in all things into the maturity of Christ (4:16). In this way and so armed with Yahweh's own armor (6:14–18; Isaiah 59:17) they will participate in the Lord's victory over the powers through the proclamation in word and deed of the gospel.

Scripture Meditation

Now in Christ Jesus you who once were far away have been
brought near through the blood of Christ.
—EPHESIANS 2:13

Thought for the Day

In Christ, the basis for cosmic unity and peace has been established, and
so as followers of Christ, we are called to bring harmony within our
spheres of influence.

Prayer

Praise be to the God and Father of our Lord Jesus Christ, who
has blessed us in the heavenly realms with every spiritual blessing
in Christ.
—EPHESIANS 1:3

AUGUST 30: NEW TESTAMENT LETTERS: EPHESIANS, A RESPONSE

Dr. Rikk Watts continued a look at Ephesians with a "re-Reformed"
interpretation of the apostle Paul's epistle, as he explained to a student.

My dear brother Tony,

Because of the impact made by the Reformation, it is not surprising
that for much of the Protestant tradition, Paul's letters to the Romans
and the Galatians are held to be the center of Paul's theology. But put
that aside for a moment and consider Paul himself.

If "justification by faith" is so central, it is difficult to explain its infrequent occurrence outside these two letters. On the other hand, what is really at the heart of Paul's ministry? Unquestionably, it is his apostleship to the nations. Is this surprising? Hardly. For at the outset of Israel's story, God called Abraham to be the beginning of a new humanity and a blessing to the nations (Gen. 12:1).

Likewise, Israel was to be an example to the nations (Deut. 4:5–6). From the diverse multitude that joined Israel's exodus (Ex. 12:38), through Rahab, Ruth, David's Philistine and international warriors (2 Sam. 15:18; 18:2; 23:39ff.), to Solomon to whom all nations came (1 Kings 4:34; 10), the vision is the same. And nowhere is this clearer seen than in Isaiah with its picture of all nations learning to walk in the ways of Yahweh (Isaiah 2), Egypt, Assyria, and Israel, brothers together (Isaiah 19:23–25), as his faithful servant serves as light to them (Isaiah 42:6; 49:6).

This it seems to me is the cosmic vision so eloquently and uniquely captured by the aptly soaring prose of Ephesians. The climax of God's divine plan, set in place from the beginning, has always been the reversal of the Fall's animosity in the formation of one, new humanity (Eph. 2:15). Jew and Gentile, at peace, reconciled to God and to one another. But there is mystery. Not only was Torah unable to restrain Israel, it also excluded the rebellious nations. Instead, it was God's son, bearing the curse of Torah in his own body, who did away with Torah's division (2:14). It was he who enabled, through the Spirit, the coming of the new creation (vv. 17–22; 4:3). He, as the first Son, is head of his body, comprising all God's sons (and daughters) who through the Spirit imitate him. Justification by faith is not the goal. It is the means.

Put another way, start with Galatians and Romans and it is difficult to explain the grandeur and universal vision of Ephesians, as the protracted scholarly debate demonstrates. But start with God's predestined plan in Ephesians, then Romans and Galatians make perfect sense. Ephesians sets forth the grand design. Galatians and Romans emerge from wrestling with the Torah's role in the formation of this new humanity. What Torah could not do—transform and unite humanity—has happened in Christ's death and the Spirit's continuing work. The Torah once divided; Jesus now unites. Torah once condemned; the Spirit brings life.

Doubtless, the Reformation was needed to challenge ecclesial corruption. But that was not the immediate context of Paul's own letter.

Should we not then release Paul from his Galatian-Reformation prison, to put his letter to the Ephesians back where it belongs: at the very heart of his vision?

Your servant in Christ,

Rikk

Scripture Meditation

[God's] purpose was to create in himself one new man out of the two [Jew and Gentile], thus making peace, and in this one body to reconcile both of them to God through the cross, by which he put to death their hostility.

—EPHESIANS 2:15–16

Thought for the Day

God's cosmic purpose is for all Christians to be bound together in love. How can we contribute to this purpose today?

Prayer

Now to him who is able to do immeasurably more than all we ask or imagine, according to his power that is at work within us, to him be glory in the church and in Christ Jesus throughout all generations, for ever and ever! Amen.

—EPHESIANS 3:20–21

AUGUST 31: NEW TESTAMENT LETTERS—COLOSSIANS

Alan Torrance, professor of systematic theology at the University of St Andrews, Scotland, offered a summary of the letter to the Colossians, as the apostle might have done so and then gave his comments in the next letter.

ear Colossians,

In our prayers for you we always thank God, the Father of our Lord Jesus Christ, for we have heard of your faith in Christ Jesus....

He is the image of the invisible God, the firstborn of all creation; for in him all things in heaven and on earth were created, things visible and invisible, whether thrones or dominions or rulers of powers—all things have been created through him and for him. He himself is before all things, and in him all things hold together. He is the head of the body, the church; he is the beginning, the firstborn from the dead, so that he might come to have first place in everything. For in him all the fullness of God was pleased to dwell, and through him God was pleased to reconcile to himself all things, whether on earth or in heaven, by making peace through the blood of the cross.

Sublime as such a revelation of Christ is to the world, my purpose in writing you is also that you are united in love, so that you will have deeper appreciation of Christ in all his glorious mystery. Because it is so easy to be distracted from gazing upon him, by religious ceremonialism, by ascetic practices, even angel worship, all of which lead actually to a depreciation of Christ himself. Actually, the more you really worship and love Christ, the more realistic will be your family life, of your mutual submission to each other. So devote yourselves to prayer, personally, for all your relationships, as well as to pray that the knowledge of Christ may become such a great missionary calling. It is in this ministry that our true friends are bonded together.

So grace be with you,

Paul

Scripture Meditation

In Christ all the fullness of the Deity lives in bodily form.
—COLOSSIANS 2:9

Thought for the Day

As all things hold together in Christ; our relationship with him shapes all our other relationships whether at home, at work, or at church.

Prayer

We always thank God, the Father of our Lord Jesus Christ, when we pray for you, because we have heard of your faith in Christ Jesus and of the love you have for all the saints.
—COLOSSIANS 1:3–4

SEPTEMBER 1: NEW TESTAMENT LETTERS: COLOSSIANS

Dr. Alan Torrance responded to the apostle's letter to the Colossians.

Dear Paul,

So let me get this right! Everything is created through Christ, is held together in Christ and thus needs to be interpreted with reference to Christ. Is this to suggest that absolutely *every* facet of creation requires to be understood in the light of the Christ Jesus—that not only the church, but our world in its totality, gender relations, race relations, our attitudes to the poor, our systems of power, our businesses, our academic, civil and political institutions and all that they do.... All this requires to be understood and rethought in the light of Christ the "head"?

And are you implying that to the extent that we fail to think in these terms we are "enemies in our minds" of Christ?

Now you're going to have to bear with me, Paul, as I'm just a simple Scotsman! Can I ask for some clarification? First, do we really need Christ to interpret creation? Creation, after all, is something to which we all have access. Are you suggesting we don't really understand it aright until we discern the full extent of the Creator's love for it and commitment to it as he stands in its midst as the one crucified within it and for it?

And why precisely do we need Christ for our reasoning about the world to be reconciled? Are you suggesting that the forgiveness he holds forth sheds light on current affairs, on how we approach political and religious strife, the spirals of retaliation and revenge that characterize international affairs?

But can't we have all this without your dramatic insistence that in Christ we have the whole fullness of the Godhead dwelling bodily? Isn't it easier to think of Jesus' place as a little more modest than you suggest, that is, more private, more spiritual and less questioning, less challenging ... and less transforming, less reconciling, less liberating, even less relevant ...!

I suppose the problem takes us back to the horns of the dilemma with which you confront us—namely, the Who question with which Jesus confronted Peter. Either Jesus is God, in which case all that you say does indeed seem to follow, or he is not, in which case, he becomes utterly irrelevant. Your letter is offensive because throughout, Christ compels us to front up to this. He graciously denies us the opportunity to count ourselves "moderates," giving him a *moderate* place within our lives and understanding. Why is this difficult? Because this means we lose the power to moderate where he is and is not to be found in our lives and in our attitudes. And to be denied *that* power is to find ourselves questioned by him—and to be questioned by him in the most radical and in the deepest possible way. And that, Paul, seems hard, seriously hard!

You end your letter by asking us to remember your chains!

May Christ's transforming presence liberate us from ours!

Scripture Meditation

Let the peace of Christ rule in your hearts, since as members of
one body you were called to peace. And be thankful. Let the word
of Christ dwell in you richly.

—COLOSSIANS 3:15–16

Thought for the Day

Can we spend this one day thinking of how Jesus Christ gives meaning
to all of reality?

Prayer

Father, give us, we pray, the eyes and the ears by which we might
see creation anew within the reconciling embrace of its risen, crucified Head. Through Jesus Christ our Lord, Amen.

—ALAN TORRANCE

SEPTEMBER 2: NEW TESTAMENT LETTERS: 2 JOHN

The second letter of John was probably written by John the apostle about the
same time as his first letter, but its focus is on the incarnation as giving all
meaning to "the truth." Dr. Barbara Mutch (b. 1959) is professor of pastoral
theology at Carey Theological College, Vancouver, Canada. She replied in the
voice of the first century to John's second epistle about living in
the light of the incarnation, as the truth of God.

*D*ear John,

All of us here in the fellowship wish to thank you for your recent letter. It was so good to hear from you and to be reminded clearly of the truth of the gospel. Naming truth five times in the opening sentences really caught our attention! Truth can so easily become a casualty of our desire to be tolerant of others, but gospel truth is not negotiable.

You well know that people of influence within the community are spreading the word that Jesus did not really come in the flesh. These people believe that the worlds of matter and spirit are in opposition to each other. They are convinced that if Jesus Christ is God in the flesh, then God crossed the boundary between spirit and matter and became changeable in nature. As a result of the way they think the world works, they have missed the whole incredible point of the Incarnation. It matters what we think about Jesus. The entire Christian faith is rooted in the historic event of the Incarnation. The mystery of God taking on human flesh, becoming a God with skin on and choosing to deal with humans in a visible way is the foundation for our faith.

The Incarnation is not just an idea to which we give our assent, though. The Incarnation is supposed to make a difference in how we live. Is that why you linked together truth and love so clearly? You love the believers in "the truth." You extended grace, mercy, and truth from God the Father and the Son to us "in truth and love." And the direct response to the good news that some of the believers of our fellowship are walking in the truth is that we all should love one another. All the commandments can be reduced to the single commandment to walk in love. If we get that right, we walk in the very way that Jesus walked. It's necessary for us to be reminded that the church of Jesus must be marked equally by truth and love. Withholding love is no more acceptable than is bad doctrine.

John, the more we think about the amazing truth of the Incarnation, the more our hearts are moved to wonder and to worship. That is likely the only proper response anyway. We look forward to seeing you in person, John. In the meantime, please know that we intend to love one another, guard the truth about Jesus, and let the Incarnation transform our lives.

Scripture Meditation

Anyone who ... does not continue in the teaching of Christ does
not have God; whoever continues in the teaching has both the
Father and the Son.

—2 JOHN V. 9

Thought for the Day

God the Father and the God the Son, Jesus Christ, can never be separated.

Prayer

Emmanuel, within us dwelling, make us what thou wouldst have
us be.

—BISHOP FRANK HOUGHTON

SEPTEMBER 3: NEW TESTAMENT LETTERS: HEBREWS

*Reverend Dr. J. I. Packer, Board of Governors' professor of systematic
theology at Regent College, Vancouver, Canada, got to the heart of Hebrews
by selecting significant verses from the epistle.*

Saints in Christ,

In the past God spoke to our forefathers through the prophets at
many times and in various ways, but in these last days he has spoken to
us by his Son, whom he has appointed heir of all things, and through
whom he made the universe.... The Son is the radiance of God's glory
and the exact representation of his being, sustaining all things by his

powerful word. After he had provided purification for sins, he sat down at the right hand of the Majesty in heaven (1:1–3).

We must pay more careful attention, therefore, to what we have heard (2:1).

We see Jesus who was made a little lower than the angels, now crowned with glory and honor because he suffered death, so that by the grace of God he might taste death for everyone (2:9).

Therefore, holy brothers, who share in the heavenly calling, fix your thoughts on Jesus, the apostle and high priest whom we confess (3:1).

Since we have a great high priest who has gone through the heavens, Jesus the Son of God, let us hold firmly to the faith we profess. For we do not have a high priest who is unable to sympathize with our weaknesses, but we have one who has been tempted in every way, just as we are—yet without sin. Let us then approach the throne of grace with confidence, so that we may receive mercy and find grace to help us in our time of need (4:14–16). During the days of Jesus' life on earth, he offered up prayers and petitions with loud cries and tears to the one who could save him from death, and he was heard because of his reverent submission. Although he was a son, he learned obedience from what he suffered and, once made perfect, he became the source of eternal salvation for all who obey him and was designated by God to be high priest in the order of Melchizedek (5:7–10).

By this new priestly order of Melchizedek, the writer intended to indicate the superiority of Christ's priestly service over the older Levitical priesthood. For Melchizedek is described in superlatives as "king of righteousness," as "king of peace," and as possessing "endless days," in an "eternal priesthood." Even Abraham, the "father of the faithful," pays homage to him alone.

Scripture Meditation

In the past God spoke to our ancestors through the prophets at many times and in various ways, but in these last days he has spoken to us by his Son, whom he appointed heir of all things, and through whom also he made the universe.

—HEBREWS 1:1-2 TNIV

Thought for the Day

Exploring the universe with the Hubble telescope to view billions upon billions of stars and their countless of galaxies, brings home the truth that this great High Priest who mediates for us, created them all!

Prayer

> Shed upon thy Church, we beseech thee, O Lord, the brightness of thy light; that we, being illumined by the teaching of thine apostle ... may so walk in the light of thy truth, that we may at length attain to the fullness of life everlasting; through Jesus Christ our Lord, who liveth and reigneth with thee and the Holy Spirit, one God, for ever and ever. Amen.

SEPTEMBER 4: NEW TESTAMENT LETTERS: HEBREWS (CONT.)

---

*Reverend Dr. J. I. Packer continued his letter containing
verses selected from the heart of Hebrews.*

He is able to save completely those who come unto God through him, because he always lives to intercede for them (7:25). Christ is the mediator of a new covenant, that those who are called may receive the promised eternal inheritance—now that he has died as a ransom to set them free from the sins committed under the first covenant (9:15).

Christ was sacrificed once to take away the sins of many people; and he will appear a second time, not to bear sin, but to bring salvation to those who are waiting for him (9:28). By one sacrifice he has made perfect forever those who are being made holy (10:14).... Since we have confidence to enter the Most Holy Place by the blood of Jesus ... and since we have a great high priest over the house of God, let us draw near to God with a sincere heart in full assurance of faith, having our hearts sprinkled to cleanse us from a guilty conscience and having our bodies washed with pure water. Let us hold unswervingly to the hope we profess, for he who promised is faithful (10:19–23).

Now faith is being sure of what we hope for and certain of what we do not see (11:1). You have come to Mount Zion, to the heavenly Jerusalem, the city of the living God.... You have come to God, the judge of all men, to the spirits of righteous ones made perfect, to Jesus the mediator of a new covenant, and to the sprinkled blood that speaks a better word than the blood of Abel (12:22–24).

Be content with what you have, because God has said, "Never will I leave you; never will I forsake you." So we say with confidence, "The Lord is my helper; I will not be afraid. What can man do to me?" (13:5–6).

Scripture Meditation

Jesus Christ is the same yesterday and today and forever.
—HEBREWS 13:8

Thought for the Day

Christ leads me through no darker rooms than he went through before.
—RICHARD BAXTER

Prayer

May the God of peace, who through the blood of the eternal covenant brought back from the dead our Lord Jesus, that great Shepherd of the sheep, equip you with everything good for doing his will, and may he work in us what is pleasing to him, through Jesus Christ, to whom be glory for ever and ever. Amen.
—HEBREWS 13:20–21

SEPTEMBER 5: NEW TESTAMENT LETTERS: ROMANS

---

*Dr. Eckhard J. Schnabel, professor of New Testament Studies
at Trinity Evangelical Divinity School in Deerfield, Illinois,
communicated the central message of the Roman epistle.*

*D*ear Christians in Rome:

Your fellow-Christians all over the world have heard of your faith! They know that you were not ashamed to believe in the gospel of God revealing himself in the life, death and resurrection of Jesus Christ, nor were you afraid to witness in your local synagogues and beyond. We still remember the events of eight years ago when emperor Claudius expelled the Jews from Rome as a result of the disturbances that resulted from your evangelistic efforts. I wanted to visit you during this difficult period when many of your leaders had to leave Rome as well, but my circumstances made a visit impossible. It seems, however, that I might be able to come to you perhaps as early as this summer, after my visit to Jerusalem. I will tell you more about this later.

You know the message that I have preached as a missionary and pastor: many of you know me personally. My upcoming visit to Jerusalem will give me another opportunity to explain the gospel message that we believe and that we proclaim so that people might find true salvation— both Jews and Gentiles. Yes, now even pagans can receive salvation: people who chose to ignore God's revelation in the created order of nature, people who worship idols in their temples, people who do shameful things and who are addicted to all kinds of perversions. We missionaries preach not only to them, however, we preach to Jews as well, as you have been doing in Rome: they need to see that their claims to moral superiority over against the Gentiles does not mean anything as they commit sins against God themselves, and they need to recognize the fact that God's new revelation in his son Jesus, the Messiah, renders their appeal to being God's privileged people on account of the Mosaic law and circumcision obsolete.

In view of God's new revelation, both Jews and Gentiles can find salvation from the wrath of God Almighty only in accepting Jesus Christ, who gave his life on the cross as a sacrifice, as God's provision for sin.

Both Jews and Gentiles are saved from the consequences of their sins, from eternal damnation, when they trust in Jesus Christ to take away their sins. When people accept Jesus Christ as divine Savior, they experience the fulfillment of God's promises to Abraham, as they trust in God in the same way that the founder of the Jewish nation trusted in God the all-powerful Creator and Giver of life. And as pagans come to faith, they experience not only the blessing of being declared righteous by God, but also the blessing of being fully integrated into God's people: as believers in the Messiah, Jesus, they are sons and daughters of Abraham in the same way that Jewish Christians are Abraham's children. The peace with God that we as Christians enjoy is a result of this acceptance into God's family, which in turn is the result of God's forgiveness of our sins who sent Jesus Christ at just the right time to die for us sinners. As God himself has removed our guilt and sin, as he has blessed us with his very presence by giving us the Holy Spirit, as he has filled our hearts with his love, we are confident that he will certainly deliver us from eternal punishment. The difficulties that we experience as Christians in our personal lives can never torpedo these divine gifts and blessings: they only strengthen our confident expectation that one day we will share God's glory in a visible way, as Jesus Christ has solved the problem of sin that was introduced into the world by Adam once and for all.

Scripture Meditation

Consider therefore the kindness and the sternness of God: sternness to those who fell, but kindness to you, provided that you continue in his kindness.

—ROMANS 11:22

Thought for the Day

Don't stay trapped inside yourself. Rise above yourself and place yourself in the hands of God who made you.

—ST. AUGUSTINE, SERMON 153

Prayer

Spirit of my Lord, lift the veil that hides the truth that giving up

self is really gaining, for of what worth is self-sufficiency if it obscures the truth of your being with me?
—SUSAN ANNETTE MUTO

SEPTEMBER 6: NEW TESTAMENT LETTERS: ROMANS (CONT.)

---

*Dr. Eckhard J. Schnabel continued his discussion on
the central message of the Roman epistle.*

It is easy to misunderstand the consequences of what happened at the cross. Yes, when Jesus Christ died on the cross, he forgave, for those who trust in Jesus, all sins ever committed—past, present and future. It would be a serious and unacceptable misunderstanding to conclude that Christians could tolerate sins in their lives, arguing that such sins have already been forgiven. Some of my opponents in the Jerusalem church use this logic as an argument against our preaching of the gospel. They insist that the Mosaic law needs to play an important part in the process of salvation: that obedience to the law needs to be emphasized as a safeguard against sin. These people fail to recognize what I emphasize in my preaching and teaching: when we come to faith in Jesus Christ we identify with his death and with his resurrection. And as Jesus died because of our sin and in order to atone for our sin, Christians can never take sin lightly: as sin has lost its power over us, as death, being the consequence of sin, has been replaced by eternal life as our destiny, we cannot play around with sin, we cannot let sin control the way we live, we cannot give in to its lustful desires.

The power by which we resist temptation and avoid committing acts of sin is not the law: the law was never given for this purpose, and the old ways of atoning for sin—worship in the temple, sacrifices, obeying the commandments—are no longer valid since God sent his Son to remove his wrath and condemnation. The power by which we resist sin is the power of God himself, the power of Christ's work on the cross, the power of his life-giving Spirit that freed us from the power of sin that leads to death. As a result of God's effective revelation in Jesus Christ, we have no obligation whatsoever to do what our sinful nature urges us to do. Since we are God's children, we will without doubt share in his glory, as no opposition and no suffering can separate us from God's love.

I continue to tell my Jewish countrymen that God's revelation in Jesus the Messiah was not some last minute idea but his plan all along. God has not forgotten his promises, he cannot be accused of having given up on his people, the Jewish nation. God has never promised that all descendants of Abraham, without exception, would have salvation, and as Jews continue to reject Jesus as Messiah it would be preposterous to blame God for Israel's failure to accept salvation. Moreover, there are Jews who believe in Jesus Christ, and I hope that as more pagans find salvation by trusting in Christ and as the life of the new covenant becomes visible in more and more communities in the cities around the world, more Jews will accept our message that the last days have arrived.

As a matter of fact, since the day of Jesus Christ's return, the day of reckoning, is drawing close, make sure that you live ever more consistently as followers of Jesus in your everyday lives, at day and at night, in your dealings with your neighbors and in your dealings with the government. Use all the spiritual gifts that God has given to you in your house-church. Get rid of any evil deeds, shed them like dirty clothes and live as those who live in the light, as people who have nothing to hide. Avoid quarreling about matters of food and drink, don't condemn Christian brothers and sisters and always remember that despite all the personal convictions that we have, we do not belong to ourselves but to the Lord Jesus Christ.

I know that you have not lost your missionary zeal, despite the upheavals in your city and in your churches. This is one of the main reasons why I want to visit you. I am presently in Corinth waiting for the end of winter. My next stop will be Jerusalem where I will be handing over funds that I collected in the churches in Greece and Asia Minor, money that the Christians in Judea need, and where I will be consulting with the leaders of the church in Jerusalem concerning my future sphere of missionary activity. I plan to leave the Eastern regions of the Mediterranean and go to the province of Spain. And this is where you come in: I hope that you will be able to help me in this new endeavor, as you know more about Spain than I do. We will talk about details once I arrive later this year, Lord willing. To him be the glory forever through Jesus Christ.

Scripture Meditation

Who through the Spirit of holiness was declared with power to be the Son of God by his resurrection from the dead: Jesus Christ our Lord.

—ROMANS 1:4

Thought for the Day

Without the recognition of Jesus Christ as the Son of God, there is no salvation.

Prayer

Grace and peace to you from God our Father and from the Lord Jesus Christ.

—ROMANS 1:7

SEPTEMBER 7: FROM AQUILA TO PAUL

Dr. Eckhard J. Schnabel wrote as Aquila to Paul the apostle.

*M*y dear brother Paul:

The arrival of your long letter was a surprise for all of us! Knowing how busy you are we felt rather privileged that you took the time to summarize for us the message that you have proclaimed for so many years now, the message that we proclaim here in Rome also.

It was sobering to be reminded of what we were before we turned to Jesus Christ. One of our recent converts, P. Turronius Claudius, became very uneasy when we read your letter out loud: when he heard you writing about foul talk, speech filled with lies, mouths being full of cursing and bitterness and destruction following people, he thought that you were describing his former life! He had been a respectable citizen, but his family knew that this had been just a facade. He was one of our Jewish business partners, a freedman of the imperial household. It was only last month that he finally accepted our invitation to dinner. We shared our conviction that the promised savior had actually come, and that his death on a cross—he had of course heard about the events in Judea and in Galilee concerning John the prophet who baptized and concerning Jesus of Nazareth, the teacher who healed the sick—was not the end of a story but the fulfillment of God's plan to save sinners from death by giving his only Son to die. He was very moved, and when Priscilla shared how she had become convinced that all this was true and how this conviction had changed her life, and the lives of so many others, he asked whether we could pray for him.

You should have seen the joy on his face! He had regularly attended the services of the *Synagoga Augustensium* and he tried to follow the Jewish traditions. But he could not control his bad temper, which made him use very foul language, especially when he conversed in Latin. He was involved in several shady business deals, and he could not stop sleeping around with the slave girls in his house. He knew that he was destroying his family. He could hardly believe when we told him God would forgive him all his sins, once and for all, if he believed that Jesus, the son of God, died for his sins—and that he would have to offer no sacrifices, perform no acts of contrition. Claudius went home that evening determined to ask his wife and family, his employees and his business partners for forgiveness.

When Claudius came to the next meeting of the church that meets in our house, he brought his wife along who couldn't explain the changes that she observed in her husband's behavior. As they came early Priscilla had time to explain the gospel to her as well. When the other brothers and sisters came, Claudius was shocked to see Paparion, originally from Akmonia in Phrygia, the slave of one of his business partners. He had not known that he was a Christian. He was even more shocked when Paparion addressed the congregation and explained how remembering the sufferings of Jesus and focusing on the love that God had poured into his heart had helped him go through a difficult week, exhorting all who were present to not let the hardships of life darken the light of their joy as children of God. Claudius is learning that ethnic and racial differences have become unimportant for us, as unimportant as social distinctions; I think he begins to enjoy the rich diversity of the people who gather in our house.

Dear Paul, we continue to learn what it means to live as a Christian. Each time one of our friends or neighbors is converted to Jesus Christ, we share in their joy. At the same time we know that the power of God's Spirit does not transform our behavior overnight. There are so many temptations. Some of our friends have to attend banquets where they offer sexual entertainment. And there are always more questions. Some of our Jewish members were not convinced by your argument concerning food and drink, just last week we had another discussion about that. But we press on. A major encouragement is the conversion of so many non-Jews: their excitement when they understand, and receive, the unconditional forgiveness of the only true God is truly contagious. We are therefore eager to hear more about your plans concerning Spain. Several of our members, I think, would be prepared to go with you.

Scripture Meditation

I am not ashamed of the gospel, because it is the power of God for the salvation of everyone who believes: first for the Jew, then for the Gentile.
—*Romans 1:16*

Thought of the Day

Christians do not copy the behavior and customs of this world: Having trusted Jesus Christ for salvation from eternal death, they let God transform their life so that they can recognize and accomplish his will, which is always good and pleasing and perfect.

Prayer

Pardon for sin and a peace that endureth,
thy own dear presence to cheer and to guide,
strength for today and bright hope for tomorrow,
blessings all mine, with ten thousand beside—
great is thy faithfulness!
—THOMAS CHISHOLM

SEPTEMBER 8: NEW TESTAMENT LETTERS: 1 CORINTHIANS

To the proudly self-sufficient Corinthians, the central theme of Paul's message
is that all of life—past, present and future —is "gifted" by God in his grace.
Canon Anthony C. Thiselton (b. 1937), emeritus professor of New Testament
Theology at the University of Nottingham, England,
provided this précis of the epistle.

Those who serve God as his ministers are agents serving with this gift of divine grace (chapters 1—4). The Corinthians are to avoid too high a view of such ministry. For "what is Paul? What is Apollos? Servants, through whom you believed" (3:5). But they are equally to avoid too low a view of Christian ministry: "Do not cheat yourselves ..., all things are yours, whether Paul or Apollos or Cephas" (3:18–23). That is to say, they need all of these ministerial resources, without picking or choosing as if from a stall in the marketplace.

After addressing some clear-cut moral issues of sexuality, idolatry, and law-suits with fellow Christians, in chapters 5—6, Paul begins his critical exposition of mutuality and reciprocity in nearly all the remainder of the letter. This begins with respect for the other in marriage (7:3–6, 32–38); then he proceeds to discuss respect by the socially influential ("the strong") for the vulnerable, and understanding on the part of the vulnerable for opportunities afforded to the wealthy to maintain their social contacts (8:1–10, 30); respect between man and woman (11:8–10); between the wealthy and their guests (the "haves") and the "have-nots" at the Lord's supper (11:17–22); and especially a use of spiritual gifts that is to build not the self (14:4), but others in love (chapters 12—14).

Hence "Body" (as [Anglican theologian Ernst] Kasemann suggests) denotes for Paul a communicable and recognizable self in interpersonal relations with others. In 1 Corinthians 15:44–57, the "self" is transformed into a progressive state of increasing glory (15:44), not least because it bears the image of Christ. Death becomes a gateway without a sting (15:55), but only because of the proclamation of the cross which has transforming, life-changing, power (1:18–25), which reaches its full climax in the transformative event of the final resurrection.

Scripture Meditation

Do you not know that your body is a temple of the Holy Spirit, who is in you, whom you have received from God? You are not your own; you were bought at a price. Therefore honor God with your body.

—1 CORINTHIANS 6:19–20

Thought for the Day

The phrase of the apostle Paul "of God" is the secret nerve of the whole of the first epistle to the Corinthians.

—KARL BARTH

Prayer

Just as I am, tho' tossed about
With many a conflict, many a doubt,
Fightings and fears within, without,
O Lamb of God, I come!, I come!

—CHARLOTTE ELLIOT

SEPTEMBER 9: NEW TESTAMENT LETTERS:
ON REREADING FIRST CORINTHIANS

*This summary response was made by Anthony C. Thiselton, who has recently
published the most exhaustive study of the epistle.*

This letter is to be recognized as more than an epistle about ethics,
unity, and a series of diverse pastoral problems. It reflects a deep inner
coherence (no less than Romans) on the gift-character of grace. This epistle has as its center the transforming, formative, shaping power of the
proclamation of the Cross. "The proclamation of the cross is foolishness
to those who are on their way to ruin … but … the power of God and the
wisdom of God … to us who believe" (1:18–25). It culminates in the
promise of the resurrection as that which equally rests upon God's sheer
gift of sovereign creativity: "How are the dead raised? God gives it a body
(a mode of existence in the public world) as he has chosen" (15:35–38).

Karl Barth hinted at this perspective in his powerful study *The
Resurrection of the Dead*, but much more may be inferred from a mass
of new research about Corinth as a Roman and entrepreneurial city in
Paul's day. Corinth was effectively destroyed as a Greek city, and re-
founded by Julius Caesar as a Roman colony in 44 BC. Its early settlers
were military veterans, freed persons, slaves, and business entrepreneurs.
The geographical situation of the city at the crossroads between East
and West, North and South, ensured that it would be the center of trade,
and the Isthmian games and the Peirene fountains ensured that it would
be a magnet for highfliers in manufacture and business. Fortunes could
be made or lost almost overnight.

This raised a major problem as well as strategic opportunity for
Paul. Many at Corinth came to regard the Gospel as a commodity to
be marketed for the benefit of consumers. They expected Paul to
behave like a paid rhetorician. Hence he declares with passion that the
message of the Cross is that which shapes the hearers and their desires
that shape the Gospel (1:18—2:5). The message, we might say today, is
not a product shaped by the desire for success, or as we might say
today of "social construction." God has "given" it. "What do you have

that you did not receive?" asks the apostle, for "by the grace of God I am what I am" (1 Cor. 4:7; 15:10).

Indeed, "gift" is the key. Paul takes the self-congratulatory term beloved at Corinth, we are "spiritual" people, with "spiritual" endowments (Greek *pneumatikoi* and *pneumatika,* 12:1), and reformulates them as "freely given gifts" (Greek, *charismata,* the rest of chapters 12—14). Where there is competitiveness and self-regard, people are hardly "spiritual" (3:1–4).

Hence the *fullest* "spiritual" mode of being is promised (even in the case of Christians) at the resurrection of the dead, when the whole person (the "body") will be raised as a spiritual *soma* (Greek term), i.e. as a mode of being wholly animated and characterized by the Holy Spirit. This, again, is not a "natural" capacity of the self (as immortality is often thought to be). It is a *gift,* which the Creator God bestows upon those who cannot themselves achieve it because they are biologically dead! Resurrection and justification by grace alone share then the same logic: all is of God, but God gives the gift to the human persons *as they are.*

Scripture Meditation

By the grace God has given me, I laid a foundation ... and some-one else is building on it. But each one should be careful how he builds. For no one can lay any foundation other than the one already laid, which is Jesus Christ.

—1 CORINTHIANS 3:10–11

Thought for the Day

Paul's message to the Corinthians still turns our world "upside down."

Prayer

God, strengthen me to bear myself,
That heaviest weight of all to bear,
Inalienable weight of care....
Yet One there is can curb myself,
Can roll the strangling load from me,
Break off the yoke and set me free.

—CHRISTINA ROSSETTI

SEPTEMBER 10: NEW TESTAMENT LETTERS: 2 CORINTHIANS

The Rev. Dr. Paul Barnett (b. 1935), formerly bishop of North Sydney,
Australia, now senior fellow of the Institute of Ancient Documents Research
Centre, Macquarrie University, New South Wales, Australia, and teaching
fellow of Moore College, Sydney, Australia, wrote, on behalf of
the apostle Paul, this summary of Second Corinthians.

I am writing this shorter version of my letter so the main points are not lost. I look forward to hearing back from you as soon as possible since I want my upcoming final visit to be a happy one.

It will be good to see you to work through the issues between us face to face. I am sure Titus will fill in the gaps.

Meanwhile I want you to know that I am a man of my word. When I did not come back to you direct but sent that tough letter instead I want you to know that I had no alternative. I stared death in the face in Ephesus at the time of the silversmiths' riot and had to flee for my life to Troas. In any case that letter has borne good fruit. You have dealt with the man who treated me so badly in my recent visit. But now it's time to restore him to the fellowship because he has expressed his regrets about what happened. But, to be frank, not all his friends have cut their ties once and for all from the local temples and prostitutes. You must be firm with these people since I don't want to discipline them when I come, though I will if it's necessary to do so.

On another matter, we really must settle money matters since they are so important to us both. My firm policy is not to accept payment for ministry. I have my own personal reasons for this; the Lord called me to preach to the Nations. How can I accept payment for doing his will, especially since I was a cruel persecutor? In any case, there is no shortage of money-hungry hucksters peddling their teachings and I don't want the Message of Christ dragged into the mud on their account. You, however, think I am getting money any way, from the support you are giving Titus. Let me assure you that I am not. You really ought to think better of me!

Is it because of your loss of confidence in me that you have stopped contributing to the fund for the believers in Jerusalem? You really must rise above your negative feelings about me. Did you know that the

Macedonians have actually asked to participate, persecuted and poverty stricken though they are? By contrast you are so well off. These Jewish believers are your brothers and sisters in Christ. One day you may be affected by famine and they will come to your aid as I am asking you to come to theirs. Remember the Lord Jesus. He was rich and he made himself poor to bring you salvation. God will honor your generosity and provide for your ongoing needs as well as provide the means for further generosity. Not least your obedience to Christ in this will connect you and them in him. So, please, finish what you so willingly began.

But, O my Corinthian children, my biggest concern is the recent arrival of the missioners from Jerusalem and your uncritical welcome of them. By now you should be able to discern true apostles from false. So I am saddened that you are taken in by those who claim to be ministers of Christ based on shallow credentials like "visions and revelations" and superior rhetoric. You are so vulnerable to superficial and triumphalist preachers. More importantly, they are seriously misleading. They claim that Moses' covenant is still operative and that we must find righteousness by self-effort. Surely you know by now that when "One died for all" he gave us the "righteousness of God." That Old Covenant was only ever an anticipation of Christ and the Spirit. True it came with glory but it never worked because of sin.

In this regard, let me pretend for the moment that I am a "fool." Please remember my many sufferings, including my "thorn" which has never left me. Can't you see that my sufferings are like those of our Lord on the cross and that they come to me precisely because I am true to the message of the cross of Christ. The genuine minister is identified by his faithfulness to Christ crucified, come what may, not in displays of religious power.

Having said all this, however, let me assure you that you are nonetheless true believers. This brings me comfort since I know that through Christ I was involved in bringing you to faith. These newcomers may come with "letters of recommendation" but you are my "letter of recommendation" that comes from Christ himself.

I don't often bare my soul but let me tell you that I love you as a father loves his children. Please love me back the way I love you.

Farewell dear friends. I look forward to seeing you soon. Take seriously the things I have written. Don't force me to come in sadness to deal with offenders. The Lord called me to be a builder not a demolisher! Let me build you up.

Scripture Meditation

For God, who said, "Let light shine out of darkness," made his
light shine in our hearts, to give us the light of the knowledge of
the glory of God in the face of Christ.

—2 Corinthians 4:6

Thought for the Day

Receiving God's love in our hearts is a mighty act of God.

Prayer

May the grace of the Lord Jesus Christ, and the love of God, and
the fellowship of the Holy Spirit be with you all.

—2 Corinthians 13:14

SEPTEMBER 11: NEW TESTAMENT LETTERS:
A RESPONSE TO 2 CORINTHIANS

In the previous letter the Rev. Dr. Paul Barnett presented a commentary on
2 Corinthians. Here he composed a brief response to
that letter from the Corinthians.

We were very moved when Titus read and explained your letter at our
monthly meeting. Many of us wept when we were reminded that you are
our father in the Lord and that you love us. Our debt to you is beyond
words. We are sorry for having doubted your promises and your obvious
self-sacrificial love for us.

So we are all very chastened and look forward to seeing you soon. Everything you have asked of us we will do, gladly so.

We have resolved to resume and complete the Collection. It will be ready when you come.

We have decided to tell the missioners to go back to Palestine. You are right. There is no going back to the Old Covenant. Christ is our righteousness and we know that we have the Spirit. This is the new and final chapter in God's book. And yes, these newcomers were all outward show and with a shallow theology. We appreciate your common-sense approach and straightforward presentation.

Gaius is preparing his guest room for you so we will all see you when we gather together. Be assured that a warm welcome awaits you when you come for your final visit. May the Lord protect you as you travel.

Scripture Meditation

Have you been thinking all along that we have been defending ourselves to you? We have been speaking in the sight of God as those in Christ; and everything we do, dear friends, is for your strengthening.

—2 Corinthians 12:19

Thought for the Day

The transparency of our relationship with the Lord helps us share the same loving relationship with others and not be mesmerized falsely.

Prayer

Lord help me to focus on Christ and not be dazzled by teachers who are all show and no substance.

—Paul Barnett

SEPTEMBER 12: NEW TESTAMENT LETTERS:
PAUL'S LETTERS TO THE THESSALONIANS

Dr. Michelle Lee is professor of New Testament Studies at Talbot Theological Seminary, Biola University, California. She summarized the two letters of the apostle Paul as she interpreted what he might have dictated.

I am writing you a single letter from my previous two letters so you may see the fullness of my concerns and love for you.

I am rejoicing greatly at the steadfastness of your faith. I was much concerned over you because I was unable to stay with you as long as I wanted to impart to you more of our faith. For this reason I was exceedingly glad to hear that not only do you still stand, but your faith has become known throughout the region.

As you know, I came to you because God had directed me through the vision of the man who called me to Macedonia. Since this calling I have experienced much that could cause me to become discouraged. I was imprisoned in Philippi and expelled from Berea, and I had very little visible success in Athens. How encouraging, therefore, it was to hear the reports of your faith! Your faith and love for one another are proof of the power of the gospel.

As you know, it is God alone that I seek to please. But preaching the gospel to you was not just a task for me, since I gave you my life as well as the gospel. I cared for you deeply, as tenderly and affectionately as a nursing mother cares for her own children.

Because I cared for you, I sought to return to you, my hope and joy. I finally sent Timothy to you, knowing that the afflictions you were suffering might cause your faith to weaken. How happy I was to find out on his return that you stand firm and long to see me as well. For this I can only rejoice and continue to pray I may see you again so that I may give you further instruction to complete your faith. I pray that the Lord will lead me to you once again and that you may continue to grow in love for each other and all people so that you may be blameless in holiness before our God and Father when our Lord returns.

For this reason I exhort you again to walk in a way that is pleasing to God, continuing to pursue his will for your life, which is your sanctification.

I urge you to walk in purity. You already love one another, but I ask you to excel still more.

What a glorious day it will be when the Lord returns! We do not need to worry about those who have died, since we do not grieve as those who have no hope. Even as Jesus died and rose again, so will those who have fallen asleep rise again. When the Lord returns from heaven, the dead will rise at the sound of his voice and the trumpet of God, and then we who are still alive will also be caught up to meet the Lord in the clouds.

This is the hope that sustains us, and we must always be ready. You know that the day of the Lord will come suddenly, just when people believe that they are secure. But you are not in the darkness, that you will be taken by surprise, like a thief in the night. You are children of the light and of the day, and are prepared with the breastplate of faith and love and the helmet of the hope of salvation. When our Lord comes, all of us, whether awake or asleep, will be together with him. Comfort and encourage one another with these words, just as you are already doing.

Although I know of your steadfastness, I want to encourage you even more in the midst of your trials, so that you will not lose heart. Be assured that your perseverance is a sign of the worthiness of your faith. God is not unjust and will vindicate you when the Lord is revealed with his angels at the judgment and glorified in his saints.

Be reassured, beloved, that the day has not yet arrived. Indeed it will not come until the apostasy and the revelation of the man of lawlessness. The mystery of lawlessness is already at work, but the lawless one will not be revealed until the restrainer is removed. He will deceive many, but you will not be deceived because you have been chosen for salvation and to gain the glory of Christ. Remember for what you have been called, therefore, and stand firm!

Pray for me, that I may spread the word of God and be delivered from evil people. Know that the Lord is faithful and will protect you as well. Follow my example in living a disciplined life and exhort those who are idle to do likewise. Do not become weary in doing good.

And may the God of peace himself sanctify and preserve you until the coming of our Lord. The grace of our Lord Jesus be with you.

Scripture Meditation

But you, brothers, are not in darkness so that this day should surprise you like a thief. You are all sons of the light and sons of the day. We do not belong to the night or to the darkness. So then, let us not be like others, who are asleep, but let us be alert and self-controlled.

— I Thessalonians 5:4–6

Thought for the Day

We must remain vigilant in the midst of an often difficult world, but Christ is faithful through all our trials.

Prayer

Lord, help me to remain faithful to your truth and not be deceived or become weary.

—Michelle Lee

September 13: New Testament Letters: A Contemporary Response to Paul's Letters to the Thessalonians

---

Dr. Michelle Lee continued with a response, appropriately received, to the apostle's message to the church of Thessalonica, yesterday and today.

Our hearts are full of joy whenever we think of you. When you first came to us, we were strangers to you and yet you gave us your very life. You worked night and day so that you might preach the gospel to us, not caring about your own comfort or well-being but only that we might know the riches of Christ and turn away from our useless idols to serve the true and living God.

We are humbled and yet rejoice that we might give you some joy by your knowing that this community that you care for so much is thriving in the midst of trials. For what temporary loss or hardship can compare with the great privilege of knowing Christ Jesus our Lord and eagerly anticipating our future glory with him? Although you were with us briefly, you taught us well, and we know that our joy and hope lie only with our Lord. We were glad to see Timothy and hope that you also will return to us soon.

We continue to try to live as you instructed us, knowing that our God desires holiness. It is not always easy to love each other and to live in harmony, but we remember the example of our Lord and your example and seek to serve one another in all things. We often fail, but through the Spirit we are learning and growing in love every day.

Your words about the return of the Lord and the resurrection of those who have fallen asleep were a great comfort to many. We mourn for those who have died because we have loved them dearly. But what an indescribable hope we have in the resurrection! One day we will be reunited and all live forever with our Lord. What great comfort we have knowing that those we loved are not lost. This is the hope that sustains us. Thanks be to God! We will do our best to be prepared always as we look for the return of our Lord, remembering your exhortation and the assurance of our faith.

We are zealous in guarding the truths you left with us. Many around us are deceived, and we encounter the works of darkness daily. But we strive to live in the peace and love of our Lord and to be a steadfast presence in our community.

We often remember your example of perseverance and love, and this encourages us daily. How much we long to see you! May the grace of our Lord be with you. We pray for you always.

Scripture Meditation

We continually remember before our God and Father your work produced by faith, your labor prompted by love, and your endurance inspired by hope in our Lord Jesus Christ.

— I THESSALONIANS 1:3

Thought for the Day

The quality of our faith is reflected in our care for our fellow believers.

Prayer

Lord, may I continue to grow in faith and in love for my brothers and sisters in Christ.

—MICHELLE LEE

SEPTEMBER 14: NEW TESTAMENT LETTERS:
PAUL'S LETTERS TO TIMOTHY

Reverend Eugene Peterson (b. 1932), pastor, teacher, writer, and translator of
The Message *used his translation to summarize Paul's first letter to Timothy.*
The apostle Paul assigned his young associate Timothy to work in the church
in Ephesus, a church he himself had gathered and pastored for three years.
But the church had been victimized by bad teachers. He wrote two letters to
Timothy, directing him in carrying out the task of sound teaching.

Timothy, my son in the faith....

On my way to the province of Macedonia, I advised you to stay in
Ephesus. Well, I haven't changed my mind. Stay right there on top of
things so that the teaching stays on track. Apparently some people have
been introducing fantasy stories and fanciful family trees that digress
into silliness, instead of pulling the people back into the center, deepening faith and obedience.

The whole point of what we're urging is simply *love*—love uncontami-
nated by self-interest and counterfeit faith, a life open to God. Those who
fail to keep to this point soon wander off into cul-de-sacs of gossip. They
set themselves up as experts on religious issues, but haven't the remotest
idea of what they're holding forth with such imposing eloquence....

I'm passing this work on to you, my son Timothy. The prophetic word
that was directed to you prepared us for this. All those prayers are

coming together now so you will do this well, fearless in your struggle, keeping a firm grip on your faith and on yourself. After that, this is a fight we're in....

Since prayer is at the bottom of all this, what I want mostly is for men to pray—not shaking angry fists at enemies but raising holy hands to God. And I want women to get in there with the men in humility before God, not primping before a mirror or chasing the latest fashions but doing something beautiful for God and becoming beautiful doing it....

You've been raised on the Message of the faith and have followed sound teaching. Now pass on this counsel to the Christians there, and you'll be a good servant of Jesus. Stay clear of silly stories that get dressed up as religion. Exercise daily in God—no spiritual flabbiness, please! Workouts in the gymnasium are useful, but a disciplined life in God is far more so, making you fit both today and forever....

Teach these things. And don't let anyone put you down because you're young. Teach believers with your life: by word, by demeanor, by love, by faith, by integrity. Stay at your post reading Scripture, giving counsel, teaching. And that special gift of ministry you were given when the leaders of the church laid hands on you and prayed—keep that dusted off and in use.... Keep a firm grasp on both your character and teaching. Don't be diverted....

And oh, my dear Timothy, guard the treasure you were given! Guard it with your life. Avoid the talk-show religion and the practiced confusion of the so-called experts. People caught up in a lot of talk can miss the whole point of faith. Overwhelming grace keep you!

Scripture Meditation

This is a trustworthy saying that deserves full acceptance (and for this we labor and strive), that we have put our hope in the living God, who is the Savior of all.

—1 TIMOTHY 4:9–10

Thought for the Day

Living in the presence of the living God puts all things into proper perspective.

Prayer

Give me, Jesus, Master Teacher, a keen sense for the truth conveyed in your life and words. And a sharp eye for discerning religious nonsense that only confuses and distracts. Amen.

—EUGENE PETERSON

SEPTEMBER 15: NEW TESTAMENT LETTERS: A RESPONSE TO PAUL'S LETTERS TO TIMOTHY

Reverend Eugene Peterson responded to Paul's letters to Timothy in a letter dated September 2, 2002.

Dear Timothy,

I have recently come across the letters that your mentor, Paul, your father in the faith, wrote to you. I sit here wondering how you felt on receiving them—they've sure put adrenaline in my blood! I've been walking around for a couple of weeks now, reading parts of them to my friends, muttering some of those sentences under my breath while going about my work, finding phrases attaching themselves to my prayers. Nobody has ever written letters like that to me! You are very fortunate to have been given that quality of thoughtful and prayerful guidance while you were working in that tangle of a congregation that Ephesus has become. It's blessing enough for me to get in on them second hand.

When I became a pastor I assumed that I would be building on foundations laid down by the "prophets and apostles." And in a basic sense, I guess that is what I have been doing. But it never occurred to me that I would have to spend so much of my time cleaning up the mess left behind by others. And now I realize that you had to do the exact same thing. And

219

in the Ephesian congregation of all places—a congregation formed under the preaching and prayers of Apollos and Paul! Of all the New Testament churches, I always thought of the Ephesian congregation as the most mature of the bunch—a "perfect church." What I've come to realize is that not even the "perfect" church stays perfect very long. Reading between Paul's lines it certainly looks like you had your hands full there.

From the numerous references Paul makes to all the loose talk and empty speculation going on in that church, there must have been a lot of either diseased or anemic words making their rounds. Noticing that, I couldn't miss the aptness of Paul's adjective "sound" or "healthy" in regard to words and teaching and doctrine. I think he used it four times in his two letters to you. What strikes me most forcibly in Paul's Ephesian assignment to you is how important words are and what a sacred trust every Christian has to teach the next generation what we have been taught—and how much Paul depended upon you to use the scriptural and gospel words accurately and seriously.

I don't think that things have gotten any better in the church or the world in the use of words than they were in your day—that's a little discouraging. But in reading these letters that shaped your life and gave urgency to the words you used and the way you used them, I feel honored to be included with you in the company of men and women who are called to use words to the glory of God.

The peace of our Lord be with you, Eugene

Scripture Meditation

Preach the Word; be prepared in season and out of season; correct, rebuke and encourage—with great patience and careful instruction. For the time will come when men will not put up with sound doctrine.

—2 TIMOTHY 4:2–3

Thought for the Day

Soundness of faith is even more vital than health of body.

Prayer

Give those that teach pure hearts, wisdom, faith, hope, and love, all warmed by prayer, themselves first training for the skies, they best will raise their people there. Amen.

—JOHN ARMSTRONG

SEPTEMBER 16: THE NEW TESTAMENT LETTERS: A RESPONSE TO THE
APOSTLE'S LETTER TO THE GALATIANS

---

*Mike Mason (b. 1952), a Canadian writer living in Langley, British Columbia,
wrote a response to Paul's letter to the Christians in Galatia, in Asia Minor,
who were being tempted to engage in Jewish practices. His emphasis
was on the vital freedom we have "in Christ."*

*D*ear Paul,

What fierce, even crude, language you use as you re-preach the gospel to people who should have grasped it already! It's amazing that such language hasn't been edited out of our Bibles.

I must admit that I sometimes feel this way toward people in my own church—people who talk a good line about their faith (such a good line that sometimes I'm taken in by it myself), but who then turn around and inflict untold damage on others by trying to make them jump through some ridiculous hoop. And it's all done so subtly, all in the name of "Christ"! I agree with you that such "faith" is utterly useless—that the moment we put anything at all ahead of unconditional love, we not only miss the gospel but we take up hammer and nails against Christ Himself.

I'm afraid, Paul, that if you were to write today to the church in North America, you would have to speak in this same shocking way. You would have to re-preach the gospel to people who think they have known it for years, people who know their theology inside out but who have lost touch with the earth-shattering freedom of the real thing.

Why did you talk so tough to those foolish Galatians? It was because you knew the power of the true gospel to set people free—so free that they would stand forever amazed and brimming with thanks before their glorious Savior. You also knew that any little kink in this gospel would change it into something else, producing exactly the sort of lethargic, hidebound religion so prevalent today. I pray that we might hear your stunning wake-up call and return to "the only thing that counts."

What impresses most is the way the power of a single word can alter one's whole life. For you state: "God, who set me apart from birth and called me by his grace, was pleased to reveal his Son in me" (Gal. 1:15–16).

Every time I read your letter to the Galatians (and I read it often; I actually became a Christian while reading this letter) I'm always surprised by this verse. What astonishes me (as so often in your letters) is the light that streams from one peculiar little word—in this case, the preposition "in."

Why didn't you write "to"? In your famous Damascus Road experience, didn't Jesus Christ appear to you rather than in you? Yet as I ponder this verse, I wonder if the crucial moment of your conversion actually came later, as you sat in the darkness of your temporary blindness and tried to make sense of what had happened on the Damascus Road. Was it then that the Son of God was revealed in you and you believed?

Ah! how great and precious is that light that shines in the dark secrecy of our own hearts! And how amazing that God Himself should come to live in us by His Spirit! Yet sadly, we can ask Jesus "into" our hearts and still relate to Him as if He's outside somewhere, distant and unreachable.

Thanks to your little word "in," Paul, I'm reminded that the essence of spirituality is not a closer walk with God, not a drawing near to God, but rather the realization that in Christ there is no more drawing near to do. It's all been done already by the One who died for us so that He might live in us.

Already we're as close to Him as we can be!

In loving gratitude, Mike

Scripture Meditation

God, who set me apart from birth and called me by his grace, was
pleased to reveal his Son in me.
—GALATIANS 1:15–16

Thought for the Day

God's gift to me is the gift of my own uniqueness before God and the
grace to be truly myself "in Christ."

Prayer

Lord, take my lips and speak through them, take my mind and
think through it, take my heart and set it on fire!
—FRANCES RIDLEY HAVERGAL

SEPTEMBER 17: NEW TESTAMENT LETTERS:
A RESPONSE TO PHILIPPIANS

*Mike Mason engaged also with the
apostle Paul's letter to the Philippians.*

Dear Paul,

Is it really possible to be always joyful? Reading your letter, I'm
moved to respond: Why not? Why not accept God's grand, stupendous
gift of life like a big chunk of watermelon, letting the sweet pink flesh
melt in our mouths, and as for the rest, spit it out? Why gnaw away dole-
fully on seeds and rind?

223

Our God is a God of absolutes. Scripture also exhort us to "always have hope" (Ps. 71:14), to "pray continually" (1 Thess. 5:17), to be "always giving thanks" (Eph. 5:20), and to "keep all [God's] commands always" (Deut. 5:29). So it is with joy.

Or consider the matter of love. Does anyone argue that we should love sometimes but not all the time? No, love "always protects, always trusts, always hopes, always perseveres" (1 Cor. 13:7).

Pondering your challenge to be always joyful, we may get stuck on that little word "always," and so overlook the key phrase that follows: "in the Lord." Nowhere does the Bible ask us to do anything in our own strength, but only in the Lord. It would be cruel to expect anyone to be always happy apart from God. But "in the Lord"—why not?

Therefore if we have Christ, why not rejoice? If we don't have Christ, let's open our hearts to Him!

This message was so important to you, Paul, that you couldn't help repeating it: "I will say it again: Rejoice!" The very word rejoice contains (in the prefix re) this idea of over again. True joy is tireless. It's like a little child squealing, "Do it again, Daddy!" to which our heavenly Daddy replies heartily, "Yes, let's do it again! And again and again!"

Joyfully yours, Mike

Scripture Meditation

Your attitude should be the same as that of Jesus Christ: Who, being in very nature God, ... made himself nothing.

—PHILIPPIANS 2:5–7

Thought for the Day

Profound revelations, as in the "self-emptying of God," are used "absolutely," for simple, daily practices of living before God and others.

Prayer

Let your love so warm our souls, O Lord, that we may gladly surrender ourselves with all that we are and have, unto you ... grant us to rejoice in your love for ever and ever. Amen.

—GERHARD TERSTEEGEN

SEPTEMBER 18: NEW TESTAMENT LETTERS: JAMES

A widow, Mrs. Elisabeth Bockmuehl (b. 1938), docent in Church History
in Chrishona Theological Seminary, near Basle, Switzerland,
reflected on the epistle of James in a letter to her friend.

*D*ear Rita,

As you know I was an only child, and so was Klaus my husband. When we married and had children, I had hoped to experience in and with my children, what it means to have a brother and sister, and I was very grateful for my three children.

Then I heard you say more than once, that I am like a younger sister, and I was very happy about that. Of course, I knew that together we are part of God's family, too. Jesus told us, that God is "Our Father in heaven"—and so Jesus must have accepted me as his little sister, too.

Then I wondered sometimes, how it must have been to be the brother or sister of Jesus—like James the Just. So I looked into the Letter of James, which may be the oldest text in the New Testament. I cannot be a physical sister of Jesus, but James was his brother. For a long time, James was very skeptical about Jesus, which seems quite natural for a brother about his sibling (John 7:2–5). James thought that Jesus was eccentric, overdoing things in his piety. He thought Jesus should fit more into his understanding of how a brother should walk, talk, work, and live. In his view, Jesus was not behaving naturally. Of course, he was right in a way, because Jesus was made and lived in the image of his Father in heaven.

It was only after Jesus died and was risen again and had appeared to James, that he came to accept Jesus as his Lord, to love him and his ways with all his heart. And so James became the leader of the young Christian church in Jerusalem, and finally he died as a martyr for Jesus.

Now, what does that all mean to me? I do belong with you, my dear friend, to the family of God. And James tells us in his letter: "Come near to God and he will come near to you," and so let us continue to go together!

With much love, Elisabeth

Scripture Meditation

My brothers, as believers in our glorious Lord Jesus Christ, don't show favoritism .
—JAMES 2:1

Thought for the Day

The practice of the Christian life is realistically tested within our families and their relationships.

Prayer

I offer myself in sacrifice, I yield myself to you, O Lord, I would have no other desire than to do your will. Teach me to pray. Pray yourself in me.
—FRANÇOIS FENELON

SEPTEMBER 19: NEW TESTAMENT LETTERS: PETER'S FIRST LETTER

The Rev. Dr. Richard A. Burridge (b. 1955) is dean of King's College, London, a New Testament scholar, and church leader. He has written widely on Jesus and the Gospels. He wrote this personal response to the apostle Peter, on the theme "Following Christ's Example," based upon Peter's first epistle, on August 18, 2003.

*D*ear Peter,

I loved your first letter from when I first read it as a young Christian. All that outburst of praise at the start, blessing "the God and Father of our Lord Jesus Christ" for our new birth really excited me (1:3–9), and then there was your vision of the church as "living stones" (2:4–6). I even played in a rock group called the "X N Trick Brick Band" because we were rather "eccentric" stones!

Yet now I am older, with years of ministry behind me. And I've got further into the later chapters, pondering your instructions to elders like me: "be examples to the flock. And when the chief shepherd appears, you will win the crown of glory that never fades away. In the same way, you who are younger must accept the authority of the elders" (5:3–5).

Like me, your letter seems to have settled down now. Isn't this rather a mixed message—or merely ordinary, conventional instructions? Is ministry really only about giving a good example? Then there are also all those instructions about being submissive: "conduct yourselves honourably among the Gentiles" and "accept the authority of every human institution" including emperors and governors (2:12–14). As for the poor slaves and women, you just tell them to put up with their masters and husbands, even when they abuse them (2:18—3:6). It's not a very revolutionary message—so how did this turn the world upside down within your lifetime?

I wonder if you have given us a clue there in 2:21: "to this you have been called, because Christ also suffered for you, leaving you an example, so that you should follow in his steps." But I thought he was the Lord, the Son of God the Father, the one who is going to return and give the crown of glory to those who have obeyed the authorities and given a good example to others. Isn't it rather a paradox—the master who has suffered, or the king who behaves like a servant? Is that really an example we can follow?

In fact, now I come to think of it, wasn't his whole ministry paradoxical like that? I mean, everyone thinks of Jesus as the great moral teacher—yet, he had a very strange group of followers. How can he teach things like "turn the other cheek" when he includes freedom fighters like Simon the Zealot in his gang? Or what about giving your money away, when you accept tax collectors like Matthew or Zacchaeus? And what he had to say about sex must have made people like Mary very uncomfortable. Then finally there was you and your big mouth, acting first and thinking later, recognizing Jesus as the Christ one minute and then trying to stop him going to suffer and die the next; how can you be inspired by the Father and then act like Satan so quickly (Matt. 16:17, 23)? Yet he called you Peter, the "rock" on which the rest of us living stones were going to be built—"rocky" stones no longer.

What was it like mixing with all this lot, everyone with their own shortcomings and problems? It must have been incredible, to have been loved and accepted by Jesus just as you were—and then to have to accept the others just as they were. Is that what the church could be again—a mixed group of mixed-up people, each with their own sins, yet gradually being made whole and new?

Perhaps that's why you wrote all that stuff at the start of your letter about being born again to a living hope and rejoicing despite the sufferings (1:3, 6). Maybe only people like that can become the living stones, no matter how eccentric we are (2:4). Is it because we have received mercy and been called out of darkness that we should show mercy to others and bring them God's light (2:9–10)? If that's the case, then suffering need not make us into a doormat—but rather the open door into the example of Christ (2:21). And as for being an elder or a minister, if that's the example we have to give the flock of God, it certainly won't mean sitting around resting on our laurels (5:2–3). If we have to accept people and forgive as Jesus has forgiven us, then I can see how that might be liberating and turn the world upside down again.

Thanks for writing, Peter, and giving the rest of us, eccentric bricks or rough diamonds, the vision of being "living stones" and following Jesus' example. If you can lead the church, then there's hope for all of us!

Keep on following on!

Richard

Scripture Meditation

Follow my example, as I follow the example of Christ.
—1 CORINTHIANS 11:1

Thought for the Day

What would an inclusive church that followed the example of Jesus look like? Would that turn the world upside down?

Prayer

Lord Jesus, give us the courage to follow in your steps and imitate your example; to suffer and not retaliate; to love, as you loved us; to forgive, as you have forgiven us; so that as we grow in the new life of living, you will grant us to wear the crown of glory with Peter and all your church. Amen.

—RICHARD A. BURRIDGE

SEASONS OF SUFFERING AND PERSONAL/PROFESSIONAL CHALLENGES

*T*aking our faith seriously may often be accompanied by some form of suffering, for it is the crucified Christ to whom we are called to be his disciples. Serving Christ in our careers often brings upon us the contempt or derision of our coworkers. And if we are truly reflecting the light of Christ, that is as it should be. Christ called us to be salt and light to those we come in contact with. Because our professional life often takes up the majority of our time, that is the arena where our beliefs are most effectively shared.

PROFESSIONAL LIFE AND ITS CHRISTIAN CHALLENGES

SEPTEMBER 20: A SLAVE GIRL'S LETTER

Harriet Ann Jacobs (1813–97) was a mulatto, born a slave, even though her maternal grandmother had been the daughter of a wealthy planter in South Carolina. Harriet was orphaned at six, learning abruptly that she was a slave owned by her master's small child. Growing into adolescence she was sexually abused by her licentious master, and ran away, hiding for nearly seven years before she managed to escape to the North. From Brooklyn she wrote her memoirs, joining a circle of antislavery activists. She wrote this letter to her Quaker friend Amy Post on June 21, 1857.

*M*y dear Friend

A heart full of thanks for your kind and welcome letter.... I would dearly love to talk with you as it would be more satisfactory—but as I cannot I will try to explain myself on paper as well as I can—

I have My dear friend—Striven faithfully to give a true and just account of my own life in Slavery [i.e., in her memoirs being sent with this letter]—God knows I have tried to do it in a Christian spirit—there are some things that I might have made plainer I know—

Woman can whisper—her cruel wrongs into the ear of a very dear friend—much easier than she can record them for the world to read—I have left nothing out but what I thought—the world might believe that a Slave Woman was too willing to pour out—that she might gain their sympathies. I ask nothing—I have placed myself before you to be judged as a woman whether I deserve your pity or contempt—I have another object in view—it is to come to you just as I am a poor Slave Mother—not to tell you what I have heard but what I have seen—and what I have suffered—and if there is any sympathy to give—let it be given to the thousands—of Slave Mothers who are still in bondage—suffering far more than I have—let it plead for their helpless Children that they may enjoy the same liberties that my Children now enjoy—Say anything of me that you have had from a truthful source that you think best—ask me any question you like—in regard to the father of my Children I think I have stated it all ... perhaps I did not tell you that he was a member of the Congress at the time.

[Editor's note: Harriet reported in her memoirs that she had two children by a neighbor's son as a teenager, stating: "It seems less degrading to give one's self, than to submit as compulsion," i.e., to her licentious master. "There is something akin to freedom in having a lover who has no control over you, except that which he gains by kindness and attachment.... There may be sophistry in all this but the condition of a slave confuses all principles of morality, and in fact, renders the practice of them impossible."]

Scripture Meditation

In Christ I could be bold and order you to do what you ought to do, yet I appeal to you on the basis of love.
—PHILEMON vv. 8–9

Thought for the Day

How slow Christians have been to learn the evils of slavery, even though the apostle wrote his letter to Philemon, to plead for the freedom of Onesimus so long ago!

Prayer

The grace of the Lord Jesus Christ be with your spirit.
—PHILEMON v. 25

SEPTEMBER 21: CONFRONTING CANNIBALISM

---

*James Chalmers (1841–1901) was a Scottish Congregationalist of the London
Missionary Society, who strove to form an indigenous church among the
primitive tribes of New Guinea. Called "The Livingstone of New Guinea,"
he explored extensively the southwest Pacific. Killed by Papuan tribesmen on
the uncivilized island of Goaribiri, he was reportedly eaten. He wrote on
October 28, 1882, to his longtime friend, John Thompson, who became the
foreign secretary of the London Missionary Society.*

The winter of heathenism reigned when we landed at the east end of New Guinea in 1878. Many who then longed and labored for the spring have gone home to God, assured that the day of joy would dawn and that some, though few, of that band would yet see the first signs of life. Generations of superstition and cruelty had produced a people sunk in crime, which had become a custom and a religion, a people to whom murder was a fine art, and who from their earliest years studied how best to destroy life.... These people had no idea of a God of love, but only of gods and spirits who were revengeful and had to be appeased, who fly about in the night and disturb the peace of homes. They lived in gross darkness and cruelty, brother's hand ever raised against brother. Great was the chief who claimed many skulls. And the youth was to be admired who could wear a jawbone on his arm as a sign that he had slain his man.

All these things were changed in 1882. For over two years there have been no cannibal ovens, no feasts, no human flesh, no desire for skulls. Tribes that could not formerly meet except to fight now meet as friends, and sit side by side in the same house, worshipping the true God. Man and woman who, on the arrival of the mission, sought the missionaries' lives, were only anxious now to do what they could to assist them, even to the washing of their feet....

The change came about in the same way, by the same means, and on the same lines as in the many islands of the Pacific. In the sameness of the Gospel there is always a freshness of true life, by which the means used becomes fresh and living, and those amongst whom the work is carried on feel the power of the life and are drawn to it. The first missionaries landed not only to preach that Gospel of divine life but also to live it, and to show to the savage a more excellent way than his own. They learned the dialect, mixed freely with them, gave kindnesses, received the same, traveled with them, quarreled with them, made friends, assisted them in their trading, and in every way made them to feel that only their good was desired....

That God is Love, seen in Christ, this was the life word we brought them. Day after day in duty's routine—not in hymn-singing, praying, preaching in public, as some imagine that missionaries spend their days—the work was ever going on. The Gospel was working its way in bush-clearing, fencing, planting, house-building, and many other forms of work, through fun, play, feasting, traveling, joking, laughing, and along the ordinary experiences of every-day life.

The gospel shows itself still the power of God unto salvation, the life and light giver to those in darkness.... But it is evident that mission work can be done only by direct contact with the people. If the gospel is to be preached throughout New Guinea, it will have to be by living in New Guinea, where the people can see, hear, and feel the glad news we have to tell them.

Scripture Meditation:

I am not ashamed of the gospel, because it is the power of God for the salvation of everyone who believes.
—ROMANS 1: 16

Thought for the Day:

Secular anthropologists are often critical of missionaries, claiming they are "interfering with native cultures," but have these anthropologists had the motive or the power to overcome cannibalism?

Prayer:

I thank my God through Jesus Christ for all of you, because your faith is being reported all over the world.
—ROMANS 1:8

SEPTEMBER 22: CONFESSIONS OF A DISENCHANTED "MISSIONARY"

Vincent van Gogh (1853–90), the famous artist, wrote this letter to his brother
Theo. At this point in van Gogh's short, turbulent life, he had lived as a
missionary aiding the Belgian coal miners, even after the missionary society
stopped supporting him. Finally, he was forced to quit. The experience harmed
his faith in religious institutions. It is said that van Gogh loved the world, but
the world did not love him back, except perhaps his brother Theo to
whom he often poured out his heart as he did here in July 1880.

So you must not think that I disavow things—I am rather faithful in my unfaithfulness and, though changed, I am the same; my only anxiety is, "How can I be of use in the world? Can't I serve some purpose and be of any good? How can I learn more and study certain subjects profoundly?" You see, that is what preoccupies me constantly; and then I feel imprisoned by poverty, excluded from participating in certain work and certain necessities are beyond my reach. That is one reason for being somewhat melancholy. And then one feels an emptiness where there might be friendship and strong and serious affections, and one feels a terrible discouragement gnawing at one's very moral energy, and fate seems to put a barrier to the instincts of affection, and a choking flood of disgust envelops one. And one exclaims, "How long, my God!"

Well, what shall I say? Do our inner thoughts ever show outwardly? There may be a great fire in our soul, yet no one ever comes to warm himself at it, and the passers-by see only a wisp of smoke coming through the chimney, and go along their way. Look here, now, what must be done? Must one tend that inner fire, have salt in oneself, wait patiently yet with how much impatience for the hour when somebody will come and sit down near it—maybe to stay? Let him who believes in God wait for the hour that will come sooner or later.

… I think that everything which is really good and beautiful—of inner moral, spiritual and sublime beauty in men and their works—comes from God, and that all which is bad and wrong in men and in their works is not of God, and God does not approve of it.

But I always think that the best way to know God is to love many things. Love a friend, a wife, something—whatever you like—you will be on the way to knowing more about Him; that is what I say to myself. But one must love with a lofty and serious intimate sympathy, with strength, with intelligence; and one must always try to know deeper, better and more. That leads to God, that leads to unwavering faith.

To give you an example: someone loves Rembrandt, but seriously— that man will know there is a God, he will surely believe it. Someone studies the history of the French Revolution—he will not be unbelieving, he will see that in great things also there is a sovereign power manifesting itself. Maybe for a short time somebody takes a free course at the great university of misery, and pays attention to the things he sees with his eyes and hears with his ear, and thinks them over; he, too, will end in believing, and he will perhaps have learned more than he can tell. To try to understand the real significance of what the great artists, the serious masters, tell us in their masterpieces, that leads to God; one man wrote or told it in a book; another, in a picture. Then simply read the Gospel and the Bible: it makes you think, and think much, and think all the time. Well, think much and think all the time, it raises your thoughts above the ordinary level without your knowing it. We know how to read—well then, Let us read!

Scripture Meditation

I have the desire to do what is good, but I cannot carry it out.
—ROMANS 7:18

Thought for the Day

Learning intellectually is not the same as relating personally.

Prayer

Unto you, O Lord, belongs righteousness, but unto me confusion of face, because you are just in all that is come upon me; for you do right, but I have done wickedly.
—LANCELOT ANDREWES

SEPTEMBER 23: ENTERING INTO THE FATHER'S LOVE

Dr. Eva Devenyi (b. 1944) is a Jew who lives in Budapest, Hungary. Many of her family perished in the Holocaust. A psychiatrist, she specializes in the treatment of autistic children. She became a Christian when she was thirty-seven, having previously been an atheist. She began her letters to the editor on December 28, 2002, and the following letter was sent on January 2, 2003.

ear James,

Twenty-one years ago, my conversion from atheism was unconnected to any denomination. It resulted from what was happening intimately within myself, of miracles and care that surrounded me. I became convinced: "somebody loves me." I had never experienced love before, and since I was given little, I was not really able to receive it, either. But at that time a quiet, warm and loving voice started to talk to me about my heart. I didn't know who he was, but felt that if I lose this voice— although it was quiet—there was no point in my going on living. Therefore, I left my medical job, convinced there was only one thing to do, "I must find God." Somebody was speaking to me, although I didn't know him, yet.

Later I bought a Bible, read the Gospels, and I was certain Jesus was not lying. If that "somebody" who was called by the name of Jesus was alive, then I wanted badly to know him. This happened about six months later. I asked to be the child of our Father, on account of Jesus, and I asked him to heal me, because otherwise I would die in the sickness I had—which he did almost instantaneously. From that time on, I knew I had a Father and a Brother. For me this is what salvation rested on, happening directly, for I knew nothing of the Scriptures, theology and doctrines. These I read much later, so Jesus did not call me by virtue of the text, as he has pointed it out to me later when the text has caused me to stumble or I misunderstood it. I didn't understand why I was baptized, either. But I gladly accepted that now I could be his child with full rights. It was only years later that I slowly came to understand doctrinally that one of the gifts and possibilities for us (perhaps the greatest gift and possibility) in Jesus' salvation is that we can become God's children, as he is himself.

I identified with the story of the leper who asked Jesus to heal him and cleanse him, as well as with Naaman, who had to wash himself in the Jordan seven times until he became clean as a little child (2 Kings 5). So, I gave up being a psychiatrist, because God said that if I was doing all the healing then he could not heal me. And during the past twenty-one years he has been healing me and training me. He has given me explanations and answers, he has told me the truth even when it was a hard truth, and most importantly he has understood me and given me a depth of under-standing that would be humanly inconceivable. And he made me understand myself. He made it easy for me to call my sins "sin," because I can always run with my sins into his wide-open arms for forgiveness and cleansing. He taught me to love my child and gave me opportunities to make amends for my sins against her. He kept healing my wounds, and he loved me, and I was only able to live with him, not without him. I could entrust my soul to him, my responsibility was always the step of response and the acceptance of his will purely out of my free will.

All that I am incapable of doing humanly has been his responsibility. For only he can heal my inner wounds that I open up before him. Again, when I wanted to forgive my parents, but felt that it was beyond me, I then entrusted myself to him to lead me down the road of forgiveness. During the course of fifteen to seventeen years he has done this. At first with much *angst*, later more and more peacefully, I also accepted that I get to know him through the healing of my own wounds. This is how I learned from him what love is—how he understands and loves me. For each of us has one's own journey. He knows our hearts and the unique road that leads each of us.

Scripture Meditation

Surely he took up our infirmities ... and by his wounds we are healed.

—ISAIAH 53:4–5

Thought for the Day

We are only real in our faith when we relate our sufferings to God's infi-nite love.

Prayer

Batter my heart, three-personed God; for you
As yet but knock, breathe, shine and seek to mend.
—JOHN DONNE

SEPTEMBER 24: WHAT IS THE LOVE OF OUR HEAVENLY FATHER?

Dr. Eva Devenyi continued her letter of January 2, 2003.

ince I now had a Father and a Brother, who drew me to himself by his Spirit, all the suffering I experienced or saw around me began to create a terrible struggle for me: What kind of a Father are you? When my second child died, I knew for sure that he was there, he even talked to me, yet our child died. But at least I knew he was with me. But right from the beginning of my conversion, I had already sensed that my wounds and sickness, as well as my greatest questions and bases of my life were all connected to my Jewish identity. That is why I asked him: what will happen to me because I am Jewish?

His answer was: "Go read Matthew!" I had to get to Matthew 5:44, and this verse jumped out for me: "But I tell you: Love your enemies and pray for those who persecute you, that you may be sons of your Father." This sounded like a promise, not like a command, since I knew perfectly well that I was unable to do anything about it, so I put the received word away deep into my soul and for twenty-one years it has not come up. I have also accepted and understood that if I can't hold my Father's hand, because who he is and what he is like have become so painfully questionable, then I am to grab hold of Jesus', who is the only one who fully knows the Father and can lead me back to him.

This is where I was when on the 28th of December when I sat down to write the letter I promised. It has turned out more like a psalm, part of which I now copy out:

I feel like I am an ant or a living speck of dust compared to the weight of the task, mainly because of the infinite, immense, impossible to be experienced measure of suffering. Maybe the words "what salvation means *for me* in the face of Holocaust" (or *Shoah*) will help. But I feel at times I withdraw looking into myself, at other times I scream in desperation. For where are my brothers and sisters? Do I dare to scream just by myself? Or do I dare to be any one of my brothers or sisters?

It was when I got acquainted with suffering that I began to fathom your greatness, my God. It is then I saw that it is only God, the one God, who is able to bear all the suffering that has accumulated in the hearts of his children who have lived in time and space somewhere, sometime. Yet seen in the light of your pain, the suffering of each one of us is a whole world of itself.

I cannot endure life unless I am close to you. Indeed, I cannot exist unless I live close to you. As one of our poets has put it: "for I neither can die nor live any more without you."[3]

For two decades now I have plagued you with the question: What did you have to do with the Holocaust? First I asked, on whose side were you? How difficult it was for me to accept that you stood on the side of the victims, and yet your heart was also aching terribly for the souls of the murderers! Then I asked: Where were you? How could you let it happen? And the most painful question of all: The children, why were the children born, if they had to suffer and die like this? Oh, my Father!

I wouldn't want to give up on getting closer to your heart. I wonder though, if I had gone through Auschwitz myself, and if my child and my grandchild had been tortured to death, would I still want to live solely in your closeness? Or would I not? Could it be that I wouldn't want to live at all, but would want to die close to you? If only love remained …! I feel that when we get to the suffering of the children, when I touch this, then I take my hand out of yours, closing my fists tight and turning my face away from you. Then I only see them, utterly terrified, but you I no longer see. Who should I run to, my Savior? You know the faces of the children and his face at the same time!

Jesus, my Savior! What is salvation for me? It is that my hand can hold the Father's hand always all throughout the unbearable questions whether I receive an answer or without it until I take my hand out of his hand, and then I can put it over into yours?

Scripture Meditation

Jesus called out with a loud voice, *"Father, into your hands I commit my spirit."*
—LUKE 23:46

Thought for the Day

So much of our present life is what St. Paul describes as "in part," and he assures us "it will be done away."

Prayer

The night is dark and I am far from home. Lead thou me on.
—JOHN HENRY NEWMAN

SEPTEMBER 25: QUESTIONING THE HOLOCAUST WITH FORGIVENESS

Dr. Eva Devenyi concluded with an additional letter sent on October 1, 2003, stating, "God did not allow me to be satisfied with my previous responses."

Dear James,

I faced two obstacles over the past nine months, trying to complete my letters to you. The first is the pain of recounting what has happened to me, and the second is a terrible resistance to go back into the hell-hole from which I have been rescued by God. For all my conscious life I had been asking, perhaps even before I was born, "why was I allowed to be born," and even "was it right that I should have been born?" I discovered other authors of the Holocaust asked the same questions. Many times I have heard it said, the Holocaust was different from other genocides. For people were killed for specific reasons—to seize territory, to fulfill nightmares of political power, etc. But in the Holocaust people were first deprived of their humanness, put outside the human race, and then exterminated like vermin.

So yesterday when I was pondering the impossibility of narrating my reflections, I believe I heard God say to me: "You glorify me precisely by the fact that you live and want to live"; indeed, "you were like a burning stick snatched from the burning" (Amos 4:11). The story of the beginning of my life probably embodies the verses in Ezekiel 16:4–6, "on the day you were born your cord was not cut, nor were you washed with water to make you clean … rather you were thrown out into an open field, for on the day you were born you were despised. Then I passed by and saw you kicking about in your blood, and as you lay there in your blood I said to you, 'Live.'" All my life, I have suffered most from rigidity, rejection and isolation. But I always receive the comfort of 2 Samuel 14:14, "Like water spilled on the ground, which cannot be recovered, so we must die. But God does not take away life; instead he devises ways so that a banished person may not remain estranged from him." When I have asked God, why do we still have children born to us when the world is becoming totally filled with such evil, the answer was clear. We bring children into this world for eternity, for them to experience it, and for God to love them in eternity. But a Christian Jewess friend then faced me with the impossible question, "how can you forgive your enemy for the Holocaust?" It was then that the darkest and most horrible night in my life of faith fell upon me. During the first days I thought I would die in it, for it was like a very painful childbirth which did not depend on me, but which I had to go through it to the end. Then the conviction grew: it was not my job to forgive the killers for Auschwitz. This is not my measure. I do not have the right to forgive in the name of six million people who were killed and another few million of those who were made sick, and yet another few million of sick and suffering second and third generation Jews. This is the right of God—maybe at the last judgment—as it will also be his right only to forgive the American slave trade, the extinction of the Indians, the atrocities of the Bosnian war, and the list could go on and on.

My only right and opportunity to forgive would be—though incapable of doing it without God's help—if I met face to face with one of the killers. This has not happened yet, although I tried to pursue it. For I sing in a Lutheran choir and for this reason I went to Germany with my choir so I could pray the "Our Father" with the German Lutherans. This was done, but impersonally, in a big group, and nobody was able to tell who was a murderer and who a victim.

But the ghastly and frightful darkness fell on me again, when I had to face the further question: "But can you forgive God that he 'allowed' the Holocaust to happen? Why didn't he save the innocent, the children, the ones who believed in him as well as the non-believers? Why did he leave them to die in such suffering? Am I able to forgive the God who made me know him as a loving Father, without whom I cannot live?" This is where I felt everything was over. The earth could no longer hold me, and heaven, where I used to long to go to him, I no longer wished to go. So to *Whom* would I go? As Imre Kertész puts it: "the sentences, which we need sooner or later will find us."[4]

Facing these questions on the days of December 29—January 1, I was unable to describe rationally what happened, but I cried telling God *everything*. I had many dreams that illuminated things for me. Eventually, I identified him, the crucified Savior in Auschwitz. Then I understood my sufferings. Are they over? I don't know. I am in his hands, and he gives more and more deeply than I could ever write or shout or imagine.

Scripture Meditation

God does not take away life; instead, he devises ways so that a banished person may not remain estranged from him.
—2 SAMUEL 14:14

Thought for the Day

Holding God's hand is more vital than all our questionings.

Prayer

See, O LORD, how distressed I am! I am in torment within, and in my heart I am disturbed!
—LAMENTATIONS 1:20

SEPTEMBER 26: GIVING COMFORT TO OTHERS THROUGH
OUR OWN LIFE OF SUFFERING

*Miss Barbara Priddy (b. 1927) has ministered to many women in
Washington, D.C. for almost fifty years. This was written to a dear friend
shortly after he was diagnosed with cancer, affecting his liver, pancreas,
kidneys, etc. She was one of a large group of friends who had committed to
praying regularly for him, and she was asked to write him.*

*D*ear Bob,

I'll never forget the night shortly before my 23rd. birthday when I was diagnosed with polio. I was paralyzed from the waist down (I had started my second year of teaching Phys. Ed. just the week before) and the masked doctor had just told me I would probably never walk again. He went on to say he didn't want to give me any false hope and abruptly left the room. I was devastated!

I had never planned to teach but desired more than anything else to join the Young Life staff. God had shown me in unmistakable ways, however, that he wanted me to teach. And so I was four days into the new school year when I became ill. There I was in isolation calling out to God to give me a word of comfort. I began to argue with the Lord that he was not hearing me because all I could think of was "Rejoice in the Lord always and again I say rejoice" from Philippians 4:4. (I knew many scriptures by heart but that verse was the only one that came—like the dripping of a faucet—over and over.) My reply to the Lord was, "I have nothing to rejoice in." Suddenly, although I did not hear his voice audibly, I knew he was saying to me "…not your circumstances or feelings but ME!" My prayer of confession at that moment was "Dear Lord, these years that I thought I was rejoicing in you was because my circumstances have been so good—so much like I had planned and hoped. Father, I do not want to spend the rest of my life in a wheelchair, but if that is your will for me, I want to be willing." At that moment that "peace that passes all understanding" did fill my heart and my mind, and I did begin to "rest and rejoice" in him.

I love this quotation from Tennyson, "More things are wrought by prayer than this world dreams of." It is a privilege to join the list of friends and loved ones who are faithfully lifting you up in prayer.

Lovingly, in Christ, Barbara

Scripture Meditation:

Rejoice in the Lord always! I will say it again: Rejoice!
—PHILIPPIANS 4:4

Thought for the Day:

When you are going to measure Christ's high grace, do not get up into a mountain, but go deep down into a valley: lower still, to the depth from which David cried.
—WILLIAM ROMAINE

Prayer:

Grant me, O Lord, that I may suffer as a Christian ... and feel pain and consolation together, that I may hereafter attain your comforts only, without any mixture of pain!
—BLAISE PASCAL

SEPTEMBER 27: NEW INSIGHTS IN REDEEMING JUVENILE DELINQUENTS

Bob Pushak is a counselor at a state institution for delinquent youth.

$\mathcal{S}$ ince I work with children and youth who are violent and have behavior problems, the Columbine school tragedy had a substantial impact on me. It forced me to reflect on the ineffectiveness of many of our mental health/social service programs and the need for more positive interventions for these children and youths. In response to the massacre, a report was commissioned by the Surgeon General of the United States, to consolidate current research on the causes and prevention of youth violence. The Report was published in 2001, giving an excellent summary of present studies. Only 20 years ago many experts in the field were indicating that nothing appears to work in treating or preventing youth violence. In recent years, however, there has been a substantial amount of progress made in both understanding the causes of youth violence and in treating and preventing this problem. The Surgeon General's report, however, indicates that this progress has had little impact on child mental health/social service programs. It states our communities are "squandering a substantial amount of money on programs that are untested or that have been shown to be ineffective"; indeed, it believes that child mental health programs are in a state of crisis because they are ineffective.

Empirical data suggests that spirituality and church involvement have a stronger overall positive impact on people's lives than the entire professions of psychiatry and psychology combined. Most therapists never realize how ineffective they really are. The Surgeon General's report also indicates that some of the most commonly used mental health programs for high-risk youth actually do more harm than good. Thus the designation of "crisis" is not an overreaction.

The most effective programs, such as Multi-systemic therapy and Functional Family therapy, however, are proving to be very difficult to disseminate. These focus on the importance of high quality parent-training, especially in group parent-training classes. But mental health professionals working individually with youth with behavior problems consistently get poor results, while professionals who give parents the right tools to intervene in their children's lives can achieve remarkable positive changes. If you know some parents who would like more information, the Surgeon General's report can be found at http://www.surgeongeneral.gov/library/youthviolence/report.html.

Scripture Meditation

In those days people will no longer say, "The fathers have eaten sour grapes, and the children's teeth are set on edge." Instead, everyone will die for his own sins; whoever eats sour grapes—his own teeth will be set on edge.

—JEREMIAH 31:29–30

Thought for the Day

Children taking responsibility for their own actions need strong parental support.

Prayer

We pray for our families, with whom we live day by day. May this most searching test of our character not find us broken and empty. By all we do and say help us to build up the faith and confidence of those we love.

—CONTEMPORARY PRAYERS FOR PUBLIC WORSHIP

SEPTEMBER 28: ENDURING A MAJOR OPERATION
BEFORE THE AGE OF CHLOROFORM

This is an account of Mrs. Davis's operation, written by a friend in a letter to Charles Wesley, on July 1, 1758, titled "An Account of Mrs. Davis Behaviour during the Operation of her breast being cut off." Chloroform was first used by Sir James Simpson in 1847. The spelling remains exactly as written, for this comes from a genuine copy in the archives of the University of Manchester.

*W*hile the Surgeon went to put his Dress on, I was left alone with her; she said 'I wish he wou'd come and do it now, for I am quite ready, and am Sure the Lord will be with me'; she was perfectly resign'd [lac] and ery compos'd, and ask'd if Mr Davis was come; when I answer'd 'no,' she seem'd Equally Satisfied; I said, 'I'm Sure God will be present: she said 'I know he will,' as I repeated these words: "Ye Souls of the Righteous appear if any are waiting around," her Soul Seem'd fill'd with prayer. When the Surgeon came in to make the Operation, she gave me one hand and ask'd me if the other must not be held; but she Stir'd neither, but only to lift them up in prayer to God. She receiv'd the first cut without a groan: when her pain increas'd she groan'd and pray'd to God, she once said 'it's very sharp pains' but did not complain; three or four times, she [lac] said aloud, 'Lord Jesus be thou my help': when the inside of her breast was taken out she ask'd if they had done cutting; I answer'd 'yes', and [illeg] some thread being call'd for, she immediately Said, 'there is some on my work basket on the table': while they Sow'd up the blood Vessel, she said 'this pain is very great', she call'd on the Lord to Strengthen her and Said 'I'm faint', and while she was going to receive some drops from the hand of a friend: I fainted away: the cause of my fainting is quite hid from me at present: For during the whole time I found my soul intirely Stay'd on the Lord, I was assur'd if she dy'd Death wou'd not Separate us from Christ; and being cinfident that every pain she endur'd wou'd be Sanctified to the Good of her Soul, I felt no degree of fear. I was intirly happy and the Language of my Soul was: 'Lord, now lettest thou thy Servant depart in peace: for mine Eyes have Seen thy Salvation'. When I recover'd my fainting, I thought I was with my Redeemer and his Love constrain'd me to Praise him aloud.

Scripture Meditation

Christ suffered for you, leaving you an example, that you should follow in his steps.

—1 PETER 2:21

Thought for the Day

As a pain-suppressant society, we cannot imagine living without aspirins, let alone without an anesthetic!

Prayer

Lord, since thou hast taken from me all that I had of thee, yet of thy grace leave me the gift ... that of being true to thee in my distress, when I am deprived of all consolation.

—MECHTILD OF MAGDEBURG, 1210-80

SEPTEMBER 29:

"A LOOK OF LONGING" IN AN INATTENTIVE WORLD

An anonymous pastor who has migrated from one denomination to another, never feeling "at home," described in self-reflection the perennial longing of the soul that is never fully satisfied.

If the eyes are a window onto the soul, then perhaps this is where we see the longings of the soul most clearly.

There is a look of longing that fills people's eyes when they feel weary or frightened by the events of their lives. I saw it the last time I watched the film "The Sound of Music." That look! That longing, hungering look that Sister Maria gives the Von Trapp mansion before she sneaks out the door and runs back to the security of the convent, afraid of the fleeting glimpses of love that have come before her. She is scared. Life seems safer at the convent than having to face the issues of intimacy that stir her soul. But before she walks out she has to have one last look. Oh, how it feels to have one last, hungering look before one turns away and tries to run from the uncertainties of the future.

It is the look lovers give each other when they are about to be separated for an untold length of time. Whether marching off to war or a new job in a strange land, a bewildering sense of distance is about to descend upon their relationship. With longing looks and desperate hugs, they try to cling to a present that slips through their hands.

Often there is an attempt to give the impression (to anyone watching) that all is calm. But the hunger in the look betrays that just below this calm veneer is an entirely different sort of swirling emotions. When the separation is uncomfortably close, lovers kiss, and cling, and go silent. Then just before they part, there is that look ... that longing look.

The longing look appears and reappears in many different circumstances if you are but attentive enough to see it. Often it lasts only seconds, yet seems to encompass an eternity. This look of longing comes not only to the eyes, but over the entire heart as you walk one last time through a house that was a home. Maybe the marriage has broken up, maybe a new job position has been accepted in a new location, maybe the person who animated the dwelling has died ... at any rate there is one last walk through before you close the door and walk away. The rooms are empty now and echo with a hollowness you have not heard since the week you moved in years and years before. But in between the echoes, you had filled the house with all the trappings of life: the moments of joys and sorrows, the laughter and toys of children, stories told, arguments resolved, meals shared, and sins forgiven. Then life takes you around one of its unexpected corners, dreams expand or contract, new challenges are accepted as old ones are resigned. But before you can walk out the door and move into the future, there is one more longing look into the past ... and this haunting realization: the past is myself.

Longing looks are accompanied with longing hearts. Such moments always come upon us when we are on the threshold of a new chapter in life, while feeling ambivalence about our readiness to leave the old. We are brought up short, realizing almost too late how quickly life passes us by. We will never be able to rewrite this chapter with all its mistakes and frustrations, or its joys and moments of contentment. Thus with a backward gaze we leap into the uncertainty of the future, hoping the net of our dreams is strong enough to catch us. Too late do we learn that the days of the present are the good old days. Our longing for something deeper and fuller sometimes makes us blind to the richness of present realities. So we play the fool to our fantasies, and temper the wisdom gained with unfulfilled longings.

Scripture Meditation

How deserted lies the city, once so full of people! How like a widow is she, who once was great among the nations!
—LAMENTATIONS 1:1

Thought for the Day

In our passage from the cradle to the grave, is our impatient and activist culture rushing us too much so that we cannot be embraced by God's present?

Prayer

Lord, with a new showering of grace and streams of mercy from on high ... the deserted cities of Israel are inhabited anew, the overgrown highways abandoned by men are trod again. Those wasting from the famine of the soul are restored by your hand.
—ST. GRIGOR NAREKATSI

SEPTEMBER 30: THE TYRANNY OF SEEKING CONTROL OF ONE'S LIFE

This letter was written on March 14, 2002, by an active parachurch leader.

It has become more apparent that anxiety plays a major role in keeping me from joy and living in the freedom of the gospel. In seeking control of my life, I often look to please others, especially God, and to "get things right." I realize that I'm afraid of weakness, or at least ashamed and embarrassed by it. The Lord says, "My grace is sufficient for you, for my power is made perfect in weakness" (2 Cor. 12:9). Paul says, "Our competence comes from God" (2 Cor. 3:5). But I run from this grace. I want to be competent, not weak … though deep down in my being the promise of this grace is what I yearn for. More than a desire to control and perform well, I crave to know that I'm loved!

This craving points to my need to be recognized, to be understood and affirmed for who I am, not for what I do.

God loves me! He celebrates me! He rejoices over me with singing (Zeph. 3:17). "He rescued me because he delighted in me" (Ps. 18:19). I deeply want to know this, to believe this reality. "I do believe; help me overcome my unbelief" (Mark 9:24).

One place to start in knowing this love more fully is in showing love more freely to my mother. She is one of the main people I've sought to please over the years. She is also one of the main people from whom I've sought recognition and understanding.

I continue to seek to know God's love as I grow in centering prayer. In re-reading M. Basil Pennington's *The Way Back Home: An Introduction to Centering Prayer,* I've been thinking about "the false self" and "the true self." I need to explore this concept more deeply.

Scripture Meditation

"I have loved you with an everlasting love; I have drawn you with loving-kindness. I will build you up again."
—JEREMIAH 31:3–4

Thought for the Day

Could it be that Christian activism reflects upon the uncertainty of truly having a Christian identity?

Prayer

In you, O Lord God, I place my whole hope and refuge; on you I rest all my tribulation and anguish; for I find all to be weak and unreliable, whatever I seek outside of you.

—THOMAS À KEMPIS

OCTOBER 1: SURVIVING IN "HELL'S HALF ACRE"

Dr. Timothy George (b. 1950), dean of Beeson Divinity School, Samford University, Birmingham, Alabama, and senior editor of Christianity Today *is a distinguished historian of the Reformation. He wrote of his childhood which as a small child he was given to two great-aunts in exchange for twenty-five dollars.*

Dear Jim,

I was born in Chattanooga, Tennessee, in 1950, and grew up in a section of that city known as "Hell's Half Acre." It was a rough neighborhood and one of the few integrated sections of the city in those days. Blacks and whites lived side by side simply because we could not afford to live anywhere else. My father was an alcoholic and my mother suffered from polio and so they left me to be brought up by my two great-aunts, neither of whom could read or write.

When I think back on those early days, two things stand out in my memory. First of all, I shall always be grateful for the special angels God placed in my life. My two great-aunts loved me unconditionally and encouraged me to learn and grow in many ways. I was also blessed with inspiring teachers in the public schools. They taught me to read and think, and they opened to me the wonderful world of books. Without these special angels I don't know whether I could have survived Hell's Half Acre.

I am also grateful for the dear Christian people who welcomed us into the family of God at Boulevard Baptist Church near our home. These are simple, unsophisticated believers, "fundamentalists" they would be called today, but I sensed among them a depth of spiritual life and community in Christ that I have seldom known since. Much of the Christianity that I know and still believe in, I first learned in that church: God is great; Jesus saves; the Bible is true; Love never fails.

Their faith was contagious and I caught it. Since then, I have traveled far and wide, have met many people and learned many things about the Christian faith that those simple believers could not teach me. But they taught me something that can never be taken away—the world through the eyes of the Savior's love.

Yours in Christ,
Timothy George

Scripture Meditation

How great is the love the Father has lavished on us, that we should be called children of God!

—I JOHN 3:1

Thought for the Day

No scholarship can truthfully supplant the child's gift of Jesus' love.

Prayer

What angel nightly tracks that waste of frozen snow.
What I love shall come like visitant of air,
Safe in secret power from lurking human snare;
Who loves me, no word of mine shall e'er betray,
Though for faith unstained my life must forfeit pay.

—EMILY BRONTË

OCTOBER 2: THE SUFFERING OF GUILT REQUIRES
MORE THAN AN ASPIRIN

Dr. June van Bruggen (b. 1943) is a psychiatrist who has practiced in North
Carolina for more than eighteen years. In this and the next two letters written
on July 7–9, 2002, she examined the range of her patients' needs.

*M*y dear friend,

As we talked yesterday about God healing our wounds, my mind traveled back in time. The well-dressed journalist buried her weeping face in her hands through much of our first session. She had spent agonizing days with little sleep or food.

My hand never reached for the prescription pad when she told her story. An illicit affair at work, her distraught husband leaving home with the children. A bitter price. Background history told me she had grown up in an openly Christian home but never really "bought into that" herself. So here came my "unpsychiatric" hunch: this woman knew at least the 10 Commandments and she was engulfed by guilt. I did not point this out to her since God's spirit seemed to have things well in hand.

I mostly just listened, then sent her home with a Bible and a two-week return appointment.

To my astonishment (feeling somewhat like Rhoda seeing Peter released from prison) this lovely lady returned with jubilant news. "I didn't open that Bible—I knew what it said. Instead, I fell to my knees and gave my life to God." And indeed, her whole life had changed. I wish all my patients needed only two appointments! But this was definitely an appointment made by God: being healed by Jesus' wounds.

Scripture Meditation

Since we have confidence ... by the blood of Jesus ... let us draw
near to God ... having our hearts sprinkled to cleanse us from a
guilty conscience.

—HEBREWS 10:19–22

Thought for the Day

Without a relationship with God, how do we deal with guilt?

Prayer

Please, my loving father God, may I hear your voice on Mondays at home and work, as well as in church on Sundays. You speak life to me!

—JUNE VAN BRUGGEN

OCTOBER 3: OUR BRAIN AS PART OF OUR BODY

Dr. van Bruggen reported an interview with another patient.

*M*y dear friend,

Along with God's healing directly, it seems that he is also pleased to use human intervention.

A postal clerk asking for help dealing with his abusive childhood came to my office. We spent many sessions as he struggled with the memories. He was coming to accept that his mother would never be able to give him the love he so desired. He also was realizing he needed to forgive her for the angry beatings, just as God was forgiving him.

But new information erupted. He arrived for a session and slumped into the chair, "There's no use in anything," he mumbled. A separate talk with his wife revealed she had barely survived his twenty years of mood swings. Sometimes he was so depressed and slept all day in a fetal position. Other times he bounded around with great plans on little sleep and the smallest thing could send him into a rage. She and the children were scared, never knowing what to expect.

The new information meant a new diagnosis: bipolar disorder (formerly called manic depression). The patient responded very well to a mood-stabilizing medicine, and continues to do well ten years later, still on his medicine.

Many things got healed: his family was no longer in fear, he could go to work every day, and stability entered his life. He also realized that his mother had the same genetic disorder as he, but her rage attacks came from never being treated.

Talking therapy, medication, obedience to God—God has so many ways of healing. I marvel (and often feel like a detective in my office as I follow the clues he is leaving).

Yours in discovery,

June

Scripture Meditation

[Jesus] welcomed them and spoke to them about the kingdom of God, and healed those who needed healing.

—LUKE 9:11

Thought for the Day

The mystery of health is far more psychosomatic than we may yet realize.

Prayer

I pray not for health or sickness, life or death; but that you would dispose of my health, my sickness, my life and my death for your glory, for my salvation, and for their usefulness to your Church.

—BLAISE PASCAL

OCTOBER 4: FAITH, BEHAVIOR, AND BRAIN CHEMISTRY

In this third letter, Dr. van Bruggen warned against seeking
a "quick fix" in our sufferings.

*M*y dear friend,

How we long for the bountiful (and quick!) healing of our miseries. But what happens when we don't see it?

There is the farmer who has been tormented lifelong by doubts that he has done enough to show God he is a true believer. The loop goes like this: "I'm desperate to know if I'm really saved. I'll call my minister (or church friend, Christian psychiatrist)" … (call) … "Yes, I see what you mean. The Scripture says my salvation is through Jesus Christ alone." … (minutes' to hours' pause) … "But what if that person is wrong? I'll call another person to check on that answer."

And the loop goes on with much misery and many phone calls. Fear of germs and prolonged hand washing is perhaps a more familiar loop in obsessive-compulsive disorder.

Since this genetic disorder seems to respond to medication enhancing our brain with serotonin, you can believe we tried many combinations of medications for two years. FINALLY, the farmer had relief. He was comfortable with God, with his family, and with himself for 3 WHOLE WEEKS!

Would that that was the end of his misery. Another illness prompted another physician to use steroid medication for a whole month. When the farmer returned to see me, many of his anxieties and doubts had returned.

He knows I am traveling with him on this hard journey. Some day he will be free of these tormenting thoughts. If not here, face to face with his for-sure Savior.

Still awaiting our full redemption,

June

Scripture Meditation

You have heard of Job's perseverance and have seen what the Lord finally brought about. The Lord is full of compassion and mercy.

—JAMES 5:11

Thought for the Day

Like the apostle we may have to live with "a thorn in the flesh."

Prayer

Ah, God! Behold my grief and care. Fain would I serve you with a glad and cheerful countenance, but I cannot do it. However much I fight and struggle against my sadness, I am too weak for this sore conflict. Help me in my weakness, O thou mighty God.

—S. SCHERETZ

OCTOBER 5: FACING UP TO DIVERSE AFFLICTIONS

The French spiritual director, Fr. Jean Pierre de Caussade, wrote to a nun on the diversity of trials we suffer; date unknown.

My dear Sister,

The sufferings about which you ask my directions are of different kinds. There are major trials, as well as the vexations of daily occurrence. These latter, because of their multiplicity, form the chief part of our treasure, if only we knew how to profit from them. But it depends upon our own efforts as we bear these little crosses we encounter daily, for by them God will enable us to destroy our self-love. Oh how blessed would we be, if we could only get rid of this accursed vanity which embitters and irritates us over every little thing, making us commit a thousand faults, and do ourselves so much harm, by the constant annoyance and inward trouble of our hearts.

Even when on occasion we have to endure still greater sufferings, remember that they will pass like everything else. Then we shall have no consolation in having borne badly with them, and derived no benefit from enduring them. On the other hand, what a great satisfaction it will be to have made virtue out of a necessity. To do this, do not speak about them more than is necessary, and then only with as few words as possible. Don't make a fuss about them, or go into details about the pain caused by them. Rather commit them all to the providence care of God, who makes all things work together for good to those who love him. This, of course, is only true for those who live by faith.

I pray God will help you to truly understand the great spiritual fruit as well as the temporal blessings you will enjoy from the holy practice of your entire resignation to all God permits you to endure. So recognize that without his permissive will, not a hair falls from our head, nor a leaf in autumn from the innumerable trees of the forest. Of course this is only recognized by faith. Could Jesus Christ have more clearly expressed it than in these words, that there is no event, great or small in the world than what he has expressly arranged by his sovereign providence? O my God! How consoling this is, and how easily we can cast off all our cares, when we learn them from you, as our loving Father. As your children, remind us that you never love us more than when you make us take bitter remedies for our cure! In your infinite goodness, have pity upon those who are sick, and in their delirium turn against you, their good Physician, and refuse the medicine intended for their health and life.

Scripture Meditation

We know that in all things God works for the good of those who love him.

—ROMANS 8:28

Thought for the Day

Our true consolations arise out of the divine grace to meet with our deepest desolations.

Prayer

O my God! How many blind and senseless people there are in the world who will not even listen to these truths, although you have revealed them in the sacred Scriptures for our present consolation and our future salvation!

—JEAN PIERRE DE CAUSSADE

OCTOBER 6: THE CRY OF A MEMBER OF THE FAMILY

During Joseph Stalin's program of collectivization, the first mass exiles of Mennonites from Siberia occurred in 1929–1930. This is a letter written on November 25, 1930 that Katya, a young deportee, smuggled out for her mother.

I have just cried my heart out. My heat wants to break for pain. I think, dear mother, brothers and sisters, that I will not see you again on this earth.... We thought things could not get worse ... and they are becoming worse and unbearable.... It is too much. There is no peace.... In the Omsk prison I managed ... but this is too much. Yesterday amid a storm and cold we had to go out ... I had to walk ... in deep snow.... (At Omsk) I always had warm feet. When we left, they took our shoes away. I am virtually barefoot.... We have not eaten in two days; no water, no bread, no soup. Today we went begging and thank God we got a few pieces of bread.... I haven't a single kopeck. Sending parcels and money doesn't help.... We get neither.... I want to endure until my pilgrimage ends ... and I can rest my weary body at a place prepared by my Lord.

There are still more people coming here, the place is overfilled.... Maybe you could send some dried bread. Hunger hurts very much. If I don't starve to death, I will probably freeze.

One day follows another and nothing changes. They only torment us further. If only the end were in sight.... If only I wasn't so tired I think I could survive a bit longer.... It's almost noon and we still have had nothing to eat or drink.... I went begging for two days without getting anything. Begging is so hard for me.... Today I searched for bread crusts.... I can hardly walk any more.... Even though I am almost dying of hunger, I hope and believe I will survive and experience the hour when we (happy and healthy) see each other again.

As long as I live no one will take this hope from me. I comfort myself with the thought that for God nothing is impossible. Should the ancient God not be able to free us from this slavery ... the right hand of the highest can change all things.... I am now going to God's school where I have already learned a lot and am daily learning. I no longer worry about the next day. If I have eaten something today I am happy and content, and give the coming day over to God. He knows what I need and where it will come from.

Scripture Meditation

O Lord, how long will you look on? Rescue my life from their ravages, my precious life from these lions.
—PSALM 35:17

Thought for the Day

How hardened we are to daily news of famine in other parts of the world, even a letter like this!

Prayer

O LORD, you have seen this; be not silent. Do not be far from me, O Lord.

—PSALM 35:22

OCTOBER 7: EXPERIENCING DECONSTRUCTION
IN A CONTEMPORARY CHRISTIAN CALLING

A friend (b. 1959) of the editor's, who wishes to remain anonymous, worked in China teaching English, trained in theology to become a church pastor for some years, and now works as a landscape gardener to support his family.

I am comforted by the words of Kierkegaard, "To suffer rightly is to have a secret with God!" So need I tell you about my confusion and angst?

Yes! The poets, Donne and Yates, as well as this writer, can rightly testify that "things fall apart, the Center cannot hold" and then everything solid melts into thin air. Along with this ephemeral age and its failing institutions, so too my self-deluded lifestyle is in process of deconstruction. Gone is the confident, self-constructed, hyper-reality I once aspired to. Naked and exposed are my precious, romantic self-absorbed notions of identity. My swollen, discursive Christian rationalism, shamelessly parading around as theology proper, is dying with the hubris of our Modern age. My incessant necessity of "doing" shut me up outside of myself, sequestering me beyond the borderland of becoming a real person. You lovingly helped kill who I thought I was, and for that I have only praise as I lie in "the recovery room."

Tragically as you know, the church has tacitly imbibed much of the spirit of Modernism, like a man who turns orange by eating an excessive amount of carrots. And because I have taken the cure, I presently am considered, in most quarters, a curious, irrelevant oddity. My passions are only marginally important to a purpose-driven, technique-oriented, professionalized church, obsessed with reinventing itself as the maker of history. It seems so odd. I am left standing alone amidst the ruins of what once seemed so alive, so vital, so real to me. Now I have been driven to the wilderness of anonymity, where my vocation can no longer issue forth from the name and skill I once exercised; rather, it can be no less than intentionally living in honest intimacy before the Triune God and his people. I am far removed from being a successful "Desert Father," yet I know the desert well. Letting go of this inordinate embrace of worldly ambitions has led me into a wilderness wandering....

263

I write anonymously, and rightly so, for I desire to live within the real name yet to be given me by God, on "a white stone." Marx spoke in a cavalier way of "people without a history" as those Third World traditional societies were considered wasted, insignificant cultures along the historical process. But faith says: only the Living God knows the process of my life and its profound significance rests in him well before any of my comings and goings. I have longed for tangible significance within the church and beyond, nonetheless, God calls me to live anonymously. To live without worldly significance ... anonymous ... nameless. Yet to live without a name frees me, breaking down my romantic notions, disturbing the still narcissistic pool that held me captive to my own self-absorption. From "faith to faith" I am being set free from my selfish preconceived notions of what my life should be. God bless you for keeping my secret....

Scripture Meditation

To him who overcomes, I will give ... a white stone with a new name written on it, known only to him who receives it.
—Revelation 2:17

Thought for the Day

Who am I? They mock me, these lonely questions of mine. Whoever I am, you know, O God, I am yours.
—Dietrich Bonhoeffer

Prayer

May I be so "joined to Christ Jesus, my Lord, as to be one spirit with him," and feel his invigorating influences continually bearing me on, superior to every temptation, and to every corruption.
—Philip Doddridge

OCTOBER 8: WHEN FAMILY LOSS DIRECTS YOUR CALLING

As the next two letters illustrate, for some people the experience of suffering can actually help to shape their professional calling, while others more directly see their profession as one of stewardship of their own gifted talents. In this letter, Miss Ellie Robson, a medical researcher in preventive medicine employed by the city of Edmonton, Alberta, described how she has been called to serve as a Christian.

I work in the health field and design new prevention programs on diverse topics from the prevention of alcohol or gambling abuse to helping prevent seniors from falling. I enjoy my work. It is creative, challenging, and extremely satisfying.

My mother died when I was 15 years of age, after 7 years of a disease, which today is preventable. I can only guess what a difference it would have made to my younger siblings and me to have had her in our lives for more years. Perhaps my mother's death helped create my interest in prevention.

In 1971–72 I took a year out of my career to attend a lay seminary in Vancouver, Canada. Coming from a liberal church tradition, many people around me discouraged me from enrolling in this program. My dad thought it was a waste of money. For admission to the college, I asked my employer for a character reference and the following note lay on my desk the next day, "Ellie is a fine Christian girl. Don't spoil her."

But God had broken into my closed up heart at age twenty-five and from then on I had a new mentor in my life, and oh, the difference to me. The year at the theological college really helped. Instead of thinking that seeing the world from a Christian perspective was more restrictive, as my dad and former employer had, I began to see it as one of the widest possible lenses. I learned to seek out the still small voice of God in making decisions and even to make decisions amongst conflicting voices. I learned to peel away the layers of my own steeled heart and openly share with others exactly where I was. I found that frequently fear was at the bottom of my own heart. I've since thought that "fear" is much more of an opposite to love than hate is, and probably determines more than it should in life.

Amazingly (to me too) I learned to become a life-long learner in terms of the things of God. With a deepened sense of the relevance of God's love in all of my life and the decisions I was making, I became more venturesome. In relationships I was less afraid to love. In work I was more willing to risk, and as a citizen I became much more involved in the issues of our day.

The confidence I now have within myself is that God continues to pay loving attention to me in all areas of my life. Therefore I gladly enter his courts with thanksgiving and listen for what he has to say to me—which turns out to be far more than I have to say to him.

Scripture Meditation

Know that the LORD is God. It is he who made us, and we are his.... Enter his gates with thanksgiving and his courts with praise.

—PSALM 100:3–4

Thought for the Day

The narrow way of the Christian faith opens upon broad horizons.

Prayer

Grant, we beseech you, O Lord God, unto all your servants, that they may continually enjoy health both of body and mind, and may be delivered from present sadness, and enter into the joy of your eternal gladness. Amen.

—ROMAN BREVIARY

OCTOBER 9: SUFFERING WIDOWHOOD CAN
FREE ONE FOR PUBLIC SERVICE

Helen Holt's (b. 1916) husband was twenty-nine when they married. Six months later he became the youngest U.S. senator at age thirty. When he died suddenly at age forty-nine, he left Helen with three small children. She wrote this letter about her life, which has since been filled with public service to her country. The week she wrote this letter, on July 20, 2003, the home of her son (a congressman from New Jersey) burned down, and her daughter's home was burglarized.

Early in my marriage to the youngest member of the United States Senate ever elected, an honest "country boy" whose integrity was the inspiration for the film, "Mr. Smith Goes to Washington," my husband was diagnosed with lymphoblastoma, a fast-growing cancer for which there was no known cure. We were devastated with no place else to turn but to the Lord.

Every morning the only visitor allowed was a close friend and pastor who came to my husband's room each day to pray with us. Suddenly I noticed that Rush was reading the Bible daily, and before long he confessed to me that he had given his life completely to the Lord. Radiation treatment was prescribed by our family doctor, but I soon discovered that hospital technicians refused to go near the old fashioned x-ray machine because they might become sterile. So, I spent the next 36 days at my husband's side assisting with this dangerous procedure.

Soon thereafter, doctors declared, much to their amazement, that Rush's cancer was in remission. Even more miraculous, three years after Rush and I had been diagnosed as "clinically sterile" because of the radiation treatment, our son, Rush Jr., was born. We knew that he was God's gift to us. Rush survived another few years until finally succumbing to the dread disease.

I was suddenly left with three small children and no income. (This was before pensions for Senate spouses.) But having passed through the "Red Sea" and seen firsthand the Lord's faithfulness in crisis, I knew without a doubt I could continue to depend upon him. I had witnessed his faithfulness to us over and over again in our 16 years of marriage, and so I too asked him to take charge of my life—just the way Rush had.

Since then, he has carried me through many more "Red Seas" and helped me to soar over the hurdles that appear along the way as I have continued to serve him in a life full of public service.

Scripture Meditation

To him who divided the Red Sea asunder His love endures forever.
And brought Israel through the midst of it, His love endures forever.
—PSALM 136:13–14

Thought for the Day

God provides a few miracles in a prolonged life of ordinariness.

Prayer

O Lord Jesus Christ, you did not come into the world to be served, but most surely also not to be just admired or in that sense worshiped. You were the Way and the Truth—and it was follow-ers only you demanded to have.
—SØREN KIERKEGAARD

OCTOBER 10: CHRISTIAN ATTITUDES THAT HELP US PROFESSIONALLY

Dean Overman (b. 1943) is a senior partner of Winston & Strawn, the oldest law firm in Chicago (founded in 1854), now with international branches. Dean has had a distinguished career, including service as a White House

fellow, assistant to Governor John Rockefeller, and leadership of the
Washington, DC office of Winston & Strawn. He wrote to
legal colleagues on August 5, 2002.

One verse which is particularly meaningful to me is: "Always be joyful; pray continually; give thanks whatever happens; for this it what God wills for you in Christ Jesus" (1 Thess. 5:16–18).

Reflecting on more than three decades in corporate law practice, I consider this verse to be particularly relevant to persons in contemporary professional life. Praying continually need not mean making constant intercessory requests of God, but rather contemplating or practicing the presence of our Lord as we move about our daily tasks. This is at the heart of what it means to abide in Christ and to allow him to abide in us.

In attempting to determine God's will for them, lawyers often think in terms of location, position, or a specific assignment. I consider this misguided. God's will is not necessarily to achieve such and such a position; but simply that, wherever we are, to know God and walk with him.

Our desire always to be in a specific location and doing something specific for God may blind us to the fact that his will is not only in specific assignments. It is not confined to a certain position. His will is that we walk with him where we are and that we take his abiding presence with us wherever we go. This requires that we continue, no matter what the task or location, to realize his presence and commune with him on a moment-by-moment basis. Brother Lawrence washed dishes and stayed in such close communion with God that his time in the kitchen was no less of a worship experience than his attendance at formal worship. Of course reaching his state of communion is not easy, but the effort is worthwhile because any increase in our communion with God will improve the quality of our lives and the quality of the lives of those with whom we work in our profession.

The changing environment in corporate law practice is causing some disillusionment among lawyers. The camaraderie and professionalism with which firms approached the central concern of the client's best interests seems to be slipping gradually away. Law is becoming more of a business than a profession. Corporate law practice is becoming increasingly specialized and fragmented. The emphasis on the accumulation of wealth and the decline in a sense of duty and purpose make lawyers, especially young lawyers, long for something deeper.

The Christian lawyer who attempts to derive meaning from his or her law practice alone will face frustration. Practicing the presence of our Lord can give authentic meaning to our professional life. If we start with our personal friendship with God and bring that into our practices, we will find a meaning which will increase our capacity to work well with our colleagues, clarify our perspective of our clients' needs, and encourage us to regard everyone whom we encounter as a person made in the image of God.

Yours Sincerely,

Dean

Scripture Meditation

You will fill me with joy in your presence, with eternal pleasures at your right hand.

—PSALM 16:11

Thought for the Day

It was said of Brother Lawrence "that the most excellent way of going to God was that of doing our common business without any view of pleasing men."

Prayer

O thou good Omnipotent, who cares for everyone of us ... your law is truth, and truth is yourself.... To you will I entrust whatsoever I have received from you, so that I shall lose nothing. You made me for yourself, and my heart is restless until it repose in you.

—ST. AUGUSTINE

October 11: A Mother's Pursuit of God as an Oblate

*Mrs. Gail Stevenson (b. 1936) discovered Christ in mid-life. She had
had a successful career in business, but in this letter she explained
to her older daughter why she had become an oblate.*

*M*y darling Daughter,

You asked me as we were talking together the other day, what it was
that made me desire to commit my life to the Lord as an Oblate.

Strangely, this is not the easiest question to answer, so I am writing this
to you, because often I find that if I let the pen move without thought, it
becomes more like prayer for me, and I too discover what it is that my
heart wants to say.

Like so many interior journeys, the moment of beginning is usually
marked by our own awareness, which I often think is like coming out of
an anesthetic after surgery. At what point are the voices and images that
you hear and touch fully clear and defined? Our desire to actualize self
anesthetizes so much of our lives that I think that the Lord awakens us
gradually until the false world fades away and all things become new.

So it was with this journey; my heart understood what my mind could
not comprehend and slowly the Lord taught me and defined this path for
me, which was and will remain as a simple journey of the heart.

I use the word *journey*, because it is just that, a continuous ongoing discovery of God and self; sometimes painful and sometimes overwhelmingly
beautiful and amazing, but most times quite everyday ordinary.

So, why be an Oblate?

Perhaps for me I needed a definition of relationship that gave me
boundaries so that I could appreciate the vast openness of God. Like one's
baptism, it became a sacramental moment of commitment that said this is
who I am, committing to whom I belong, and making a public declaration
that made my inner self aware of how serious this really was and is.

It was choosing a lifestyle that was not in reaction against something,
but a step in the direction towards "Someone." That someone being God
changed everything that I saw, or did, or wanted to become.

The word *desire* is a big word in the monastic tradition. This is one of
the questions that you are asked when you make your promises. What is

it that you desire to become. I think that says it all. If the heart desires God whole and completely, then the journey towards that desire is what really counts. It is not so much where you have come from, but where you are going, and if the heart desires a spiritual home, then our steps—no matter how faltering—will be to where our lives now become directed.

You asked what the difference was between a Sister or Nun and an Oblate, and the best response that I can give you is that each is "a calling." Without a calling there is no journey. A Sister is called to live a fully committed lifestyle within the monastic walls, with vows of poverty, obedience and chastity. An Oblate promises to follow a rule of life that allows a life of commitment that must be lived in relationship to an Order, but not living within their midst. The two are in relationship with each other, and perhaps if the circumstances of an Oblate's life were different she would have been called into the Sisterhood. But this should not be seen as second best, because this is a calling too.

I realize that this can be quite threatening to you, as you have expressed that you felt in the beginning that you were losing me as a Mother, as my love for Jesus takes me more and more into the life of a contemplative. But now, you have seen that this is not really happening.

God opens our hearts to love more, accept more, to suffer more and live more fully. The simpler that life becomes the more room there is in loving each other. I am so glad you are free to ask the question, and I hope that in the answer we can share more of what God has in store for us both, individually and collectively. For we share the same Heavenly Father, the same love of Jesus, and the same Holy Spirit walks with us and guides us each on the path he has set before us. My walk is special to me, and so is yours. Thanks be to God, who has placed us where we are, and who continually asks us the question "What is it that your heart desires?" As a Mother I shall love you always, and may the Love of God give you as much love as you can experience.

Your loving Mother

Scripture Meditation

The LORD came and stood there, calling as at the other times, "Samuel! Samuel!" Then Samuel said, "Speak, for your servant is listening."

—I SAMUEL 3:10

Thought for the Day

"What is the journey that your heart desires?" asks the Lord.

Prayer

*I come, O Lord, naked, offering who I am alone, without excuse
I stand. I offer my nothingness in exchange for "your everything."
I commit myself to you, knowing only your holiness can clothe
eternity. Amen.*

—GAIL STEVENSON'S PRAYER OF COMMITMENT

OCTOBER 12: LIVING WITH WAR—WITHOUT AND WITHIN

*Stuart W. Bowen was legal advisor to George W. Bush when he was governor
of Texas; he then served as assistant counsel in the White House when he
wrote this letter on the first anniversary of the September 11 attacks.*

*D*ear Jim:

We are at war. The first shots of this latest and strangest of conflicts
were seared onto our collective consciousness a year ago through
repeated televised visuals of planes and flames, and clouds of smoke,
dust, and death. I stood that morning on the ground floor of the west
wing of the White House transfixed by those visuals, and coming to the
"surrealization" that we were indeed at war.

Then I was told to run. They said something unseen may be bearing
down on where I stood. Fear joined my feelings and then ruled over
them for the rest of that morning—all still so surreal in my alternately
hazy and vivid recollections. I remember that some sort of prayer went

out before each of my quick steps down Pennsylvania Avenue and then up 17th. I knew I was out of Eden then, the Agent behind me at the Gate like an Angel with a sword.

The terrorists had surreptitiously planned great atrocities and chillingly carried them out, killing some 3,000 innocents. The evildoers, as The Koran or the President might call them, committed these horrors in the name of a god they believed they served. How wrong they were—and how wrong in so many ways.

It is now an almost unseen war, and the signs of the damage are only occasionally in view. It is a war of gathered intelligence and a war of secret weapons; and a war of nameless opponents who continue to fight despite the futility of their cause. It is a war of paradox where both bombs and relief fall from the sky. And it sounds and seems like spiritual warfare, which it surely must also be.

True, we are at war. And equally true, I am at war. Within my heart and soul—how do the two overlap?—there rages a surreptitious struggle between what the Bible calls the Flesh and the Spirit. Nominalists say those are words alone, but for me, they alone have meaning to describe the true combatants within. One seeks my certain downfall, while the other is my true home. In this war, too, there is intelligence and secret weapons and nameless opponents. And there are paradoxes of action. In this war, too, I must trust my Leader—who is my Savior—to show the way. And I must train and prepare for the unexpected and dwell on that which is good. I know that my enemy's cause is futile. But I know also that he is dangerous. There is a banner over me that speaks the victory of Love. My heart yearns to follow that call. By his grace, I shall follow; and I shall go up in glory and not in flames.

Scripture Meditation

In my distress I called to the Lord, and he answered me. From the depths of the grave I called for help.
—JONAH 2:2

Thought for the Day

Be prepared to fight today's battles within and without!

Prayer

"See, O LORD, how distressed I am! I am in torment within.... Outside the sword bereaves."

—LAMENTATIONS 1:20

OCTOBER 13: AN OPERA SINGER REFLECTS UPON DEATH

Born in the Philippines to a Chinese family, Grace Chan (b. 1964) was trained as an optometrist. But she found her voice was her true vocation and has entered a successful career as an opera singer. She has become fascinated with death, for death is the great dramatic theme of opera. After her debut in Toronto, the National Post *critic praised her: "with her no holds barred death scene producers should be running to cast her as the Old Prioress in Poulenc's* Dialogues of the Carmelites.*" She wrote this letter about her profession on October 7, 2002.*

I have always been fascinated by death. It was around me every-where since I was young. Relatives, acquaintances, friends, dying; sickness, accident, assassination; young, old, middle-aged. Perhaps because of ancestor worship, Chinese families are particularly prone to be surrounded by many superstitions about death. Around death, too, are multiple stages for me to view—the people stage, the religious stage, the music and theatrical stage where the best and sublime music flowed from the pen of the masters. I witnessed the sick and the dying, fighting in bitterness to the end, or the prepared, ready to go home, even the living dead that walk around us in their unreality! I sing at a lot of funerals, too, and I've witnessed the laments of grieving loved ones or of relieved detractors who survive them—religious rituals and superstitions—people can be closest or furthest to God in death!

Oftentimes I wonder about my own death. On the human physical level, I am aware of daily deaths in my own body. Dead skin, dead cells, dead possibilities in a woman's monthly cycles, etc. On the subject of my final death, I have wondered about finding a burial plot. Taking Robert Fulghum's suggestion that from the point of finitude, we number our days and live rightly, I recognize on the spiritual level the need to die daily to self, when I make daily choices to follow Christ's example of humility and sacrifice. I die to my need to control, of vengeance, of greed, of sinful pleasures. And on the subject of my final death the scenario only brightens! Resurrection and eternal life with my God, no more pain, no more tears. Death is only gain for a Christian who struggles with the constant clash in the realms of spirit (heaven) and earth.

Not too long ago, I was to perform a role that brought many of these interesting elements to the fore. I was to play the role of a dying mother who would later come back in spirit to admonish, remind, instruct her daughter every time she strayed from family expectations. In preparation for the role, I conferred with a medical doctor friend. I had to research on the physical ways (and its corresponding structural, neurological significance) of dying. The opera opens with my death scene. I have to be armed with enough information before the director discusses and decides what actual precipitating "illness" my character would die of. The scene opens with all my women neighbors taking vigil and have begun their mourning chants (which means there is public knowledge/acceptance of my imminent death). But then, I have still ten minutes of music to sing, so I can't be having my last breath, and I need to be careful not take huge and hearty "youthful" breaths as required by singing. When I choose my "disease" and its corresponding body movements, then I'll practice the moves and find a way to sing, how to relapse slowly, and when is the precise moment life is extinguished and how it is convincingly identified—visually, dramatically, and musically. As a performer, I must draw together every aspect of mind, body, inner spiritual content, melding athleticism with intellect, memory, creativity and emotion.

I had twelve shows—twelve attempts at dying! The experience afforded me a special exercise to reconsider my thoughts and emotions. Knowing that my Redeemer lives, and that I shall rise with him on that day, allows me to serenely close my eyes, WILL to let go, then to dissipate into a peaceful and blissful countenance and die!

Scripture Meditation

Where, O death, is your victory? Where, O death, is your sting?
—I Corinthians 15:55

Thought for the Day

We must all learn to die, in fact, to die in the absolute sense of the word; for the fear of the end is the source of all lovelessness and it arises only where love itself has already faded. How did it come about that mankind so lost touch with this bringer of the highest happiness to everything living that in the end everything they did, everything they understood and established, was done solely out of fear for that end?
—Robert Donington

Prayer

Father, into your hands I commit my spirit.
—Luke 23:46

OCTOBER 14: MUSIC IN THE CHRISTIAN LIFE

As music has become such a profound influence in Western culture, so it should also be taken seriously within the life of the Christian. Reverend Dr. Jeremy Begbie (b. 1956), vice principal of Ridley Hall at Cambridge and associate professor of theology at the University of St Andrews, writes on this issue in a letter dated August 10, 2002. He is an accomplished musician.

I'm often approached by Christians who are anxious about music's emotional power, especially in worship. Most of all, they seem to be worried that music's huge subjective power will get in the way of the objective focus of worship—God and his glory. Worship too easily turns into a wallowing in our own, unholy emotions.

That kind of suspicion has a long history. Augustine and Calvin—to mention a couple of Christian giants—both had it. The trouble is that it often goes with two assumptions that need challenging. The first is this: the more objective worship is, the less subjective it is. Fortunately the Gospel itself demolishes this. God wants to renew the whole of us. So the more we are objectively focused on God, the more subjectively we'll be involved, emotions included. We learn a deeper joy than we knew was possible. We learn to be angry as never before. We learn to cry as we have never cried before. (Just read the Psalms!) And music in worship can play a key part in this subjective renewal.

The second assumption is that music does no more than mirror or copy our emotional states. We have an emotion and then express it directly in music. Surely, the objectors say, we want to avoid this in worship since most of us are in emotional chaos!

In fact, music rarely copies our emotional life. At its best, it focuses or concentrates it. In everyday life, our emotions are indeed messy, unfocused, confused and cloudy. They also come and go. Music, I believe, offers us intensely focused emotional sound-patterns, so that when we hear the music, we can identify with it as if to say: "yes, that's it; that's how I really want to feel, deep down."

Imagine a Scottish piper winding a poignant lament over a windswept graveside. He takes our muddled and inchoate grief, refines it in sound, giving it a new intensity and vitality. I hear purified remorse, distilled sorrow. I identify with what I hear, and discover more of what I really want to feel. I believe that great music—perhaps all great art—does something like that.

Isn't this just the vicarious dynamic we ought to find in Christian worship? We don't know how to pray, we don't know how to worship (Romans 8:26). But Christ prays for us (Romans 8:34), and the Spirit prays in us (Romans 8:26). They take our confused muddled, messy, all-over-the-place prayers and make something of them in the face of God the Father. Our prayers are focused, our heartaches and longings condensed, our joys purified — and in time we find out what it is we really ought to be praying.

Yes, of course, music needs careful handling, but does it not have extraordinary powers to take us into the life and love of the Trinitarian God, powers we need to appreciate, celebrate and explore to the full?

Scripture Meditation

The Spirit helps us in our weakness. We do not know what we ought to pray for, but the Spirit himself intercedes for us with groans that words cannot express.
—ROMANS 8:26

Thought for the Day

Worship expressed musically reminds us that subliminally, as well as consciously, we seek to adore our God.

Prayer

I will sing a new song to you, O God; on the ten-stringed lyre I will make music to you, to the One who gives victory to kings.
—PSALM 144:9–10

OCTOBER 15: LETTER TO A YOUNG MUSICIAN

Reverend Dr. Jeremy Begbie wrote to a young musician about his own struggles and experiences as a professional musician.

*Y*ou know your trade well — you have played for many years, practiced for hours, walked on to many concert platforms, sat up late waiting for reviews, taught unwilling teenagers. And now that most supreme life-changing event of all — you have come to know Jesus Christ. A huge vista of opportunity opens out before you, for you are now in touch with that supreme Composer of unlimited creativity. What can I say as you stand on the brink of this adventure?

First, ask yourself: whose opinion matters now? Musicians sometimes say to me "I don't care what anyone thinks of me or my music-making." This turns out to be nonsense. Everyone cares what somebody else thinks. The question is: who is the somebody? You reply — "the Lord." Fine. But we always hear the Lord's voice to some extent through other people, especially other Christians. You say: "can't we trust the Bible?" Of course we can. But remember that the way we read the Bible is always affected to some extent by what other people tell us about it. (And that is quite right. When you learn a Beethoven score, don't you get advice, or listen to others play it?) In short, we need to ask: Who are we going to trust to help us hear the authentic voice of Jesus? Choose at least two wise and experienced Christians, and meet with them regularly. Let them pray with you, journey with you, encourage you, challenge you. And make sure at least one of them is a musician, someone who knows your world.

Many Christian musicians give up their faith because they are pulled in a hundred directions by ungodly forces in the music business. When you are faced with an awkward decision — whether to use your time in this way or that, to accept this invitation or that, to meet with this agent or that — you will need wise friends. Make sure they are at hand.

Belonging to a church is not an option. Musicians and artists have a funny habit of thinking they're too special, too creative, too "cutting-edge" to be a committed member of a church. So they sit on the sidelines and talk much about the ideal fellowship that will take them seriously enough and give them limitless "room." Don't get caught up in this "prima donna" posturing. The perfect church exists only in heaven. Get stuck in now, and love your partners in Christ as Christ loves you — unconditionally. They need you and you need them.

At the same time, beware of pastors who see you only as a potential music director. When I first came to faith at the age of nineteen, having trained as a musician, I was often told: "Wonderful, now you'll be able to put all your energy into Church music." Well, music in worship needs to be good. Make sure you give a portion of your time there. But remember that God's horizons are much wider. Try to work out what it means to be a Christian musician in the world and for the sake of the world—that's where Christians live out their lives, after all. It means composing music with the distinctive aroma of the Kingdom. It means playing in such a way that the audiences are taken beyond you and your personality and begin to hear something of the beauty of God. And it means much more besides—but that is for you and your wise friends to work out together.

Scripture Meditation

Praise the LORD. Praise God in his sanctuary.... praise him for his surpassing greatness. Praise him with the sounding of the trumpet, praise him with the harp and lyre, praise him with tambourine and dancing, praise him with the strings and flute, praise him with the clash of cymbals. Let everything that has breath praise the LORD. Praise the LORD.
—PSALM 150

Thought for the Day

See your profession as an opportunity to see and praise God through wide-angled lens!

Prayer

I confess with thanksgiving, that you have made me in your own image, that I may direct all my thoughts to you, and love you. Lord, make me know you aright, that I may more and more love, and enjoy and possess you.
—ST. ANSELM

OCTOBER 16: THE MOTIVE OF A CHRISTIAN NOVELIST

---

*Walker Percy (1916–90) was a Catholic novelist who diagnosed the modern
malaise but was misunderstood by his critics in his literary works, such as* The
Moviegoer, *which won the National Book award. He expressed this
misunderstanding in a letter to his friend, mentor, and fellow
Catholic novelist Caroline Gordon.*

ctually I do not consider myself a novelist but a moralist or a propagandist. My spiritual father is Pascal (and/or Kierkegaard). And if I also kneel before the altar of Lawrence and Joyce and Flaubert, it is not because I wish to do what they did, even if I could. What I really want to do is to tell people what they must do and what they must believe if they want to live. Using every guile and low-handed trick in the book of course....

The problem which almost throws me all the time is this: How does a Catholic fiction writer handle the Catholic faith in his novel? I am not really writing to get your answer because I think I already know it—that you don't worry about it—do what Augustine said: love God and do as you please. But this doesn't help much. (Actually the only reason I can raise the question now is that I can see the glimmerings of an answer.) Dostoevsky knew the answer.

But to show you that I am not imagining the problem: *The Moviegoer* was almost universally misunderstood. Its most enthusiastic admirers were precisely those people who misunderstood it worst. It was received as a novel of "despair"—not a novel about despair but as a novel ending in despair. Even though I left broad hints that such was not at all the case. [The main character] Jack Bolling says, for example, that as far as his search is concerned, he is not inclined to say how it came out, since like Kierkegaard he does not believe he "has the authority to speak of such things." Also, when one of the children asks him at the end, if it is true Our Lord will raise up on the last day, he replies simply: yes.

... When the holy has disappeared, how in blazes can a novelist expect to make use of it? Holderlin said that God had left us, and I think that one can give this a Catholic reading that though he has not left us, his name is used in vain so often that there remains only one way to speak of him: in silence. Perhaps the craft of the religious novelist nowadays consists mainly in learning how to shout in silence. That plus what Jack Bolling called learning how to place a good kick in the [pants]. As far as I'm concerned, the latter comprises 90% of my vocation and my next novel shall be mainly given to [that purpose] for Jesus' sake.

Scripture Meditation

Go and tell this people: "Be ever hearing, but never understanding; be ever seeing, but never perceiving." Make the heart of this people calloused; make their ears dull and close their eyes.
—Isaiah 6:9–10

Thought for the Day

Being a Christian in a hostile environment makes us more conscious of what it should be "to be a Christian," whereas for Dante it was almost unconsciously that he was one.

Prayer

O Lord, strengthen and support all persons unjustly accused or underrated. Comfort them by the ever-present thought that you know the whole truth, and will in your own good time make their righteousness as clear as the light.
—Christina Rossetti

OCTOBER 17: LIVING FATHERLESS IN GENERATION X

As a college lecturer in business ethics in Finland, Juhana described his generation to the editor in a letter written July 15, 2002.

*Y*ou are an orphan," you said, after I had shared my story with you the first time we met. I had never thought about it this way, but I knew instantly that you were right. I had just seen myself as a "divorce-kid" when I was only six years old. Then, when my mother died at age of fifty-five after struggling five years with cancer, I thought as a twenty-three year old student, "at least I still had my father."

But of course I never really "had" him. After my mother left him, he found it difficult to be in contact with me, as this meant being in contact with my mother too. So we met irregularly, even if we still lived in the same small town for several years after the divorce. But this situation left me with the typical question of a divorce-kid: "Why did my parents have to divorce?" It was with this painful question in mind that I remember sobbing myself to sleep time and time again. The subconscious answer to the question was of course, that "there had to be something wrong with me that caused my parents to divorce." It helped only marginally to know that my mother had only lost her faith in my father's ability to quit drinking (incidentally he did stop drinking at the time of the divorce and is now celebrating his 30th AA-anniversary of non-drinking).

What does growing up without a father do to a child? Certainly one is without the "fifty percent" of the emotional and moral support that an individual needs as part of his development. There has to be a reason for why God designed two parents for each of us. As someone born in 1968, I am part of the somewhat debated Generation X, raised more by its peers than by its parents. In my Finnish context this is easy to see, not only as a result of the breakdown of the family in our generation, but also against the backdrop of certain socio-historical factors.

Tens of thousands of families lost their fathers in our two wars against the Soviet Union (the Winter War in 1939–1940 and the Second World War 1941–1945). Alcoholism was with us already before the wars, but it was accompanied with increasing work-a-holism after the WWII, as Finland had to pay her "war-debt" to the allied nations as part of the peace pact. All these factors combined contributed to fatherlessness of major proportions.

"It is hard to give what you have not received yourself." My father was only sixteen years old when he lost his own father to cancer after the wars in 1949. This was deeply traumatic for him and can be seen as the major factor triggering his alcoholism. Tragically then, his own father-lessness led to the curse his own children have had to suffer from. His

first marriage—of which my older half-brother and -sister were born—
ended up with a divorce as did his second, of which I am the only child.
His third marriage has lasted but I am not sure how much real mental
presence he has been able to provide to my younger half-brother, the
only child from my father's third marriage.

Hence we, my father's children have grown up without much of the
affirmation and support a father can provide. I can see this in my own
insecurity. We have compensated, as survivors, in excelling in our careers.
But we are still hungry for the love and acceptance of our parents. What
are we to do when we realize that our biological parents may never be
able to deliver what we long for? At least in my case it seems evident,
that it was the wounds—caused by the biographical factors described
above—that also made it possible for our Heavenly Father to "break in."
Through my own wounds Christ, the Wounded Healer, has entered my
life and showed what his wounds are accomplishing. May we keep the
flag of discipleship flying by being Christ's presence for others. As someone coming from Finland I know that this flag carries a cross. But it is in
this sign that we shall be "fathered" indeed.

Yours in him,

Juhana

Scripture Meditation

*You did not receive a spirit that makes you a slave again to fear, but
you received the Spirit of sonship. And by him we cry, "Abba, Father."*
—ROMANS 8:15

Thought for the Day

Since you are a son, God has made you also an heir.... Now that you
know God—or rather are known of God.
—GALATIANS 4:7, 9

Prayer

*Eternal Father of my soul, let my first thought today be of thee, let
my first impulse be to worship thee. Let my first speech be thy name.*
—JOHN BAILLIE

SEASONS OF SPIRITUAL GUIDANCE
AND DIRECTION

*J*ust as the classical world was "big" on mentoring, so the Christian church has had a long tradition of valuing spiritual guidance—call it what you will: the role of the "Abba," spiritual friendship, confession, spiritual direction, eldership, godly counsel. Today we seek it in more ecumenical ways than ever before, so we start appropriately with a letter on the importance of being ecumenical in spirit, in order to benefit from the communion of all the saints.

SPIRITUAL GUIDANCE AND DIRECTION

Archbishop Nerses Pozapalian (b. 1928) is in charge of the publications of the
Armenian Church in the Holy See of Etchmiadzin, near Yerevan, the capital
city of Armenia. He has trained all the bishops of the Armenian Church and
was the senior candidate to become the Cattolicos (or head of the church,)
some six years ago. However, he felt called of God to step aside and permit his
own former student to be elected instead; he sees his role to be a selfless
mentor of his theological alumni. In September 2001, the Armenian Church
celebrated 1700 years of existence with special celebrations including the
building of a new cathedral. He wrote the editor soon after that event.

𝒟ear Professor Houston!

I am still remembering your recent visit to the Holy See of Etchmiadzin and the Church of St. Gayane, where I am in charge of the publications of the Holy See. How nice it was to meet you and discuss about many different matters concerning all Christian churches at this time a year after we have celebrated seventeen hundred years of our own church's history. Facing the twenty first century, we realize it will be a difficult century indeed. Together we discussed especially about the Ecumenical movement, which was by the grace of the Holy Spirit, established in 1948 in Amsterdam, immediately after the Second World War. I believe that those leaders who established this movement were fulfilling a long expected dream, which belongs to all Christendom. I believe that the ecumenical movement became a reality, because in many countries Christians of good faith have worked for many centuries in pursuit of this dream....

In the Armenian Church, for example, from the 12th and 13th centuries Saints Nerses Shnorhaly and Nerses of Lambron were advocates for Christian Unity and for the establishment of Christian Nurture for the minds and in dialog with diverse Christian communities.

Now the Ecumenical Movement has been established, and in Geneva it has its headquarters, but it seems to have become only a selective movement of a group of ecclesiastical and lay leaders. But this doesn't reach to the bottom where there are the ordinary lay people. The twenty first century will have to be a century where there is a relational reformation of the Church, where the Ecumenical spirit and its ideal of unity reaches to the lowest levels of society, so that it can become not only a movement for the upper classes of society, but for the poor and hidden levels of society also; indeed, at the grass-roots!

At the present moment the world is in turmoil, so we Christians have to find new ways and means to restore the desired tranquility to the world, in order that we may give hope and faith to the peoples of the world. Everywhere secularization dominates over the Churches and our communities. We must have then a special message for ordinary people.

I am very happy, that I was born in a Christian family. My mother's godly influence has always been with me, as well as that of my father and sisters. Our family was a pious one. Before eating, before sleeping and before starting on anything, we used to pray. Of course the family environment in which I grew up, has always helped me to devote myself to my Church. God alone knows how much I have been useful.

Hope this letter finds you in good health and Spirit. With God's blessings and with the Love of the Holy Spirit, I remain faithfully yours, Archbishop Nerses Pozapalian

Scripture Meditation

Now you are the body of Christ, and each one of you is a part of it.
— I CORINTHIANS 12:27

Thought for the Day

We are most united when we are most devoted to the crucified Lord, who in his three-personed deity is yet one God.

Prayer

This we pray in the name of your awe-inspiring, mighty and holy oneness and the lordship of your three-fold person.... Through you, O merciful Lord, all things, in all ways, for all people, are possible.... Amen.
— ST. GRIGOR NAREKATSI

OCTOBER 19: A CHRISTIAN REFORMER BEFORE THE REFORMATION

John Wycliffe (c. 1324–84) was a translator of the English Bible, master of Balliol College, Oxford, and promoter of the Lollard cause for church reform. Equally content with being a village pastor, his sermons were biblical, simple, and pastoral in intent. This letter is part of the letter he sent Pope Urban VI near the end of Wycliffe's life, explaining his physical inability to obey the summons to the trial of his reforming spirit in Rome.

I have joyfully to tell all true men the belief that I hold, and always to the pope. For I suppose that if my faith be rightful and given of God, the pope will gladly conserve it, and if my faith be error, the pope will wisely amend it. I suppose over this, that the gospel of Christ be part of the body of God's law. For I believe that Jesus Christ gave in his own person this gospel, as very God and very Man, and by this it surpasses all other laws. I suppose over this, that the pope be most obliged to the keeping of the gospel among all men that live here. For the pope is the greatest vicar Christ has here on earth. For greatness of Christ's vicars is not measured by worldly greatness, but by this, that this vicar follows more Christ by virtuous living; for thus teaches the gospel. That this is the sentence of Christ and of his gospel I take as belief, that Christ from the time he walked here was most poor man of all, both in spirit and in possessions, for Christ says he had nowhere to lay his head.

Over this I take as belief that no man should follow the pope, nor any saint now in heaven, but inasmuch as he followed Christ. Even James and John erred, and Peter and Paul sinned likewise. Of this I take as wholesome counsel, that the pope leave his worldly lordship to worldly lords, as Christ gave him, and move speedily all his clerics to set the same example, for this is what Christ exemplified, and taught this to his disciples.

Scripture Meditation

Be imitators of God, therefore, as dearly loved children and live a life of love, just as Christ loved us and gave himself up for us as a fragrant offering and sacrifice to God.

—EPHESIANS 5:1–2

Thought for the Day

Self-sacrifice is the basis for the continual reform of life

Prayer

We grant meekly that we have sinned in thought, in word, and in deed; but we know that God's grace is much more than all our sin.

—JOHN WYCLIFFE

OCTOBER 20: "REFORM" IMPLIES A CHANGE OF MIND

Jean Gerson (1363–1429), chancellor of the University of Paris, was a conciliar reformer who sought church reform through the medium of church councils, rather than by the authority of the pope. Writing against the Great Schism (1378–1417) when a pope in Avignon was pitted against the pope at Rome, he was also critical of scholastic theology that was not pastoral in intent. He wrote the following letter to Pierre d'Ailly, his mentor and predecessor as chancellor, on April 1, 1400, from Bruges.

Reverend father and special lord,

I turn the powers of my mind to our condition and order, if there is any order at all in this our time of tempest. I can consider the general disaster of the church, which is so much to be pitied because its size and merits have been diminished in a reduction of religious feeling. One can only weep, and according to the advice of Ezekiel (9:4), sigh over all the abominations that take place rather than think of help or hope for some remedy ... for a raging corruption of sins has filled the entire body of Christianity. It has such deep roots in the hearts of men ... that it seems as if one can only despair of providing human counsel or aid. For it is as if the advice of elders, speech from the prophet, law from the priest ... have all disappeared....

Someone might ask what it is about the present situation that makes it worse than before? There are many factors which cannot be explained. Doubtless, conditions get daily worse when everyone adds something to the heap of iniquity, and no one reduces it. If you are in doubt, then take a look at the hateful schism. Here is seen the evident passivity of former pastors, to allow the worst customs gradually to take root, so that as Seneca says, remedy is impossible when vices habits. I speak from experience!

... Preaching the word of God is the greatest medicine for spiritual illnesses. It is the specific duty of prelates to do so, but these men neglect to do so, as if it were a superfluous task, distasteful and beneath their dignity. So preaching of God's word is handed over to I don't know whom. Lacking knowledge and their immoral way of life, they have contaminated what should be treated wisely, turning the divine word, as trivial song, fable, and mockery for those who listen (cf. 2 Tim. 4:4).

The prelates are entirely to blame, protecting their interests at great expense, with lawyers, defenders, prosecutors, and other officials, who they maintain [with] lavish salaries. All this is done plundering their flock....

Has it come to the point that strictness within every discipline has been so erased from the church that those who profess even the most ascetic religious professions can sin more freely than deacons or secular clerics once could do?

Scripture Meditation

O God ... *according to your great compassion blot out my transgressions.*
—Psalm 51:1

Thought for the Day

"Superbia" is the great academic sin of assuming one's knowledge makes one superior to others and so live in a privileged, churched arrogance.

Prayer

Dear Father, may your name be hallowed in us. I confess that I
have dishonored you, and with pride and the quest for my own
honor and glory, I blaspheme your name.... Amen.
—MARTIN LUTHER

OCTOBER 21: COUNSEL FOR THE DESPONDENT

---

*Martin Luther (1483–1546), founder of the sixteenth-century Protestant
Reformation and translator and commentator of the Bible in the vernacular
(common language), promoted the Lutheran piety of the laity. He suffered
most of his life from fits of depression. Much of his spiritual counseling
is expressive of his sensitivity to those likewise depressed in their
sufferings. He wrote to Matthias Weller on October 7, 1534.*

Your dear brother has informed me that you are deeply distressed and
afflicted with melancholy. He will undoubtedly tell you what I have said
to him.

Dear Matthias, do not dwell on your own thoughts, but listen to what
other people have to say to you. For God has commanded men to comfort their brethren, and it is his will that the afflicted should receive such
consolation as God's very own. Thus our Lord speaks through Saint
Paul, "Comfort the fainthearted" (1 Thess. 5:14) and through Isaiah:
"Comfort ye, comfort ye my people. Speak ye comfortably" (40:1–2).
And elsewhere our Lord indicated that it is not his will that man should
be downcast, but that he should rather serve the Lord with gladness and
not offer him the sacrifice of sorrow. All this Moses and the prophets
declared often and in many places. Our Lord also commanded us not to

be anxious, but to cast our cares upon him, for he careth for us, as Saint Peter taught from Psalm 55.

Inasmuch then, as God desires everyone to comfort his brother, and desires that such comfort be received with a believing heart, be done with your own thoughts. Know that the devil is tormenting you with them, and that they are not your thoughts but the cursed devil's, who cannot bear to see us have joyful thoughts.

Listen then to what we are saying to you in God's name: Rejoice in Christ, who is your gracious Lord and Redeemer. Let him bear your burdens, for he assuredly cares for you, even if you do not yet have all that you would like. He still lives. Look to him for the best. This is the greatest sacrifice in his eyes, for as the Scriptures say, no sacrifice is more pleasing and acceptable than a cheerful heart that rejoices in the Lord.

When you are sad, therefore, and when melancholy threatens to get the upper hand, say: "Arise! I must play a song unto the Lord on my [organ] (be it the Te Deum laudamus or the Benedictus), for the Scriptures teach us that it pleases him to hear a joyful song and the music of stringed instruments." Then begin striking the keys and singing in accompaniment as David and Elisha did, until your sad thoughts vanish. If the devil returns and plants worries and sad thoughts in your mind, resist him manfully and say, "Begone, devil! I must play and sing unto my Lord Christ."

Scripture Meditation

Encourage one another and build each other up, just as in fact you are doing.

—I Thessalonians 5:11

Thought for the Day

We minister most effectively to others from our own wounds and handicaps.

Prayer

Dear Lord God, I am your creature—fashioned by you and placed here by your will. I have suffered grievous difficulties and borne great trials. Give me grace that I may truly recognize that I

*am yours and you are my Father. May I wait upon you for help
and security. Amen.*

—MARTIN LUTHER

OCTOBER 22: WHY THE CELEBRATION OF THE MASS
WAS CONDEMNED BY THE REFORMERS

---

*The collection of more than six hundred letters written by John Calvin
(1509–1564) begins in 1528 and continues to his death. For twenty-three years
he maintained frequent correspondence with the daughter of the French King
Louis, Jane Duchess of Ferrara, who had married an Italian prince. When
Calvin visited her in her youth, she began to develop Reformed sympathies,
but her husband kept her a prisoner until she relented and made a public
appearance as a Catholic. After his death she returned to the French court, but
religious wars kept her in constant danger. In this first letter, which Calvin
wrote to Jane in October 1541, he showed her the false doctrine
implicitly practiced, repeating in every mass the once-for-
all sacrifice of Christ for our salvation.*

*M*adame,

I humbly beseech you that you would take in good part my boldness in
writing these present thoughts, trusting that you do not interpret my plain-
ness of expression as the result of being rash, or being full of self-conceit;
rather it comes from pure and true affection for your service in our Lord.
For I have observed in you such fear of God and such disposed faithfulness of obedience, that independently of the high rank which he has
vouchsafed you in society, I do so value the graces which he hath put upon
you, even to such an extent that I would think myself accursed should I fail
to be frank with you. I say without pretense or flattery but in sincerity of
heart, speaking as in his presence who knows all our secret thoughts.

… Now, Madame … I come to the present matter.… In so far as the mass is a sacrifice, appointed by men for the redemption and salvation of the living and the dead, as their canon bears, it is an unbearable blasphemy by which the passion of Jesus Christ is quite overthrown and set aside, as if it were of no effect whatsoever. For we uphold that the faithful have been purchased by the blood of Jesus, and have obtained thereby the remission of their sins, righteousness, and the hope of eternal life. This belief implies that the blessed Savior, in offering up himself to the Father, and presenting himself to be our sacrifice, has offered himself as an eternal sacrifice. By him our iniquities have been purged and cleansed, and we ourselves have been received into the grace of the Father, and made partakers of the heavenly inheritance. This the Apostle declares very fully in the Epistle to the Hebrews.

If then, the death of Jesus is not acknowledged as the only sacrifice which has been once made for all, and thus has eternal efficacy, what more remains except that it be effaced entirely, as being altogether ineffectual? I know well that these liars, to cover their abomination say that they make the same sacrifice which Jesus has made; but from that statement there arise several blasphemies. For that sacrifice could be made by no one except by Christ himself. And the Apostle says that if he is now sacrificed all over again, it follows that he must suffer still. Therefore, you can see that one of two things must result: either one acknowledges the horrible blasphemy of the mass, or one detests it. For in approving it, one tramples under foot the cross of Jesus. How much it is contrary to the Supper of Christ, I leave you to consider for yourself, after you have read in Scripture the words of its institution. But the crowning desecration which they commit, is the idolatry which they perpetuate by adoring a creature instead of God, a thing which is altogether inexcusable.

Scripture Meditation

Day after day every priest stands and performs his religious duties; again and again he offers the same sacrifices, which can never take away sins. But when this priest [Jesus Christ] had offered for all time one sacrifice for sin, he sat down at the right hand of God.

—HEBREWS 10:11–12

Thought for the Day

Since Christ's work as Redeemer has been completed, no religious acts or traditions should ever be interpreted as additional needs required of us.

Prayer

Grant, Almighty God, ... that being confirmed in faith and united to you by that sacred bond, we may yet constantly abide under the restraint of your word, and thus cleave to Christ, your only begotten Son, who has joined us forever to himself. Amen.

—JOHN CALVIN

OCTOBER 23: THE GRACE TO BE A FAITHFUL WITNESS

John Calvin used to write letters of encouragement to every convert to the reformed faith who awaited trial in prison. Five young Frenchmen, who had completed their theological studies in a seminary in Lausanne, were treacherously betrayed and imprisoned on their return to Lyons. After a lengthy trial, they were condemned to be burned at the stake. This was Calvin's first letter to them written on July 7, 1553.

My Brethren

... Now, although [the news from your prison is] naturally sorrowful to bear, and more so because of the love we have for you in God, yet we must submit ourselves to the will of this kind Father and sovereign Lord. For not only do we consider his way of dealing with us to be just and reasonable, but we also accept it with a gentle and loving heart. For it is right and profitable for our salvation, ... patiently waiting until he fully reveals it to be so. Besides, we have much to rejoice [about], even in the midst of our sorrow, for God has so powerfully helped you by strengthening you by his Spirit. Also your confession of his sacred truth is far more precious to you than even your own lives. Yet alas, we know only too well how difficult it is for us to forget "the self."

That's why our gracious God has to put forth his strong arm; then, for the sake of glorifying him, so we do not fear torments, shame, not even death itself. So, as he has girded you with his power to sustain the first assault, you need to ask to be further strengthened more and more as you face further conflict. Since God has promised us victory in the end, do not doubt that having already imparted a measure of his strength, you will have more ample evidence of it in future. For God does not make a beginning only, to leave his work imperfect....

This is especially so when he honors his people in appointing them to maintain his truth, and lead them by the hand into martyrdom. Then he never leaves them unequipped with the necessary weapons. Meanwhile, remember to look up to see that everlasting kingdom of Jesus Christ. Think whose cause it is that you are fighting. Then that upward gaze will not only help you to overcome all temptations which come from the weakness of the flesh, but it will also make you invincible to all the wiles of Satan—whatever he may devise to darken God's truth. It is by his grace that I am confident you are so settled and grounded, that you take no risks, but truly are already the valiant champions of Jesus Christ.

So you can affirm, "I know whom I have believed."... So I shall beseech God to grant you the grace to be stayed upon him, to never waver, and grow the stronger. May he protect you, and give you such assurance of his security, that you are able to despise all that is of the world. My brethren greet you very affectionately, and so do many others.

Your brother,
John Calvin

Scripture Meditation
If God is for us, who can be against us?
—ROMANS 8:31

Thought for the Day

It has been the frequent testimony of many martyrs that only in the final surrender of their lives to God did they receive the transcendent power of God.

Prayer

Grant, Almighty God, that as you have given us your Only Begotten Son to rule us ... may we be perpetually safe and secure under his hand against all attempts of the devil and of the whole world.... Amen.

—JOHN CALVIN

OCTOBER 24: THE COSTLINESS OF FOLLOWING JESUS

One of the great saints of the Reformation was M. de Falais, a nobleman with whom Calvin had a lifelong correspondence. For his faith he relinquished his wealth and property, moved into exile, was falsely accused by his enemies, and suffered many sicknesses. Calvin also wrote many letters to Falais's wife who accompanied him into poverty. This letter was dated September 1545.

Monsieur,

Although I don't know your present state of mind or body, I have confidence in God that whether you are sick or well, God gives you the necessary strength to overcome your trying situation. For you are no novice in the fight, since for a long time now the Lord has been preparing you for it.... For when you determined to follow Jesus Christ, you were prepared also to take up your cross, knowing that he has honored us to be crucified in sin to glorify us with himself. Even when you were living comfortably in your own mansion, and in the peaceful enjoyment of your property, you would then have had the courage to give up everything had the Lord called you to do it. You are among those Paul would recognize, as "those who use the things of the world, but are not engrossed in them" (1 Cor. 7:31). You have become an example to many in setting your affection on things above, not upon the things of this world. Thus, you continue to glorify the name of the Lord in your manner of life.

Indeed, ... having set our affections on things above, and making ourselves poor, to depend only on him, we are tested. Then the fruit of this spiritual poverty will be to bear patiently the loss of worldly goods without any regret.... I realize you are not ignorant of these things nor need wordy exhortations from me about this way of poverty. It is for the love I have for you that I write of these things ... as I also suffer in your person.... Even if everything should be taken from you, there would still remain the consolation to yield ourselves entirely to him. For it is certain that having the Son of God, we suffer no injury in being deprived of all else.... My wife who is sick in bed asks also to be kindly remembered to you....

Your humble brother, servant, and assured friend,

John Calvin

Scripture Meditation

Those who use the things of this world, as if not engrossed in them. For this world in its present form is passing away.

— 1 CORINTHIANS 7:31

Thought for the Day

Setting our affections on things above gives us a superlative orientation for our lives.

Prayer

Grant, Almighty God, that since the depravity of our nature is so great that we cannot bear prosperity without some wantonness of *the flesh ... grant that we may profit under the trials of the cross ... and never glory in ourselves, for all true and real glory is laid up for us in Thee.... Amen.*

—JOHN CALVIN

OCTOBER 25: TEMPTATIONS OF A YOUNG CHRISTIAN

Ignatius of Loyola (1491–1556), a contemporary colleague of Calvin in Paris, sought to see God in all his actions and to use all of creation for the "greater glory of God." Within his Spanish Catholic culture he desired to be a true knight for God, adopting the spiritual exercises of Ludolph's Life of Christ *into his own teaching. Nearly seven thousand of his letters have survived. Some of these letters were addressed to Teresa of Rejadell, a Benedictine nun in Barcelona, with whom he corresponded for thirty years until her death in 1553. From Venice he wrote to Teresa on June 18, 1536.*

Your letter, which I received some days back, has caused me much joy in the Lord whom you serve and wish to serve even more, and to whom we must ascribe everything good that we see in a creature.

You ask me ... to undertake the care of your soul. It is true that without my deserving it, his Divine Majesty has for many years now given me the desire to give as much satisfaction as I can to all men and women who walk in the way of his will, and also to serve those who labor in the service owed to him. And since I have no doubt that you are one of these persons, I long to be where I could demonstrate what I say through deeds.... I will be very glad to tell you my definite opinion in the Lord. If on a given point I seem severe, it will be less against yourself than [me].

... The enemy is causing you confusion [on two issues]. First, he is persuading you to have a false humility. Second, he is causing in you an excessive fear of God, on which you dwell ... too much. Concerning the first: It is the enemy's general practice with persons who desire and are beginning to serve God our Lord to create obstacles ... so he says, for example: "How are you going to live a whole lifetime of such penance, with no pleasure from friends, relatives, or possessions, leading such a lonely life, with no respite? After all, you can save your soul in other ways, without such hazards."

... Then the enemy tries his second weapon: pride and vainglory. He tells the person that he possesses much goodness and holiness, and exaggerates more than he deserves. If the servant of God resists these arrows, the enemy comes with his third weapon—i.e., false humility. When he sees how good and humble the Lord's servant is, how even while fulfilling all that the Lord commands, he still thinks it is worthless and focuses on his own weakness and has no thought of self-glorification, the enemy then injects the suggestion that, if the person adverts to anything that God our Lord has given him by way of deeds or resolves and desire, he sins through another species of vainglory because he speaks approvingly of himself.

In this way, the enemy tries to get the person not to talk about the good things he has received from his Lord, so that he will not produce fruit in others or in himself. It is always a help then [to] remember what one has received from the Lord already, to then move on to still greater things.... If you reflect, you will realize that these desires to serve Christ our Lord do not come from yourself, but are given to you by the Lord. And so when you say, "The Lord gives me strong desires to serve him," it is the Lord himself in whom you boast, since you do not attribute the grace to yourself.

Scripture Meditation

We are God's workmanship, created in Christ Jesus to good works, which God prepared in advance for us to do.
—EPHESIANS 2:10

Thought for the Day

Moral self-reliance creates much confusion of religious life.

Prayer

Lord, all belongs to you. Dispose of these gifts according to your will. I ask only for your love and grace.

—Ignatius of Loyola

OCTOBER 26: SIN IN THE CHRISTIAN'S LIFE

Ignatius of Loyola continued his first letter to Teresa of Rejadell. Just as there is reference to "sin" on almost every page of the Bible, so in the confessional ministry of the priest there is the issue that in spite of our conversion, baptism, and church membership—we are still "sinners." While Luther stressed the rigor of personal mortification, and Calvin more positively stressed the central importance of "vivification," of benefiting from the "new life in Christ," Catholic mentors inherited the medieval theory that at baptism all sin was cleansed away. So then categories of sin that reappeared after baptism became classified: "minor," compensated by virtues; "venial," incurring penance; and "mortal," which could lead to perdition. None of this is biblical, so such moral guidance led Ignatius to explore the continuum of the soul's journey from interior desolation toward consolation, now widely popularized in "Ignatian spirituality." Perhaps in this letter Ignatius was putting blame on the devil instead of questioning Thomist moral theology.

*W*hen [the devil] encounters a person who has a delicate conscience (no fault in itself) and sees that the person not only repulses mortal sins, and venial sins so far as he can (for they are not all in our power), but even tries to repel every semblance of slight sin, imperfection, or defect, then the enemy attempts to throw this excellent conscience into turmoil by charging sin where there is none and defect where there is perfection, so that he can confound and distress us. Often, when he cannot get a person to sin and has no prospect of doing so, he will at least try to torment the person.

To make it somewhat clearer how this fear is produced, I will mention, although briefly, two lessons which our Lord either first gives or secondly, permits.

The first lesson he gives is in interior consolation; this dispels all confusion and draws a person to every form of love of the Lord. In this consolation, he gives some persons light, and to others he reveals many secrets. With this divine consolation, all hardships are a pleasure and all labors repose. This consolation does not dwell in us uninterruptedly, but always follows its definite periods as has been ordained, all for our own progress.

Then, when we are left without this consolation, the second lesson comes. That is when our ancient enemy sets up every possible obstacle to turn us aside from what we have begun. He sorely afflicts us … frequently causing us to be sad, even without our knowing why we are sad. So we cannot pray devotedly, we cannot contemplate, we cannot even speak or hear of the things of God our Lord with any interior taste or relish.… If the enemy sees us weakened and downcast by these accursed thoughts, he suggests that we are utterly forgotten by God our Lord. We begin to think we really are totally separated from our Lord, and that all we have done and desire to do is worthless. Thus he tries to leave us totally discouraged. So then, we must see that in our fear and weakness, we are dwelling excessively on our miseries, submitting abjectly to his lying suggestions.

Thus we must note which is his offensive tactic. If it is consolation, then we must abase and humble ourselves, remembering the trial of temptation will soon come. If it is desolation, then come darkness or sadness, which we must oppose, without being affected too much by it. Instead we must wait patiently for the consolation of the Lord, which will disperse all confusion and outer darkness.

Scripture Meditation

You, my brothers, were called to be free. But do not use your freedom to indulge the sinful nature; rather, serve one another in love.
—GALATIANS 5:13

Thought for the Day

We must take our emotions seriously, not trusting in them but only in God's grace.

Prayer

May the grace and peace of Jesus Christ our God and Lord be felt always and increase in our souls. Amen.

—IGNATIUS OF LOYOLA

OCTOBER 27: LIVING WITHIN THE LOVE OF GOD

Francis de Sales (1567–1622) broke with the moral rigidity of Thomism to believe optimistically in the intrinsic gift of love placed within the human soul. As the Catholic missionary bishop of the See of Geneva, he was charged to spearhead the Counter-Reformation. He preached winsomely of "the two arms of love," those of prayer in loving God and of friendship with one's neighbor. He practiced this theology by writing personal letters each day. This letter was addressed to Mademoiselle de Soulfour on July 22, 1603.

Mademoiselle,

My brother has just brought me one of your letters, a letter that makes me praise God for the spiritual light he has shown you. If your clouds have not disappeared completely, don't be surprised. Spiritual fevers, like physical fevers, usually have after-effects which are useful to the recovering patient, destroying other infections which caused the illness. They remind us of our recent illness, make us fear a relapse, ... hold us in check, and warn us to take care of ourselves until we have a complete recovery.

... Know patience is the one virtue which assures us most of our reaching perfection, patience with others, but also with ourselves. To aspire to the pure love of God we need to be more patient with ourselves than with other people.... This is to nurture humility. For we are weak creatures who scarcely do anything well. But God, who is infinitely kind, is satisfied with our small achievements and very pleased with the preparation of our heart.

And what do I mean by "the preparation of our heart"? According to Scripture, "God is greater than our heart," and our heart is greater than the whole world. When our heart by itself in meditation prepares the service it should give to God ... to honor him, serve the neighbor, mortify our exterior and interior senses, and do similar good disciplines, it can performs marvels....

All this is still little on the scale of God's grandeur—so infinitely greater than our heart—yet it is ordinarily greater than the world, and greater than natural actions.... So I recommend to you holy simplicity, in just anticipating each day.... We are only to make provision for enough manna for the day, and no more. So don't doubt that God will provide more for us tomorrow, the day after that, and all the days of our pilgrimage.

Scripture Meditation

Aim for perfection, listen to my appeal, be of one mind, live in peace. And the God of love and peace will be with you.
—2 CORINTHIANS 13:11

Thought for the Day

Since God's love is like the sunshine, who of us has a monopoly on its diffusion?

Prayer

I thank and praise our God for the blessing you are pleased to give us through the exchange made possible by our perfect friendship.
—FRANCIS DE SALES

OCTOBER 28: THE ISSUE OF "CHRISTIAN PERFECTION"

Occasionally Francis de Sales would draft short memos on topics anticipatory of common issues asked by correspondents. Then he would use this memo as the need arose. The following memo is an example, which was reproduced in a number of his letters.

Everyone is obliged to strive for the perfection of Christian life, because our Lord commands that we be perfect and St. Paul says the same. Perfection of Christian life consists in conforming our wills to that of our good God, who is the sovereign standard and norm for all actions. So in order to acquire perfection we must always consider and recognize what God's will is in everything that concerns us, so that we can flee what he wants us to avoid and accomplish what he wants us to do.

There are some matters in which it is clear what God's will is, as in what concerns the commandments or the duties of one's vocation. That is why we must always seek to carry out well what God expects of all Christians, as well as what our own vocation requires of us in particular. Anyone who does not do this much with care can possess nothing but a fraudulent devotion.

There are still other matters about which there is not doubt whether God wills them, such as trials, illnesses and chronic conditions. That is why we should accept them with a good heart, and conform our will to that of God who permits them. Anyone who can arrive at the point of not only supporting them patiently but even of willing them, that person can be said to have acquired a great conformity. Thus, the death of relatives, various losses, illnesses, dryness or distractions in prayer—these give us opportunities to grow in perfection.

But we must go further and see this will not only in great afflictions but even in little reversals and minor inconveniences that we will always meet with in this unhappy life.

In this regard many people make a mistake because they prepare themselves only for major affliction and remain totally without defense, strength or resistance when it comes to small ones. Actually it would be more understandable to be less prepared for major afflictions which happen but rarely, and to be prepared for the little ones which come up every day and at every moment.

I will give you an example of what I mean: I prepare myself to suffer death patiently—which can happen to me but once—and I do not prepare myself at all to put up with the inconveniences I encounter from the moods of those I am with or the pressing spiritual demands which my work brings me and which arise a hundred times a day. And that is what makes me imperfect.

Scripture Meditation

When perfection comes, the imperfect disappears.... Now I know in part; then I shall know fully, even as I am fully known.
—1 CORINTHIANS 13:10, 12

Thought for the Day

Christian perfection is expressive of responsive growth in divine love, not in human achievement.

Prayer

May God be your very heart, mind, and soul ... in his merciful love.
—FRANCIS DE SALES

OCTOBER 29: LEARNING TO GROW GENTLY IN CHRIST'S LOVE

In March 1605, Francis de Sales wrote to Madame Brûlart, reaffirming the spiritual value of gentleness and daily patience in living close to Jesus. She was the wife of the president of the Burgundian Parliament, an energetic, anxious woman, with whom he exchanged many letters after they first met in 1602.

In spite of your great desire to attain perfection and the pure love of God, you complain your life is quite mixed up with faults and imperfections. My response is that it is impossible to completely empty ourselves of "self." So as long as we live here below, we must always "bear" with ourselves ... and be patient, acknowledging we can't overcome in one day all the bad habits we have acquired in a lifetime because of our spiritual carelessness.... God left in several of his dear disciples many marks of their evil inclinations for some time after their conversion.... So ... blessed St. Peter stumbled many times after his initial calling, and on one occasion failed totally and miserably by denying the Lord.

... So be of good heart, and gradually train your will to follow God's will, wherever it may lead you.... Especially, you must stop acting hypocritically with your inner struggles, or at least, do so in moderation, ... so gradually correct such outbursts, moderating them every day.

As for your desire to see your dear ones make progress in the service of God and in their longing for Christian perfection, I praise this desire of yours greatly.... But to tell you the truth, I am always afraid that in these desires ... there may be traces of self-love and self-will too ... so we may not leave enough room in our hearts for humility, resignation, gentleness of heart, and the like. Or again, the intensity of these desires results in anxiety and over-eagerness, so that we are not submitting ourselves to God's will as perfectly as we should ... so pursue your intent gently and quietly, without upsetting those with whom you would like to share your desire for perfection. Don't even tell them what you hope for, because, believe me, this could do more harm than good.... Sow seeds gently ... gradually implanting holy inspirations and reflections in their minds. Pray about it too, then you will do more good than you could do in any other way.

Scripture Meditation

Let your gentleness be evident to all. The Lord is near.
—Philippians 4:5

Thought for the Day

Christian gentleness inspires great hope in God's love.

Prayer

O God, perfect us in love ... fill our hearts with your joy and shed abroad in them your peace which passes all understanding.... Make us long-suffering and gentle ... through Jesus Christ, our Lord.

—HENRY ALFORD

OCTOBER 30: LET JESUS LIVE WITHIN THE MESS OF YOUR EMOTIONS

Jane, Baroness de Chantal (1572–1641), met Francis de Sales in 1604 as a young widow. They corresponded regularly in letters until his death. In 1610, they cofounded a congregation for women in Annecy, the Visitation of Holy Mary, without the austerities of the conventional convents. With graciousness, gentleness, and tender concern for each other, she provided spiritual direction for the community. She wrote this letter to Sister Péronne-Marie de Châtel in a sister community at Lyons on February 9, 1616.

In my judgment, all your reluctance to speak to me, all your inhibitions and difficulties are for your greater good; so much so that you have an obligation not to act upon such feelings. Instead, every day you should determine to resist and fight them. Even if you fall—even fifty times a day, don't let it surprise or worry you. Instead, ever so gently set your heart back in the right direction and practice the opposite virtue.

My darling Péronne, speak continuously words of love and trust to our Lord, even when you have committed a thousand faults, as much as if you had committed only one. Do try to remember what I have said to you so often on this subject, and put it into practice for the love of God. Know that out of this weakness of yours, he will bring forth both his glory and your perfection. Never doubt this. No matter what happens, be gentle and patient with yourself.

Once in a while, if you feel particularly weak, without courage and confidence, make yourself say the opposite affirmations of what you are feeling. Say with conviction: "My Savior, my All, despite my feelings of misery and distrust, I place all my confidence in you; you are strength for the weak, refuge for the miserable, wealth for the poor; you are indeed my Savior who has always loved sinners." But, dearest, say these or similar words resolutely, without self-pity or tears; then turn your attention to something else. The Almighty will never let you slip from his arms, for he holds you firmly. Don't you see how very gently he comes to your rescue?

Scripture Meditation

Be completely humble and gentle; be patient, bearing with one another in love.

—EPHESIANS 4:2

Thought for the Day

I am as human as anyone could possibly be!

—FRANCIS DE SALES

Prayer

O my Lord, I am in a dry land, all dried up and cracked by the violence of the north wind and cold; but as you see, I ask for nothing more; you will send me both dew and warmth when it pleases you.

—MADAME DE CHANTAL

OCTOBER 31: A REFORMED CHURCH REQUIRES A REFORMED PRIESTHOOD

---

*Pierre, Cardinal de Berulle (1575–1629), was ridiculed by the worldly
Richelieu as leader of the "devout party" in France. Actually, Berulle felt much
more deeply the challenge of the French Huguenots as he sought a kind of
"Copernican Revolution" within Catholic spirituality. As Francis de Sales had
focused upon a "lay spirituality," Berulle felt called to reform the clergy. He
founded a theological institute in Paris, the Oratory, in 1611. In this letter he
described the ideal nature of the priesthood to a priest of the Oratory.*

Father,

... You should know that the church is divided into two parts and both
of them are holy, if we consider its institution and origin. One is the
people, and the other is the clergy. One receives holiness, and the other
brings it about. In the period closer to its birth, these two parts brought
forth many virgins, confessors and martyrs who blessed the church, filled
the earth, populated heaven and diffused everywhere the odor of the
sanctity of Jesus.

This holy body, animated by a Holy Spirit and governed by holy law,
has lost its fervor and diminished in holiness through the corruption of
the ages. This slackening began in its weakest part, the people. Then,
from among the people, some withdrew to preserve in themselves the
holiness proper to the whole body. These were the monks who, according to Saint Denis, constitute the highest and most perfect part of the
people. They were governed by priests in the early church, receiving
from them direction and perfect holiness, to which they aspired in an
extraordinary way.

At that time holiness dwelt in the clergy as in its fortress, and it struck
down idols and worldly impieties. At that time the clergy, composed of
prelates and priests, radiated only holy things and dealt only with holy
things, leaving worldly things to the worldly. At that time the clergy bore
nobly the mark of God's authority, holiness and light: three beautiful
jewels in the priestly crown joined together by God's design for his
anointed ones, his priests and his church.

... However, time which corrupts all things, brought about laxity in
most of the clergy. These three qualities: authority, holiness and doctrine,

which the Spirit had joined together, were separated by the human spirit and the spirit of the world. Authority has remained in prelates, holiness in religious and doctrine in the schools. In this separation God preserved in different segments of his church what he had joined in the clerical state. Such is the plan of God and the institution of his Son, Jesus. Such is the excellence of our state. Such is the power, light and holiness of the priestly condition.

However, alas! We have fallen from it. The evil of the world in which we live has demoted us from this dignity. It has passed into foreign hands.… It is God's will and plan for us … to reclaim our inheritance, to recover once again our rights, to enjoy our legitimate succession, to have the Son of God as our portion, to share in his Spirit, and through his Spirit to share in his light, holiness and authority, which are communicated to prelates by Jesus Christ and through them to priests.

Scripture Meditation

Our inheritance has been turned over to aliens, our homes to foreigners. We have become orphans and fatherless.

—LAMENTATIONS 5:2–3

Thought for the Day

Do we not see the same need for ecclesial reform today?

Prayer

O Jesus Christ, my Lord and my God, my life and my Savior! … I join myself to you by the bond of perpetual servitude … begging you to give me more grace and power to be united to you in a greater, holier and closer bond.

—PIERRE DE BERULLE

ALL SAINTS' DAY

NOVEMBER 1: THE FEAST OF ALL SAINTS' DAY
---

*After a radical change in his own life, Jean-Jacques Olier (1608–57),
companion of Vincent de Paul, founded the Society of St. Sulpice in Paris. He
devoted himself to spiritual direction in which he deeply influenced many of
the aristocracy. In this undated letter to an unknown correspondent, he
explained why the Feast of All Saints is the most important
in the Church's calendar.*

*D*ear Sir,

Since you have asked me to write on the mystery of this day, consider
it to be the great feast of God the Father, God the Son, and God the Holy
Spirit. That is why in my morning prayers today, I thanked the Lord that
he gave you the desire to learn about this, since the Feast is even greater
than those of Easter or the Day of the Ascension. For it celebrates the
completion of our Lord's mission [as expressed in his prayer of John 17].
It is what the apostle refers to in Ephesians 4:13, "until we all reach unity
in the faith and in the knowledge of the Son of God, attaining to the
whole measure of the fullness of Christ." Christ then appears as the perfect man, having accomplished through his members the fullness of his
purposes in his glorious body. For on this holy day, his members appear
in anticipation of their eternal perfection, according to the divine purpose of God the Father, accomplished in Christ the Son, according to
what Proverbs 8:31 expresses as "rejoicing always in his presence" … yet
also "delighting in mankind." Jesus Christ would remain unsatisfied
without the full accompaniment of all his members. So while his resurrection and his ascension were both glorious, yet the completion of his
mission lies with the accompaniment of all his saints.

This Feast is even more glorious because it reveals the life hid in God,
the filial life between the Son and the Father, now extended to the sons
of God. For first of all, it is the Feast of the Son, and of the Body of
Christ, the Church. Then secondly, it is also the Feast of God the Father,
revealing the beauty of his life in eternal relationship with his Son, now
revealed in time, in the Incarnation. Likewise the apostle speaks of the

saints in Christ: "you died, and your life is now hidden with Christ in God. When Christ, who is your life, appears, then you also will appear with him in glory" (Col. 3:3–4). But you may ask, if God has created so many millions of living things, how can we imagine what our new life will look like — now hid in Christ — when we appear with him in eternal glory! … Certainly it will be expressive of his eternal light and love, leading us to praise as the psalmist concludes his doxology: "Let everything that has breath praise the Lord!" (Ps. 150:6).

But thirdly, this is the Feast of the Holy Spirit, for his saints are the temple of the Holy Spirit. It is in this blessed fellowship of the Holy Spirit, where community is true unity. All sacrificial worship is offered to the Father through the Spirit, who unites us all in one consummation.… So by the Holy Spirit we rejoice in all that God has accomplished … asking him to reign over us … and seeking to renounce all that we are in ourselves, to be united in the Three in One.… Of course we continue to struggle because of the fleshly nature we still possess, but one day the victory will be finally accomplished in Christ, to enter into our full and final freedom.

Scripture Meditation

It was [Christ] who gave some to be apostles, some to be prophets, some to be evangelists, and some to be pastors and teachers, to prepare God's people for works of service, so that the body of Christ may be built up until we all reach unity.
—EPHESIANS 4:11–13

Thought for the Day

Christian maturity is seeing the Self-as-the-Other, never self-contained.

Prayer

Father, … I have given them the glory you gave me, that they may be one as we are one.
—JOHN 17:21–22

SPIRITUAL GUIDANCE AND DIRECTION (CONT.)

NOVEMBER 2: HUMILITY AS THE BASIC NEED OF THE CHRISTIAN

Jean-Jacques Olier also founded six seminaries in different cities of France.
He wrote frequently on the essential, basic Christian need of humility, of
poverty of spirit, and of taking up the cross to follow Jesus.
He wrote this letter to a church prelate.

By God's grace, you have been shown your need of humility. This is where mutually we can understand each other. For I see this need as basic to my own needs before God. It is the basis of the life of Jesus Christ entering within us. Humility is the power for all the true virtues. It is a mystery indeed, infinite indeed, but its result is to give depth to the soul, as well as innumerable side effects. It is expressed in the Gospels, as like the treasure hid in the field, the grain of mustard seed that grows into a large tree with its branches, fruits and shelter. It is what the apostle Peter says: "let your inner being have the unfading beauty of a gentle and quiet spirit" (1 Pet. 3:4). The deep thinker, John of Climacus, does not identify humility with any one trait, such as awareness of one's sinful nature, the knowledge of God, the joy of a docile spirit, the acceptance of humiliating circumstances, the public confession of one's sins, the need of being unconscious of one's goodness, even of contrition, and many other traits we commonly associate with humility. Humility is expressive of all of these, and more, for it is the basis and source of them.... It is the expression of the vivification of God's Spirit operating within our lives. This results in an unchanging gentleness, an insurmountable patience, an inviolable chastity, sobriety that is always the same, in a word that you have become godly. It is only when you have received this grace of humility that you will desire to be absorbed in reflecting all the virtues, as well as discerning the traits of vices, which might otherwise molest you.

To be able to resist the temptations of the flesh, and to learn their tendencies, as the ways of the "old man," the following are basic questions to keep before you:

1. Do we constantly thank God for all his benefits in our lives?
2. Do we ask him constantly to keep us thankful?
3. Do we do all things in his love?
4. Do we avoid any longings that may not be of God?
5. Do we avoid correction, or subtly restrict the desires of our heart for God?
6. Do we avoid our own rebuke, by being over-critical of others?
7. Are we jealous of others, when they are praised?
8. Do we overlook the imperfections of our friends, to recognize our own?
9. Can we accept being overlooked by others, because we live a hidden life in Christ?
10. Or do we continue to fester with resentment against others, because God is forgotten?

Scripture Meditation

Your beauty should not come from outward adornment.... Instead, it should be that of your inner self, the unfading beauty of a quiet and gentle spirit.

—1 PETER 3:3–4

Thought for the Day

How basic is humility in the lives of the saints yet how rare in our society!

Prayer

My soul glorifies the Lord and my spirit rejoices in God my Savior, for he has been mindful of the humble state of his servant.

—LUKE 1:46–48

NOVEMBER 3: A HEART ENLARGED FOR CHRIST'S LOVE

Jacques-Benigne Bossuet (1627–1704), bishop of Paris, tutor to the
Dauphin of France, and outspoken supporter of the rights of the French
church against the papacy, was a controversial leader. But he wrote many
letters of spiritual direction, especially when he was a young priest. This was
one of a series of letters he wrote in 1662 to a young lady of Metz.
It expressed deep insights and his own devotional ardor for
Jesus Christ and for the unity of the Church.

It is vital, my dear daughter, that you ardently desire to love Jesus Christ. As you have urged me to write you regarding this desire, all day yesterday I was thinking about my response.

The desire to love Jesus Christ is the beginning of holy love, which opens and dilates the heart unreservedly to give one's self entirely to him. It is this desire for such love that is infinite, which can never end....

The first disposition of the heart which desires to love is an appropriate admiration for the object of one's love. This is the first wound one receives in the heart by holy love [as Teresa of Avila described]. For with compunction, one is pricked with the pre-occupation of the matchless beauty of Jesus Christ, and so for him alone.... One exclaims with the lover in the Song of Songs, "How beautiful you are, my darling! How beautiful!" (1:1) ... or as the Psalmist exclaims, "Great is the Lord, and most worthy of praise" (Ps. 48:1).

The second disposition is to recognize the incomparable beauty of Jesus Christ, expressed by both his strength and weakness. "My Beloved is radiant and ruddy, outstanding among ten thousand" (Song of Songs 5:10). Paradoxically, we see the radiance of his glory, yet also the bloodiness of his sufferings.... Thus he is uniquely presented to us as the center of both glory *and* scorn, of strength *and* weakness. It is beauty before his Father, beauty equal as God, yet also beauty in his humanity. It is likewise expressed in his miracles, and yet also in his sufferings. It is expressive of his ascension into the heavens, and yet also of his descent into hell....

The third disposition is to adore Jesus Christ, as now being ascended into the heavens, to be seated at the Father's right hand in all his Majesty. Yet he bears the nail prints in his hands and the spear thrust in his side as expressive of his love. He is served by celestial spirits, yet also by us as his ministers in his holy Church.

Thus each of these dispositions of holy love has infinite profundity, opening out the heart to receive new capacities to love and to adore. What a glorious blessing then, to have a heart which adores Jesus, and so it is opening out into more ecstasies of love!

Scripture Meditation

My lover spoke and said to me, "Arise, my darling, my beautiful one, and come with me. See! The winter is past!"
—SONG OF SONGS 2:10–11

Thought for the Day

How corrupted can the "first love" for Christ become in ecclesial ambitions!

Prayer

O Lord, my God, fountain of all true and holy love; who has made me, and preserved me that I might love you; give to your servant such love that whatever happens adversely to flesh and blood, in your service, I may not feel it … my God and everlasting hope. Amen.
—JEREMY TAYLOR

NOVEMBER 4: HAVING A ZEAL FOR CHRISTIAN MISSIONS

John Eudes (1601–1680) knew and was influenced by both Berulle and Olier.
He was most inspired by the Pauline theme of the life lived "in Christ Jesus."
He founded the Congregation of Jesus and Mary in 1643, creating five
seminaries to further the work of priestly reform initiated by the Oratory. He
developed a "heart theology," centered on the love of Jesus and Mary. He was
an indefatigable "home missioner," conducting a series of missions
in France. He reported his results in this letter of July 23, 1659,
to Blouet de Camilly, a recent entrant to his congregation.

My dearest Brother,

I cannot begin to describe the Lord's blessings upon this mission. They are innumerable! Because of this I have not preached in church now for some time, although it has grown a great deal. For on Sundays we are blessed with an attendance of over 15,000. There are twelve confessors but fifty would not be enough.... We hear only the weeping and groaning of poor penitents, and the fruits brought forth by the confessors are indeed wonderful. The sad thing we can only listen to the confessions of a fraction of those desirous. Some wait over a week for confession, and still cannot have their wish. All this is overwhelming us. They fall on their knees before the priests, crying and begging them to hear their confession. We have been now here in Vasteville and Valledieu for six weeks. The missions are a great good, and clearly necessary. To put obstacles to them is very wrong, so if only those who have been hindering us in the diocese knew what harm they were doing! "Father forgive them." We pray the Lord to send more workers for the harvest. For what are so many [theological] doctors and teachers doing in Paris, while souls are perishing in their thousands for lack of those who could stretch out a hand to save them ...? I should be off to Paris to shout in the Sorbonne and the other colleges: "Fire, fire, fire! ... Leave Paris, doctors, bachelors, reverend Fathers, all you priests, and help extinguish the fires of hell!"

Your brother, John Eudes

Scripture Meditation

All authority ... has been given me. Therefore go and make disciples of all nations.
—MATTHEW 28:18–19

Thought for the Day

Has not the harvest always been plentiful, but the workers few?

Prayer

Ask the Lord of the harvest, therefore, to send out workers into his harvest field.
—LUKE 10:2

NOVEMBER 5: A LIFE HID "IN CHRIST" IS SAFEGUARDED

Samuel Rutherford (1600–1661) was a Presbyterian theologian and clergyman who was twice placed under arrest. During his pastoral ministry at Anworth on the Solway Firth in Scotland, he was exiled to Aberdeen for his "extreme Calvinism." Forbidden to preach, his ministry became one of comforting and encouraging many correspondents. Some of his correspondence was published in 1664 under the name Joshua Redivivus, a veiled reference to having been Moses' spy surveying the Promised Land, as the Scottish Covenanters also saw themselves. He wrote to Lady Jane Kenmure, a Campbell, who had made a tragic marriage to a most unsuitable man, as well as having lost several children at birth.

*M*y prayer to our Lord for you is, that you may be sick of love for Him, who died of love for you, ... I mean your Saviour Jesus. And O sweet were that sickness to be soul-sick for Him! And a living death it were, to die in the fire of the love of that soul-lover, Jesus! And, Madam, if you love Him, you will keep His commandments; and this is not the least one of the least, to lay your neck cheerfully under the yoke of Jesus Christ. For I urge your Ladyship did first contact and bargain with the Son of God to follow Him upon these terms, that by His grace you shall endure hardship and suffer affliction, as the soldier of Christ. They are not worthy of Jesus who will not take a blow for their Master's sake.... I persuade you your sufferings are but like your Saviour's (yea, comparably less and lighter), which are called but a "bruising of His heel" (Gen. 3:15), a wound far from the heart.

Your life is hid with Christ in God (Col. 3:3), and therefore you cannot be robbed of it. Our Lord handles us, as fathers do their children; they lay up jewels in a place, above the reach of the short arms of their children, else the children would put up their hands and take them down, and lose them soon. So our Lord has done with our spiritual life. Jesus Christ is the high coffer in which our Lord has hid our life; we children are not able to reach up our arms so high as to take down that life and lose it; it is in Christ's hand.

O long may Jesus be Lord Keeper of our life! ... Then, Madam, as long as this life itself is not taken, all other troubles are but touches of the heel! I trust you soon will be cured.

Scripture Meditation

I know whom I have believed, and am convinced that he is able to guard what I have entrusted to him for that day.
—2 Timothy 1:12

Thought for the Day

When our identity is committed to Christ, then we are most secure.

Prayer

My prayer to our Lord is, that you may be sick with love for Him, who died for love of you.

—SAMUEL RUTHERFORD

NOVEMBER 6: A CONFESSION OF PERSECUTED FAITH

John Bunyan (1628–88), celebrated author of Pilgrim's Progress, *was a dissenting preacher and teacher. He defended his cause for being twice imprisoned, leaving a young wife and family almost destitute. This letter was a preface to the reader on the publication of his* Confession of my Faith, *and a* Reason of my Practice in the Worship of God, *written in 1672.*

*T*o the Reader, Sir:

I marvel not that both yourself and others think my long imprisonment strange, or rather strangely of me for the sake of that; for verily I should also have done it myself, had not the Holy Ghost long since forbidden me. Nay verily, that notwithstanding, had the adversary but fastened the supposition of guilt upon me, my long trials might by this time have put it beyond dispute; for I have not hitherto been so sordid as to stand to a doctrine right or wrong; much less when so weighty an argument as above eleven years imprisonment is continually dogging of me to weigh and pause, and pause again, the grounds and foundation of those principles for which I thus have suffered; but having not only at my trial asserted them, but also since, even all this tedious track of time in cold blood, a thousand times, by the word of God, examined them, and found them good, I cannot, I dare not now revolt or deny the same, as pain of eternal damnation....

And that my principles and practice may be open to the view and judgment of all men, (though they stand and fall to none but the word of God alone). I have, in this small treatise, presented to this generation *A Confession of my Faith, and a Reason of my Practice in the Worship of God;* by which, although it be brief, candid Christians may, I hope, without a violation to faith or love, judge I may have the root of the matter found in me....

Faith and holiness are my professed principles with an endeavor, so far as in me lieth, to be at peace with all men. What shall I say? Let mine enemies themselves be judges, if any in these following doctrines, or if aught that any man hath heard me preach, doth or hath, according to the true intent of my words, savoured either of heresy or rebellion....

Scripture Meditation

I love the LORD, for he heard my voice; he heard my cry for mercy. Because he turned his ear to me, I will call on him as long as I live.

—PSALM 116:1–2

Thought for the Day

May I clearly discern when I suffer for the sake of the Gospel and when I suffer from my own personal deficiencies

Prayer

O LORD, truly I am your servant; I am your servant ... you have freed me from my chains.

—PSALM 116:16

NOVEMBER 7: BECOMING A "REFORMED PASTOR"

*Richard Baxter (1615–91) was the Puritan's pastor to pastors. He coined the
phrase "mere Christian," to express the basic ecumenicity that every Christian
should share in spite of religious wars and other conflicts. His parish of
Kidderminster became a model for other pastors to follow, visiting each
household regularly as he echoed in this letter to young pastor,
Abraham Pinchbecke, on July 5, 1754.*

ear Brother,

Having this opportunity of writing you by Mr. Warren, I shall now give
you my thoughts ... viz. the managing of your ministerial work.

1. Still look to your ends, not only that they may be right (the glory
   of the Redeemer, the winning and saving of souls), but also that
   your intention to that end be frequently and seriously acted, seeing that you must be animated to and in the means of grace.
2. Pray for your people as well as study them.
3. Let them perceive by all your dealing with them that your heart
   is set upon them for their salvation....
4. Study to preach to them as plainly, seriously, and movingly as
   you can speak. Let both your language and tone be as familiar
   as possible. Preach to them as you would discourse with them;
   and studiously avoid an affected, strained, alien tone. To these
   ends: Dwell much on the fundamental truths, about sin, misery,
   redemption, the nature and way of salvation.... Study the most
   convincing way of preaching ... that they be forced to confess
   that it's reasonable ...; in dealing with their sins, be sure to meet
   the greatest and most damning unbelief, hardness of heart, pride,
   worldliness and sensuality (or flesh-pleasing); and suspect that in
   every man; drive home every truth with resolution and practice.... [Then Baxter listed twelve social tips that had helped his
   ministry]: be moved with compassion ... converse privately ...
   study well your own heart ... ponder seriously the greatness and
   weight of the truths being preached ... when [your] heart is very
   dull ... read inspiring books till [your] heart grows warm again;
   especially seek recourse to God through Christ by believing,

earnest prayer; in preaching and relating publicly be sure to show love to your hearers as much as you can. Preach rather with tender, melting affection than with anger and disdain. Assure them frequently, of your duty to be their teacher and guide. Deal with all private or questionable sins as secretly as you can. Take all opportunities to be with them in their afflictions ... be as merciful and bountiful as your estate can afford. Keep a private meeting for yourself every week ... and see your people well spend the Lord's day.... Remember also the health of your body ... and lastly do not weaken or dampen your spirits by too much sadness or melancholy ... this is all in haste I can give you (which little I shall yet find much in the practice myself).... So I remain your loving brother, Rich. Baxter

Scripture Meditation

Keep watch over yourselves and all the flock over which the Holy Spirit has made you overseers.
—ACTS 20:28

Thought for the Day

The Gospel cannot be communicated personally enough.

Prayer

O you who are the gracious Father of spirits, you have sworn that you delight not in the death of the wicked, but rather that they turn and live; deny not your blessing to these persuasions and directions.... Amen.
—RICHARD BAXTER

NOVEMBER 8: CULTIVATING BEING HEAVENLY-MINDED

Richard Baxter was an intensely productive writer, authoring nearly two hundred books, which is why he apologized in this pastoral letter to his Kidderminster flock that he should ever "have become thus public, and burden the world with any writings of mine." He explained how he came to write this wonderful classic in this dedicatory letter of January 15, 1649.

y dear Friends,

If either I or my labors have any thing of public use or worth, it is wholly (though not only) yours. I am convinced by Providence that it is the will of God it should be so. This I clearly discerned in my first coming to you ... in my forced absence from you (in the Civil war).... The offers of greater worldly accommodation, with five times the means which I receive from you, was no temptation to me once to question whether I should leave you: your free invitation on my return, your obedience to my doctrine, the strong affection which I have still towards you above all people, and the general hearty return of love, which I find from you, all of these persuade me that I was sent into this world; especially for the service of your souls....

The Lord has forced me quite beyond my own resolution to write this treatise and leave it in your hands.... Being in my [military] quarters far from home, cast into extreme languishing [by the sudden loss of about a gallon of blood, after many years suffering weakness of general health], and being without companionship, and no books except the Bible, living in continual expectation of death, I turned my thoughts to my Everlasting Rest. Through extreme weakness, my memory being imperfect, I took up my pen and began to draft my funeral sermon, with some personal helps for my own meditations of heaven. In this condition, God was pleased to present himself to me for about five months away from home, where having nothing else to do, I pursued this work, which grew to what it has now become [i.e., more than a thousand pages, instead of one or two sermons! Baxter then enumerated ten directions for his parishioners].

1. Labor to be people of knowledge and sound understanding. A sound judgment is much conducive to the soundness of heart

and life. A weak judgment is easily corrupted ... so read much of the writings of the old divines....

2. Do your utmost to get a faithful minister, when I am taken from you....

3. Let all your knowledge turn into affection and practice; keep open the passage between your heads and hearts, that every truth may go the quick. Spare no pains in working out your own salvation....

4. Be sure you make conscience of the great duties you have to perform in your families. Teach your children and your servants the knowledge and fear of God. Pray with them daily and fervently....

5. Beware of extremes in the controversial points of religion. When you avoid one error take heed not to run into another error.... There is a true mean in the doctrines of justification and redemption.

6. Above all, see [that] you are followers of peace and unity, both in the church and among yourselves.... He who is not a son of peace is not a son of God....

7. Above all, be sure you get rid of the pride in your hearts. Don't forget all the sermons I have preached to you against this sin. For there is no sin more natural, more common, or more deadly....

8. Be sure to keep the mastery over your flesh and the senses. Few ever fall away from God, but [that] the cause is pleasing the flesh.... "Make no provision for the flesh, to satisfy its desires" (Rom. 8:5, 6, 7; 13:4)....

9. Accept the great duty of reproving and exhorting those around you ... yet don't punish without due process.

10. Lastly, be sure to maintain a constant delight in God, and a serious spirituality in all your worship. Think it not enough to delight in duties, if you do not take delight in God.... Live a constant readiness and expectation of death; and be sure you get acquainted with this heavenly conversation, which this book I [have] written to direct you ... until we may together enter into Everlasting Rest.

Your most affectionate, though unworthy teacher, Richard Baxter

Scripture Meditation

Make every effort to live in peace with all men and to be holy.
—HEBREWS 12:14

Thought for the Day

As witnesses for Christ, we can only communicate what we have ourselves lived in personal experience.

Prayer

> To the God of mercy, do I offer my most hearty thanks, and pay
> the vows of acknowledgement which I oft made in my distress,
> who has not rejected my prayers ... and has supported me in
> these fourteen years in a languishing state, in which I scarcely
> ever had an hour free from pain, and who has over twenty times
> delivered me, when I was near death.... My flesh and my heart
> failed, but God is the strength of my heart for ever.
> —RICHARD BAXTER

NOVEMBER 9: LIVING DAILY IN PRAYER

*Pierre Poiret (1646–1719) has been called "the only mystic of the French
Reformed Church." He studied theology at Basle and studied mysticism for
eight years under Antoinette Bourignon, a contemporary mystic living in
Hamburg. He left behind many books, including the seven-volume* L'Economie
Divine. *He had a large influence on the German romantic mystics.*

*M*y dear Friend,

... I don't want your mind ordinarily engaged in prayer, for then your head would soon be exhausted, and would invent a thousand unnecessary imaginations. But I would have you ask for one particular grace, that of continual prayer.

And that you may know what is prayer, and that it is not difficult but that on the contrary nothing is sweeter or pleasanter, remember it is not in vocal phrases, nor in meditations nor mental aspirations that it is to be found. True prayer consists in a spiritual conversation between man and God. And this elevation of mind or colloquy with God is the true prayer, compared with which none other is valid.

God never asks the impossible from man. If one had always to be at church, man would die for lack of the necessities of life; and were one obliged to be always on one's knees, the body could not bear this constant fatigue. And if one had always to meditate with one's head one would break down for one could neither eat, drink nor sleep. But God asks only for this conversation to continue always between Himself and the soul, and it can continue when you are working, eating, drinking, writing, even sleeping. So you see it is perfectly possible to pray without ceasing, as Jesus Christ taught us. For myself, I could not live without this continual prayer, and I would prefer death to being without it for an hour, for all pleasures other than this conversation bore me and are, indeed, mortal afflictions to me. That is why I keep always in this prayer, and I do not think you have ever seen me leave this conversation to enjoy any other pleasure. From this you can see that it is perfectly possible and good and pleasant always to pray, for anyone who is in such continual prayer is never melancholy. Do not therefore try and speculate upon the mysteries of God nor his relations with man but just talk continually to him.... All the religions in the world cannot give us union with God: we must find it for ourselves.

Scripture Meditation

Pray in the Spirit on all occasions with all kinds of prayers and requests. With this in mind, be alert and always keep on praying for all the saints.

—EPHESIANS 6:18

Thought for the Day

Prayer is the breath of the Christian, as vital as the need to breathe.

Prayer

My God, my Father and Preserver, who of your goodness has watched over me during the past night and brought me to this day, grant that I may spend it wholly in the worship and the service of your most holy name. Let me not think or do, or say a single thing which tends not to your service and submission to your will.

—JOHN CALVIN

NOVEMBER 10: DIRECTIONS FOR HOLY LIVING

Francois de la Mothe Fenelon (1651–1715), bishop of Cambrai, tutor to the Duke of Burgundy, the Dauphin's son, and friend of Madame Guyon, was embroiled in much political persecution over his interpretation of the devotional life. If Francis de Sales was "the harmless Dove," Francois Fenelon was as "wise as the serpent," because of his familiarity with "the ways of the court." His letters were marked by boldness and directness in getting to the heart of each issue of personal character. So they have an ongoing relevance and personal application. Like Francis de Sales, he jotted memos of key thoughts for his letters to communicants, indicated by the following spiritual directions.

1. The principal instrument, or means of our perfection, is contained in this one expression of God to Abraham, "Walk in my presence, and be thou perfect."

2. The presence of God calms the mind, gives sweet repose and quiet, even in the midst of our daily labors; but then we must be resigned to him without any reserve.

3. When we have found God, there is nothing worth looking for in men: We must then give up our very best friends, for the good friend is in the heart, the spouse who is jealous, and will have every thing else put out.

4. It does not require a great deal of time to love God, to draw near and enjoy his presence, to lift up our heart to him, or to adore him at the bottom of our heart, nor to make him an offering of what we do and suffer; for the very Kingdom of God is within us, which nothing can molest.

5. When the hurry and distraction of the senses, and the wanderings of the imagination, hinder us from getting into a quiet and composed frame of mind, let us at least calm ourselves by the integrity of our will, and the very desire to be composed is enough. We must also turn our minds inward to God, and do whatsoever he would have us, with a pure and upright intention.

6. We must endeavor from time to time to excite in us a desire to be devoted and resigned to God, contemplating him with mind and will to love him. Let us also desire that our senses may be consecrated fully to him.

7. Let us take care we be not occupied too long, either outwardly or inwardly, about unprofitable things, which create such distractions both of heart and mind, and draw them so much out of themselves, that 'tis with difficulty they can be brought again to be inward enough to find God....

8. When we perceive in ourselves a strong and very eager desire after any thing whatsoever, and find that our humor and inclination carries us too precipitately to do any such thing, be it only to say something, to see an object, or go anywhere, let us strive to moderate ourselves, and request of God, that he would stay the precipitation of our thoughts, and the commotion we are under, because he has said, that his Spirit abides not in hurry and commotion.

Scripture Meditation

I know, O LORD, that a man's life is not his own; it is not for man to direct his steps.

—JEREMIAH 10:23

Thought for the Day

The more our life is wholly the Lord's, the simpler it becomes.

Prayer

Govern all by your wisdom, O Lord, so that my soul may always be serving you as you will, and not as I may choose.... Let me die to myself, so that I may serve you, and live for you, who is yourself the true life. Amen.

—TERESA OF AVILA

NOVEMBER 11: CONSEQUENCES OF SELF-CENTEREDNESS

Francois Fenelon often wrote letters of reprimand on such issues of pride, as illustrated by the following letter to a lady at the court.

So take care not to be pre-occupied with unprofitable things, either outwardly or inwardly so, which distract both heart and mind, and focus so much attention upon themselves, that we have difficulty in being inward enough to find God....

When we perceive in ourselves an obsession for something—whatever it is—becoming fixated by it, try to moderate it—whatever it is. Let us then ask God, that he would keep us from such violent impulses and strong tensions, because his gentle Spirit is peaceful and patient.

Scripture Meditation

When Abram was ninety-nine years old, the LORD appeared to

him and said, "I am God Almighty; walk before me and be
blameless. I will confirm my covenant between me and you."
—GENESIS 17:1–2

Thought for the Day

When the Kingdom of God is within us, our heart can be his throne.

Prayer

Lord … I offer myself in sacrifice; I yield myself to you; I would
have no other desire than to accomplish your will. Teach me to
pray. Pray yourself in me. Amen.

—FRANCOIS FENELON

NOVEMBER 12: THE ONLY REMEDY IS RENUNCIATION OF "SELF"

Francois Fenelon had plenty of opportunity in the court of Louis XIV to
observe the ambitions and egotism of those around him.
So he wrote this letter from much experience.

So long as we are centered upon ourselves, we shall be vulnerable to the contradiction, wickedness, and injustice of others.
Our temper will bring us into collision with other tempers; our
passions will clash with those of our neighbors. Our desires have
so many tender places exposed to the arrows of the jealous
around us. And our pride, which is incompatible with that of our
neighbors', rises like the waves of a stormy sea; everything to
arouse, attack, and to rebuff us. So we become exposed on all

sides, because of passionate sensitivity and jealous pride. Expect then, no peace within us, when we are at the mercy of a mass culture of greedy, insatiable longings, for the empty unfulfilled, and touchy "me." So in our dealings with other people, we are like a bed-ridden invalid, who cannot be touched anywhere without feeling pain. A sickly self-love cannot be touched without screaming; the mere tip of a finger seems to scarify it! Then add to this, the roughness of neighbors in their ignorance of their disgust at our infirmities (at the least as great as ours toward theirs), and you soon find all the children of Adam tormenting each other, each embittering the other's life. And this martyrdom of self-love you will find in every nation, every town, every community, every family, often between friends.

The only remedy is to renounce "the self." If we set aside—and lose sight of—"self," we shall have nothing to lose, to fear, or to consider; and then we shall find that true peace which is given to "people of good will," to those who have no will save God's, which has become theirs. Then others will not be able to harm us, no longer able to attack us through hopes or fears, for we shall be ready for everything, and refuse nothing. This is how we then become inaccessible and invulnerable to the enemy. Others can only do what God permits, and whatever God permits others to do against us becomes our will, because it is God's. So doing, we shall store our treasure so high that no human hand can reach to assail it. Our good name may be tarnished, but we consent, knowing that if God humbles us, it is good to be humbled. Friendship fails us: well! it is because the one true Friend is jealous of all others, and sees fit to loosen our ties. We may be worried, inconvenienced, distressed; but accepted as from God, it is enough. We love the Hand which smites; there is peace beneath all our woes, a blessed peace. We will that which is, we desire nothing which is denied us; and the more absolute this self-renunciation, the deeper our peace. Any lingering, possessive wishes disturb it. If every bond were broken, our freedom would be boundless.... Powerless indeed are they; even though they can destroy life, their day is soon over! They can but break the earthen vessel, kill that which voluntarily dies daily. Anticipate somewhat the welcome deliverance, and then the soul will escape from their hands into the bosom of God, where all is unchanging peace and rest.

Scripture Meditation

Those who live according to the sinful nature have their minds set on what that nature desires; but those who live in accordance with the Spirit have their minds set on what the Spirit desires.
—Romans 8:5

Thought for the Day

Freedom from "self" is the only true freedom.

Prayer

Lord, I know not what I ought to ask of you; you alone know what I really need. You love me better than I know how to love myself. O Father, give your child what he himself does not know what to ask. I dare not ask for either for crosses or consolations. I simply present myself to you.
—Francois Fenelon

November 13: Jealousy Requires Straight Talk!

In this letter to a high-placed lady living within the intriguing, backbiting society of the court, Francois Fenelon rebuked her spirit. No wonder he incurred so many enemies from the directness with which he wrote to such aristocrats!

It is out of jealousy you are offended by the faults of M—; actually, you are more annoyed by her good qualities than by her faults. All this is very horrible and unworthy; but it is what proceeds out of your heart.

God is allowing you to realize this, to show you how much self-esteem you have, and to teach you never to depend upon your own goodness. Your self-love grows desperate, when you find yourself yielding to such vehement, shameful jealousy on the one hand, and on the other, find yourself so full of distractions, weariness, and coldness for the things of God. But God often carries on his work in souls by the emptying them of self, by dint of taking away every possible resource left to self-conceit and complacency. You want to feel good, upright, strong, incapable of doing wrong? If so, you are all the worse for having that impression. Rather you need to feel abject, know yourself to be bad, unjust … indeed, to see nothing but weakness in yourself, abhor and distrust yourself, having no hope except in God alone. Then you have to bear patiently with yourself. Moreover, as these are all involuntary things that are troubling you, which you don't want to have, these feelings help to humiliate you, because you really don't want to entertain such evil thoughts.

So the important thing is don't give up communicating. Communion is the best remedy for weakness, tempted souls, who in spite of all the efforts of self-love, actually long to live in Jesus Christ. So go on living upon Jesus Christ, and live for him. The essential thing is not to seek strength, but lowliness. Allow yourself be brought low … never relying upon human wisdom and courage. Learn to tolerate others by dint of having so much to tolerate about yourself! You fancied you were fully in control of yourself, but experience has shown that you have allowed a moody, peevish, and insecure self-love to control you! So I hope you will give up any idea of self-guidance, and rather become wholly guided by God.

Scripture Meditation

Out of the same mouth come praise and cursing. My brothers, this should not be. Can both fresh water and salt water flow from the same spring?

—JAMES 3:10–11

Thought for the Day

May our overactive prejudices act as a rearview mirror to look within ourselves.

Prayer

Lord … I open my heart to you. Behold my needs, which I know not myself; see and do according to your tender mercy. Smite or heal; depress me or raise me up; I adore all your purposes without knowing them. I am silent. I offer myself in sacrifice.

—FRANCOIS FENELON

NOVEMBER 14: HAVING OTHERS ON OUR HEART

John Brown (1722–87) was a dissenting minister from the Church of Scotland who established a theological institute in Haddington for pastors. He had an encyclopedic mind, as this story told of the French explorer La Salle humorously indicated.

I desire to sympathize with you in your affliction. Experience hath made me know how hard it is to part with a pleasant child. God hath in his dispensation shown you that "vanity of vanities, all that cometh is vanity." There is no certain source of pleasure besides Christ. When we come into life, we are much in the same situation as you were when you got home—we find created joys on their death bed. May we put as little trust in them as they deserve! … What you have met with on this occasion appears to me an evidence, so far as I can see into the secrets of Jehovah, that God has at once taken your child to Himself, and, in some measure, taken your child's room in your heart. If, when young ones are in such danger here, God hath taken your daughter to educate her in heaven, if she is gone to Christ, your best Friend above, is she any worse? Rather, is she not far better? Do you well to be angry that God has dealt so graciously with her? Learn from the death of children to pant for the ever-living God; to consider them, and all created things, as mere loans,

337

which God may recall at pleasure. Esteem nothing but Christ your proper possession; all things beside him give us the slip.

As to the note at the service of the table, of which you spoke, it was to this purpose: "When the savages of Louisiana were going to murder Robert Cavelier La Salle, or his Italian friend, he told them that, such was his regard for them, that he had them all in his heart; and would they murder a man who loved them so well? At the same time applying a small looking-glass to his breast, he desired them to look, and see if it was not so. It is said that the poor savages, observing their own image, had their barbarity melted into the most tender compassion and love; they would not for the world have hurt him or suffered him to be hurt by others."

Now, believing communicants, Jesus bids you look into his heart, and see yourselves there. "Behold," said he, "you were on my heart from eternity, when I undertook for you; then My delights were with the sons of men, and I rejoiced in the habitable parts of the earth. Lo! You were on my heart on Calvary, when it was melted as the wax with the wrath due to your crimes! Behold you are on my heart, now that I am in the midst of the throne, while I appear in the presence of God for you and prepare a place for you!"

Scripture Meditation

I will put my laws in their minds, and write them on their hearts.
I will be their God, and they will be my people.
—HEBREWS 8:10

Thought for the Day

Just as God uses bereavement to draw us closer to him, so his intimacy helps us to love others more widely.

Prayer

May the Lord make your love increase and overflow for each other and for everyone else, just as ours does for you.
— 1 THESSALONIANS 3:12

NOVEMBER 15: THE CHRISTIAN ON A JOURNEY

Gerhard Tersteegen (1697–1769) was a member of the Pietist Movement,
which combined the Lutheran emphasis on biblical doctrine with the Puritan
emphasis on individual piety and a vigorous Christian life. Employed as a
weaver in the textile mills of Mulheim, he was much influenced by Pierre
Poirot as well as Madame Guyon. His world-denying spirit gained him the
title of "radical pietist," but the pastoral ministry of his many letters reveal him
as a devoutly, single-minded Christian. His characteristic theme of being
"on pilgrimage" was expressed in this first letter.

*M*y dearly beloved brother!

… We are not at home here, but rather on a journey. We have to love
one another as pilgrims [on the way] to the native country in eternal salvation. We cannot continually stay together on the journey. This would
have to be considered as delay and misery. A good many people should
want to keep themselves in the presence of pious people in this wretched
world, in order to rejoice, find strength and edification in the good things
together with them. This is precisely what we want to do, but as fellow
pilgrims (that is), as long as God keeps us together here, in anticipation
of an eternal and perfect fellowship. We cannot and do not want to stay
here forever. One has to die earlier, the other one later, that is to finish
the arduous journey and to go home to the father, to whom we all have
aligned our heart and countenance. What then does it matter if the one
arrives several days earlier? This deep truth, that we do not have a lasting city here, but rather that we should search for the future one, the
Lord wants to teach us through sickness and death of his children. We
always want to remember our home and learn in time to direct our heart
and walk toward the place where we will be forever.

Let us love one another warmly, you children, but not as children of
this world but of the one that is to come! Let us love one another in the
same way we will love one another in eternity. Let us see each other in
faith, not as we look now for a few days in imperfection, but as we will
look some day forever in our father's kingdom, namely perfectly beautiful and without reproach. To eternity! To eternity! Here, here our sweet
savior Jesus is waiting for us, here, here countless angels are waiting for

us, so many saints and so many of our dear friends, who went before us, here, here we will without ceasing remain in the presence of Christ and without ceasing in the presence of one another.

Let us console one another with these words! Amen. May Jesus reign and control all our hearts. Your obliged, weak brother ...

Scripture Meditation

Here we do not have an enduring city, but we are looking for the city that is to come.

—HEBREWS 13:14

Thought for the Day

The reality of God grows as the world's claims become more illusionary.

Prayer

O Lord, your hands have formed us, and you have sent us into this world, that we may walk in the way that leads to heaven and yourself, and may find rest in you who are the Source and Center of our lives. Look in pity on us poor pilgrims in the narrow way; let us not go astray, but reach at last our true home where our Father dwells.

—GERHARD TERSTEEGEN

NOVEMBER 16: GOD ALONE CAN FULLY INTEGRATE US

Gerhard Tersteegen also emphasized that the Christian life is essentially simple and integrated when it is wholly committed to God, as he wrote in the following letter.

*G*od alone is our peace. In him my dearly beloved brother!

As the opportunity arises I feel called to write back to you a few lines in response to your letter, with which I was very pleased. I fully agree with the truths that you have expressed in it, and with the mood of your soul, that comes out in it. May the Lord be praised and glorified for his intimate and faithful leading he provides to us. Let us then love this God sincerely and purely!

God is the highest and sole unity. Therefore we do not need to be surprised that when you let go of yourself completely in order to surrender to him, the simpler your whole life will become, and the closer you will get to him who is our resting place. All the manifold, the physical, and the intellectual then become arduous. If we want to give the Spirit room, everything else must fall off. You can no longer think and contemplate or use reason as you did earlier. You can no longer consider rules and regulations except for the one that says to forget all rules. You can no longer speak as much as you used to because it seems that you can say big things, indeed everything in one word. All religious exercises melt into one single exercise that embraces everything, and in which you can wait without repeating or changing it for hours and days. Everything is good, everything is new, and just like there is no yesterday and tomorrow but only a today in eternity, so a soul that has come intimately close to God can no longer think back and forward. It is as if you were to experience a moment that lasts forever.

You can no longer reign yourself and your affairs, both physical as well as intellectual ones, according to your own wisdom, but rather you have to abandon yourself. In one word you have to become and remain a little child. A child really only lives if it completely surrenders to its mother, which is what the Apostle had in mind when he said: I live but now it is not I. For what I live now in the flesh, I live in faith through the Son of God. Blessed is the one, whose spirit has met and put on God's intimate love and presence. (Blessed is the one) who without resistance allows himself to be dragged away by this unifying strength. He is like a surging river that on its way to the ocean has gained a considerable current. It flows gently over the sand, so that you hardly notice its current, and yet it flows unstoppably, driven to reach its goal. It is true that in passing it occasionally moistens an arid field, or that it powers a mill, or that it transports a boat for the best of others. But the driving force of the river is always in charge. Its waters soon enough flow back together from its diversions and various arms, and its course continues toward the ocean, in which it wants to lose itself. For a soul that at least to some degree has experienced God's influence to its very bottom surely and unquestionably knows that it can find its element only in God and in complete surrender to his influence. If it (the soul) wants to be active in itself, if it wants to seek light or differentiation through reason and thereby stand still, it will not be satisfied by the dark, general light of faith in its spirit—it will immediately fall into a state of doubt and restlessness and find itself caught in a corner, feeling that it has to come out of itself in order to return to its element, which it can only find in surrendering to God through the Spirit. Oh, how arid and reprehensible everything else becomes that is considered, done or received outside the One. Lord, may you alone remain forever our all-sufficient object.... Peace be with you and in you, my beloved brother.

Your obliged brother, in the Lord.

Scripture Meditation

I will lead them beside streams of water, on a level path where they will not stumble.

—JEREMIAH 31:9

Thought for the Day

The humblest of God's people can fructify the lives of others beyond all their dreams.

Prayer

O come, Thou Holy Spirit, and kindle our hearts with holy love; come, Spirit of Strength, and arouse our souls to hunger and thirst after you.... Arise, O Spirit of Life, that through you we may begin to live ... as the heart of God longs to see us, renewed in the image of Christ, and going from glory to glory.... Amen.

—GERHARD TERSTEEGEN

NOVEMBER 17: PASTORAL LETTERS ENGENDER UNITY OF FAITH

John Newton (1725–1807) belonged to the Augustan era of belles lettres,
himself one of the most distinguished Christian writers of letters. "Yes," he told
a friend toward the end of his life, "the Lord saw I should be most useful by
them." In an age of religious dissent, John Newton expressed wisdom, a passion
for godliness, and yet, like Richard Baxter, a desire to avoid the "party spirit" as
a "mere Christian." This truth is illustrated in this letter to Rev. Francis Okeley
who gave up a promising academic career at Cambridge to become a
Moravian pastor in Northampton. Newton wrote him on April 3, 1759.

How welcome your correspondence is to me! I know not if heart was ever more united to any person, in so short a space of time, than to you; and what engaged me so much was the spirit of meekness and love (that peculiar and inimitable mark of true Christianity) which I observed in you. I mean it not to your praise. May all the praise be to him, from whom every good and perfect gift comes, who alone makes the best to differ from the worst.... All who conversed with you greatly regret your speedy departure.... I hope to hear soon and often from you.

I number my Christian correspondents among my principal blessings— a few judicious, pious friends, to who, when I can get the leisure to write, I end my heart by turns. I can trust them with my inmost sentiments, and I can write with no more disguise than I think. I shall rejoice to add you to the number, if you can agree to take me as I am (as I think you will) and suffer to commit my whole self on paper, without respect of names, parties, and sentiments. I endeavor to observe my Lord's command, to call no one master upon earth; yet I desire to own and honor the image of God, wherever I find it. I dare not say I have no bigotry, for I know not myself, and remember to my shame that formerly, when I ignorantly professed myself free from it, I was indeed overrun with it ... but I strive and pray against it. And thus far, by the grace of God, I have attained, so that I find my heart as much united to many who differ from me, in some points, as to any who agree with me in all. I set no value upon any doctrinal truth, further than it has a tendency to promote practical holiness ... "in things necessary." What are these? I answer, those in which the spiritual worshippers of all ages and countries have agreed. Suppose it ran something in the following manner: I believe that sin is the most hateful thing in the world; that I and all human beings are in a state of wrath and depravity, utterly unable to sustain the penalty, or to fulfill the commands of God's holy law; and that we have no sufficiency of ourselves to think a good thought. I believe that Jesus Christ is the chief among ten thousand; that he came into the world to save the chief of sinners, by making a propitiation for sin by his death ... that he is now exalted on high ... and that he ever lives to make intercession for us. I believe that the Holy Spirit (the gift of God through Jesus Christ) is the sure and only guide into all truth, and the common privilege of all believers; and that under his influence, I believe that the Holy Scriptures are able to furnish us thoroughly for every good work. I believe that love to God, and to man for God's sake, is the essence of religion, and the fulfilling of the law; and that without holiness no man shall see the Lord; that those who, by a patient course in well doing, seek glory, honor, and immortality, shall receive eternal life; and I believe that this reward is not of debt but of grace, even to the praise and glory of that grace, whereby he has made us accepted in the Beloved. Amen.

I pretend not to accuracy in this hasty draught; they are only outlines.... I only add my prayers, that the Lord may be with you, and crown your labors of love with success, that you may hereafter shine among those who have been instrumental in turning many to righteousness. I am,
John Newton

Scripture Meditation

It is by grace you have been saved, through faith.
—EPHESIANS 2:8

Thought for the Day

Amazing grace! How sweet the sound!
That saved a wretch like me.
—JOHN NEWTON, "AMAZING GRACE"

Prayer
Jesus! My Shepherd, Priest and King;
My Lord, my Life, my Way, my End, accept the praise I bring!
—JOHN NEWTON

NOVEMBER 18: SUSTAINING FRIENDSHIP WITH A MELANCHOLIC

John Newton became rector of the parish of Olney, Bedfordshire, in 1766,
living close with the poet William Cowper (1731–1800) and ministering there
for eleven years. He was very sensitive to Cowper's fits of depression, such as
when Cowper accused Newton later in 1783: "You do not know what I have
suffered while you were here, nor is there any reason you should.... The friend
of my heart, the person with whom I had formerly taken sweet counsel is no
longer useful to me as a minister, no longer pleasant to me as a Christian, was
a spectacle that must add the bitterness of mortification to the sadness of
despair." Yet Cowper added in 1795, "There is no day in which you are
excluded from my thoughts." Here in this letter dated May 6, 1780, Newton
tried his best to cheer up his friend Cowper.

My dear Sir,
You will have no reason to apply me Luke 8:42. For when you pipe, I
am ready to dance; and when you mourn, a cloud comes over my brow,
and a tear stands a-tiptoe in my eye. I observe [that] your letters usually
begin and end in the allegro strain, and you put the most serious part in
the middle; as this seems the fittest place for it, I will try to imitate you,
though it be something, if either my beginning or my close should enti-
tle me to your smile, except you smile at the presumption of your
humble imitator, and recollect the fable of the frog who tried to imitate
the ox....

Do not wonder [that] I prize your letters. Beside the merit which friendship puts on them, as being yours, you always send me something I should value from a stranger. Some thoughts in your last I shall be the better for, if it be not my own fault. How wonderful is that tincture, the inexpressible something, which gives your sentiments when you speak of yourself so gloomy a cast, while in all other respects it leaves your faculties in full bloom and vigor! How strange that your judgment should be clouded on one point only, and that a point so obvious and strikingly clear to everybody who knows you! How strange that a person who considers the earth, the planets, and the sun itself as mere baubles, compared with the friendship and favor with God their Maker, should think the God who inspired him with such an idea, could ever forsake and cast off the soul which he has taught to love him! How strange it is that you should hold tenaciously both parts of a contradiction. Though your comforts have been so long suspended, I know not that I ever saw you for a single day since your calamity came upon you, in which I could not perceive as clear and satisfactory evidence, that the grace of God was with you, as I could in your brighter and happier times. In the midst of all the little amusements, which you call trifling, and which I be very thankful you can attend to in your present circumstances, it is as easy to see who has your heart, and which way your desires tend, as to see your shadow when you stand in the sun.

Most affectionately yours, J.N.

Scripture Meditation

To the weak I became weak, to win the weak. I have become all things to all men so that by all possible means I might save some.
— I CORINTHIANS 9:22

Thought for the Day

Commitment to friendship requires consistent means of communication, regardless of emotional swings or fits of depression like those of William Cowper.

Prayer

Now to him who is able to establish you by my gospel ... to the only wise God be glory forever through Christ Jesus! Amen.
—ROMANS 16:25, 27

NOVEMBER 19: THE DEVOTIONAL STUDY OF SCRIPTURE

Henry Venn (1724–97) was an Anglican clergyman and a friend of John Newton. Like Newton, Venn also had a collection of his pastoral letters published. Here he wrote to encourage a young clergyman, Jonathan Scott, in his preparations for ministry, on November 6, 1765.

To secret prayer you will join devout study of the Bible; because it is our infallible guide, and the treasury of a truth necessary to salvation. But the riches laid up there are not to be found by proud or careless minds: none possess them, till they dig for them as for silver, longing to know the will of God, that they may do it. To superficial readers of the Bible, it presents little more than a great number of duties, which must be performed; and sins, which must be renounced, with insupportable pains, in failure of obedience. To such readers it also presents passages of excellent use, when believed, because they at once rouse the selfish soul of man to seek reconciliation with God, and help from Heaven, and sweep away every refuge of lies, under which love of sin leads us to take shelter.

But earnest and devout readers of their Bible discover much more: They discover the tender heart of Christ; the efficacy of his blood, to cleanse from all unrighteousness; and a variety of spiritual blessings, which are the present reward of being true-hearted in his service. I am at a loss for words to express how much solid knowledge, transforming your mind into the Divine image, you will certainly gain by persevering in diligent prayer, year after year, for the true interpretation of God's blessed Word, that you may be made wise and holy. A pattern is plainly set before us, in these memorable petitions: may they come from our hearts, and ever dwell upon our tongues! "I am a stranger upon earth (very soon to leave it; therefore its riches and honors cannot profit me); O hide not thy commandments from my, which will enrich me for ever! Open thou my eyes, that I may see wondrous things in thy Law! Thy hands have formed and fashioned me; O give me understanding, that I may know thy Law!"

This method of reading the Bible must be continued through life, especially while the capital truths of the Bible are before our eyes. By this means we have an absolute security from abusing any part of the Word of God. And those who dare despise persevering prayer to be taught by the Spirit of God what is contained in his holy Word, as if they knew enough, fall into pernicious errors. For example, they wrest some passages of Scripture, to contradict others. Or grow violently zealous for doctrines, but very cold respecting that heavenly mind, which those doctrines are revealed to produce. Our profiting will then only appear, when, after the example of David and St. Paul, we pray from deep conviction that we cannot be properly affected with what we believe, unless we are divinely taught; and that if any man thinks that he knows anything as he ought to know, that man knows nothing.

Scripture Meditation

I rejoice in following your statutes as one rejoices in great riches.
—PSALM 119:14

Thought for the Day

Nothing reveals our relationship with God more than how distortedly or appreciatively we handle the Scriptures.

Prayer

I will praise you with an upright heart as I learn your righteous laws.

—PSALM 119:7

NOVEMBER 20: LEARNING TO SEE THE BEST IN OTHERS

Charles Simeon (1759–1836), a friend of the Clapham Group, was an
Anglican clergyman in Cambridge who informally taught homiletics to
theological students, eventually becoming mentor to many clergy throughout
the country. This letter to a friend was dated July 7, 1817.

*L*ast night Mr. D. represented to me in strong terms the (supposed)
ill behavior of Mr. — — — to his pupils; and particularly to Mr. B., to
whom he refused lately to give his hand.

The longer I live, the more I feel the importance of adhering to the
rules which I have laid down for myself in relation to such matters.

1. To hear as little as possible what is to the prejudice of others.
2. To believe nothing of the kind till I am absolutely forced to it.
3. Never to drink into the spirit of one who circulates an ill report.
4. Always to moderate, as far as I can, the unkindness which is
    expressed towards others.
5. Always to believe that if the other side were heard, a very differ-
    ent account would be given of the matter.

I consider love as wealth; and as I would resist a man who should come
to rob my house, so would I resist a man who would weaken my regard
for any human being. I consider, too, that persons are cast into different
molds; and that to ask myself, what would I do in that person's situation,
is not a just mode of judging. I must not expect a man who is naturally
cold and reserved to act as one that is naturally warm and affectionate;
and I think it a great evil, that people do not make more allowances for
each other in this particular. I think religious people are too little attentive to these considerations; and that it is not in reference to the ungodly
world only, that that passage is true, "He that departs from evil makes
himself a prey"; but even in reference to professors also; amongst whom
there is a sad proneness to listen to evil reports, and to believe the repre-
sentations they hear, without giving the injured person any opportunity
of rectifying their views, and of defending his own character.

The more prominent any person's character is, the more likely he is to
suffer in this way; there being in the heart of every man, unless greatly

subdued by grace, a pleasure in hearing anything which may sink others to his level, or lower them in the estimation of the world. We seem to ourselves elevated in proportion as others are depressed. Under such circumstances I derive consolation from the following reflections:

1. My enemy, whatever evil he says of me, does not reduce me so low as he would, if he knew all concerning me that God knows.

2. In drawing the balance, as between debtor and creditor, I find that if I have been robbed of pence, there are pounds and talents placed to my account, to which I have no just title.

3. If man has his "day," God will have his. See 1 Corinthians 4:3, the Greek.

Yours sincerely,
C. S.

Scripture Meditation

Submit to one another out of reverence for Christ.
—EPHESIANS 5:21

Thought for the Day

We can tolerate much from others when we are wholly trusting in God and not in them.

Prayer

Lord, let me have no will of my own; or consider my true happiness as depending ... on anything that can befall me outwardly, but as consisting altogether in conformity to your will.
—HENRY MARTYN

NOVEMBER 21: LIVING APPROPRIATELY WITH THE WORLD

Charles Simeon was asked by the Duchess of Beaufort how he might guide
her in living within the English court. He replied on May 13, 1823.

*M*y very dear Madam,
On the subject of your grace's letter, I have always felt myself incompetent to advise those who move in the higher walks of life. I know in a measure what the blessed word of God says in relation to our separation from the world, and I know in a measure the line of conduct that befits my own situation in life; but when I come to mark with precision the line that has to be observed in your high station, I feel, and [have] ever felt, myself unequal to the task. My own habits, instead of inspiring me with confidence in relation to others, only make me the more diffident. I am a man of some firmness and decision of character; and from the first moment that I set myself to seek the Lord, I gave up myself wholly to Him, and separated myself altogether from the world. I had no one to control me; my situation favored it; the people about me had not (as far as I could see) one particle of what I judged to be the only true wisdom; and therefore I walked with Him only who had chosen and called me to be His servant. And to this hour I have ever persevered in this course. I feel, and have ever felt, that I had no talents for the world, no taste for the world, no time for the world; and therefore, except as an ambassador from the Lord, I have had for forty-four years almost as little to do with the world, as if I had not been in the world.

It was easy therefore for me to draw my line broad, and to make as little distinction for others, as I have made for myself. But it does not appear to me that this would comport either with wisdom or with love. The difference between young and old ministers, in general, consists in this: that the statements of the old are crude and unqualified, whilst those of the latter have such limitations and distinctions, as the Scriptures authorize and the subjects require. The doctrine of salvation by faith alone and of predestination, etc., are often, as is well known, so stated, as to become a stumbling-block to thousands; whilst, when Scripturally stated, they approve themselves to those who have been most prejudiced against them. And this, I think, particularly distinguishes the statements of ministers respecting overcoming the world. A person who views the subject broadly, and without reference to the different circumstances of men, finds it easy to adduce strong and sweeping expressions, and to require a full conformity to them, without any modification whatever. But one who takes into his account all the varieties of situation in which Christians move, and all the diversities of circumstances under which they may be placed, will feel it his duty to consider what those situations and circumstances call for, and what influence they ought to have on the conduct of those who are found in them. They will be led to distinguish between the spirit and the letter of a command, and to modify the latter, whilst in the strictest possible way they adhere to and require the former.

... I am, my dear madam, your grace's most truly affectionate and devoted servant,

C. Simeon

Scripture Meditation

Do not love the world or anything in the world.

—1 JOHN 2:15

Thought for the Day

In reacting against legalistic strictures over "worldliness," have we become indifferent to the influence of "the world" over our way of life?

Prayer

May God of His infinite mercy give me more abundantly to experience a heavenly disposition; and may all that I have written be blessed of Him to producing of this holy disposition in others. Amen, and Amen.

—CHARLES SIMEON

NOVEMBER 22: THE FATHER OF AN ILLEGITIMATE CHILD

John Keble (1792–1866), ordained in 1815, had been a brilliant scholar at Oxford but rejected senior academic posts to lead the life of a rural parish priest and later became an adviser of the Tractarian or Anglo-Catholic Movement. Some of his many pastoral letters were published after his death. Since he faced the world with all its range of human circumstances, it should come as no surprise that he could write this letter.

*D*ear Sir,

I wish to say a few words to you on a very painful matter.... I fear it is impossible for you to deny that you are the father of — —'s child, and I do beseech you to consider what a heavy burden this ought to be on your mind. You are not an ignorant person, brought up amongst unprincipled people: you cannot but know that, however lightly the world may treat such sins as these, the Bible speaks plainly, and says, they who do such things, cannot inherit the kingdom of God; and that these are the very sinful lusts which you renounced in your Baptism and Confirmation, so that now you have, by indulging in them, cast away the blessing of your Baptism, and ought not to have a moment's peace of mind, until you have some good ground to believe that you are in God's sight a true penitent (Matt. 7:7–10; Luke 11:5–13; Matt. 18:1–14).

You ought not to be easy for this plain reason, that if you should die before such a change has taken place in you, you are sure to be lost forever. You cannot deny this without contradicting a great many plain words of God. Then, besides the danger of your own soul, what a burden it is to have to answer for the souls of others, unhappy partners in such sins; innocent, perhaps, until corrupted by you; or if they had gone wrong before, plunged by you into deeper wickedness. Remember our Lord himself says, "Whoso [sic] shall be the cause of sin to one of these little ones, it were better," etc. Think what it must be to meet them at the last day, and to feel that you are the cause of their ruin—the devil's agent to prepare them for his kingdom, and not only them, but all others whom such bad example tends to corrupt.

Now I do not at all suppose that you ever intended all this mischief; nor do I doubt that, as a good-natured young man, you are sorry for the present misery of this young woman; but the mischief you see is done: you were carried away by your passion, in spite of good instruction; and however sorry you may be now, surely experience must have taught you to mistrust yourself for the future. Surely you must feel that if you do not now turn over a new leaf entirely, and seek God's pardon and help, a truer and better way than you have hitherto done, there is no chance, but that you will go from bad to worse: and what will be the end? For the sake of your parents and for your own sake, I beseech you to think on these things now; as you know as well as I do, that the time will soon come when you will wish you had thought about them....

But, in any case, repentance after such things must be a long and painful business, and particularly it will be quite necessary to make up our mind not to care for the foolish laughter of those who make a mock of sin.... Do let me have the comfort of knowing that you intend to repent in earnest.

Scripture Meditation

The way of the unfaithful is hard.
—PROVERBS 13:15

Thought for the Day

Is the abdication of church discipline today a sign we do not truly love sinners enough?

Prayer

Lord, without you, I can do nothing; with you I can do all ... if I lose sight of you, bring me back quickly to you, and grant me to love you better, for your tender mercy's sake.
—E. B. PUSEY

NOVEMBER 23: ADVICE TO ONE SUFFERING FROM VANITY

Edward Bouverie Pusey, friend of John Keble, was an Anglican scholar, leader
of the Oxford Movement, and Regius Professor of Hebrew at Oxford. Pusey
House was founded two years after his death to honor his memory.
He wrote many letters of spiritual counsel. This one was written
to an unknown recipient, around 1877.

And now, since you have made me in a sort a spiritual adviser, I will mention two things to you, and you will not be mortified at my naming them, or at my having seen or heard of them. Not to keep you in suspense, I would say at once (with all affection for your general character), that there is one prominent fault, which people at least do not like to be charged with, though so many have it, over self-esteem, or to speak very plainly, vanity! Knowing very little of your early life, I have no grounds, as I have no reason to judge, how much of a fault this is; nor could I say precisely, on what it turned, what was its principal subject. I might suspect, perhaps, even "personal appearance," or something about the person or connected with it, was a subject (as it is a most capricious quality, and as they said of an eminent German linguist, [Friedrich] Schegel, that he was vain of everything which was his, down to his elbow-chair). This you can tell far better than I can: whether it be this, or conversation, or general ability, or acquirements, or whether it floats about different things, it will in some shape or other, constitute your trial for some time. And it is of course a very important one, because it has a tendency to corrupt everything we do, by infusing self-satisfaction into it. It is easier to write than to say this, though you will believe I have some reluctance even in writing it; but having seen good sort of people in whom it has grown up even to advanced life, and knowing what a bane it is to spiritual progress, and a hindrance altogether, I could not but think it right to name it. It is often useful that a person should know that any given quality is perceptible to others; it makes them realize more the degree in which it is in them; and I doubt not that, in earnest as you are about yourself, you will set yourself vigorously to correct it.

—E. B. PUSEY

Scripture Meditation

Do not be arrogant, but be afraid.

—ROMANS 11:20

Thought for the Day

Your only penance must be in speech, to utter nothing consciously fostering yourself, and to pause before speaking to pray, when you are in danger or perceive yourself so to be.

—E. B. PUSEY

Prayer

Empty me, O Lord, of self, and fill me with You.

—E. B. PUSEY

NOVEMBER 24: PRAYER AND DOUBT ARE INCOMPATIBLE

John Sergieff, known as Father Ivan or John of Kronstadt,[5] was an Orthodox priest who spent six years as bishop of St. Petersburg and then retired to spend the rest of his life in obscurity as a spiritual director or starets, writing to thousands of correspondents throughout the Russian empire and also overseas. His favorite theme was the life in Christ as the source of all blessings for the inner life. In this letter on prayer, his constant topic, he challenged his readers about their doubts.

*I*f you wish to ask God in prayer any blessing for yourself, then before praying prepare yourself to seek for undoubting and firm faith. Take all means to remove doubt and unbelief. For it will go ill with you, if during prayer itself, your heart begins to waver in its faith and does not stand firm. For in so doing, you will have offended the Lord, and God does not bestow his gifts on such. "And all, whatsoever you shall ask in prayer, you shall receive" (Matt. 21:22). So if you doubt, you will not receive.... "But when he asks, he must believe and not doubt," says the apostle James, "because he who doubts is like a wave of the sea, blown and tossed by the wind. That man should not think he will receive anything from the Lord" (James 1:6–8). The heart that doubts God is punished, and becomes depressed and even further contracted by further doubt. So never anger God with your doubts, especially those of you who have already experienced many, many times, the omnipotence of God.

Indeed, doubt is a blasphemy against God, an insolent lie of the heart, or of a lying spirit that nestles within the heart, against the spirit of truth. Fear it as you would a poisonous snake, or rather despise it, and take no notice of it! For remember that during your prayer time, God is waiting for your affirmative answer to the challenge he makes inwardly to you: "Do you believe I am able to do this?" (Matt. 9:21). Your response should be from the depth of your heart: "Yes, Lord."

Let the following reflections help you in your doubts. Firstly, I am only asking God about things that already exist, because he has created all things. I am not asking about imaginary things that have no existence. "For through him all things were made, and without him nothing was made, that has been made" (John 1:3). Moreover, nothing happens without his permissive will, so that God "calls things that are not, as though they were" (Rom. 4:17). Secondly, I ask of God what is possible, because what is impossible for us is possible for God, so God can do for me what I might think was quite impossible. It is our misfortune that our faith is hindered so often by the short-sightedness of our own reason. Human reason is like a spider that catches the truth in the web of its own judgments, arguments and analogies. Whereas faith embraces and sees suddenly what human reason can only arrive at circuitously. Faith is the communication between one spirit and another, while Reason is the means of communication between the spiritually sensual and the spiritually material.

Scriptural Meditation

With man this is impossible, but not with God; all things are possible with God.

—MARK 10:27

Thought for the Day

Without faith it is impossible to please God.

—HEBREWS 11:6

Prayer

Thou, O Holy Spirit, are a treasury of blessings! All the blessings of the soul, all that constitutes the true life, the peace and joy of the heart, come from Thee!

—JOHN OF KRONSTADT

NOVEMBER 25: TEMPTATIONS OF THE INTERNET TODAY

Rick Smith, a counselor who specializes in issues of drug addiction, reflected on a new issue of addiction, the Internet, in this letter of August 12, 2002.

I have been reflecting on the new ways the Internet can impact us. It is an amazing entity. It arose as the desire of the U.S. military contractors to communicate more easily with the Pentagon. It has since gained a life of its own, and has been growing as an underground culture at an astounding rate. Internet users pride themselves on the fact that there is no central organization that runs this interconnected web of telephone wires. Gradually the business potential for the Internet has become apparent. But significantly, the first profitable business venture was not book or clothing sales, but pornography. This is a problem for Christians, more than we may realize or acknowledge. For while its potential for promoting more personal and loving communications, it has become a very damaging avenue for sinful perversions. It appears to damage human relations in three primary ways: as an addictive response; as disrupting existing intimate relationships; and as pornography.

Internet addiction can rob a person in the same way as drugs or alcohol can do. Some users can get so involved in the Internet, that they disregard normal human activities and relationships. While some carry the bumper sticker on their car, "my dog is my best friend," the laptop has become even more so, for some perverts. Then they start to replace normal human emotional responses and personal relationships with all the richly complex ways we relate with other human beings … with a machine instead.

Internet "romantic" affairs are a sufficiently large problem for marriages, that it has become a topic for research. What is intimate about sitting and staring at a computer screen and typing words on a keyboard? Yet for some reason, this activity is breaking up marriages. There is something about the Internet form of communication that simulates and stimulates a form of false intimacy. It does not set social boundaries, to create shame, to inhibit the exercise of one's fantasies, that even a brothel or night-club may do.

For the same reason the Internet was early recognized as a way of delivering pornography more efficiently, and less open to exposure before others. But in whatever form it is delivered, pornography is a violation of the personal qualities for which human relationships were intended. For it becomes a form of idolatry of the human body, instead of being iconic of the rich fullness of personal relationships in friendship and true love of each other.

The Christian has to wonder whether the inner consciousness of too many Christians remains too shallow and unrooted, when instead, it should be "rooted and grounded in divine love," as the apostle prays we should be.

Scripture Meditation

Dear friends, do not believe every spirit, but test the spirits to see
whether they are from God, because many false prophets have
gone out into the world.

—1 JOHN 4:1

Thought for the Day

Ambiguity between the powers of good and evil will intensify as technology is further extended.

Prayer

I pray that you, being rooted and established in love, may have
power, together with all the saints, to grasp how wide and long
and high and deep is the love of Christ, and to know this love that
surpasses knowledge.

—EPHESIANS 3:17–19

NOVEMBER 26: EXPANDING HORIZONS IN PSYCHOLOGICAL RESEARCH

*Rick Smith continued to write on recent findings of the Psychological
Associations of North America in this letter of August 14, 2002.*

Psychological research is now a huge enterprise in the Western world.
Most research in social psychology tends to address conflict resolution, not
forgiveness. For forgiveness is interpreted as a pro-social strategy, not
intrinsic in itself. So I was intrigued to find in the calendar of presentations

at a recent national conference there was a seminar on forgiveness. It grew out of research on some victims who were observed, to be able to return to life, because they were able to forgive their perpetuators.

The first study examined children at a childcare center. The results showed that when asked to forgive their playmates, they responded positively within 10 to 65 seconds. It was also found that friendship between victims and offenders tended to be greater than with adults.

This seems to highlight Christ's observation that we as adults need to enter the Kingdom of God as little children. The second study attempted to discover the components of forgiveness. They found five features: that it was an active process; it occurred between individuals; it occurred willingly; it required a decision that an unjust event had occurred; and forgiveness involved relinquishing negative cognitive, emotional and behavioral response. It would appear that forgiveness is not a simple human response.

The third study examined moderating factors in the ability to forgive. One factor was the ability to exercise empathy. Another was the ability to take perspective more selflessly. Good self-esteem was another positive factor. This contradicts a popular view that to forgive implies weakness. While a negative view of oneself was found to create inability to forgive. Curiously, being "religious" did not correlate at all with the ability to forgive.

Altruism as associated with forgiveness, has become a new field of study. In the past, those with an evolutionary bias in researches into human behavior gave altruism no function in humanity's survival. There was no apparent scientific foundation for a truly selfless act. But a new technology, FMRI, or Functional Magnetic Resonance Imaging, now allows researchers to examine brain operations while an individual thinks, feels and acts. This research identified the areas in the brain that were triggered when altruistic acts were performed; it was the area where rewards were processed. The conclusion accepted by the researchers was that the human being is hard-wired to co-operate. Could this be basic to the relational qualities of being human, to love, forgive, care and form friendships and communities? Rather than being simply tool-making creatures, or even more intelligent than other primates, could it be that being language communicants and even altruistic, we really are made in God's image and likeness for purposes of fellowship, human and divine?

Scripture Meditation

Whoever pursues righteousness and love, finds life, prosperity and honor.

PROVERBS 21:21

Thought for the Day

Whatever true insights are gained of the human condition, these will always be consistent with God's Word.

Prayer

My God, here I am, my heart devoted to you. Fashion me according to your heart.

— BROTHER LAWRENCE

NOVEMBER 27: A RENEWED CALL TO CHRISTIAN COMMUNITY

Dr. Larry Crabb is a professional counselor and author of many books on fostering deeper relationships for contemporary Christians through New Way Ministries in Littleton, Colorado.

We're hiding relational inadequacy behind success in everything else. We don't know how to connect as persons. And it's leaving us troubled, sometimes to the point of despair, and alone. We have become a community of the unbroken, unknown, and untouched.

Western Christendom knows how to orchestrate mass worship and stage big events. And that's good. God often moves in large gatherings. But we are in danger of allowing the visible success of corporate Christianity to dull our longing for relational Christianity, for the joyful, hard work of intimate friendship. We're better at big events than soul fellowship.

Hebrews tells us to give ongoing deliberate attention to how one Christian can arouse the passion for love and holiness that is in the soul of another (see Heb. 10:24). Method-centered recovery groups, professionalized helping, highly touted "breakthroughs" in Christian counseling, and overly structured lay counseling and discipleship programs are getting in the way.

They're keeping us from seeing each other as persons, as beings designed for relationship rather than as rebels to merely scold or psyches to technically fix. And they're interfering with meeting each other in community, as broken, restored, grateful, forever-dependent followers of Jesus. They're getting in the way of radically depending on supernatural resources to relate to each other the way the Trinity relates which, in our case, requires us to see through mutual ugliness to redeemed beauty.

The spiritual journey is not about projects. It is not reducible to manageable programs for getting things done or for making us who we should be. It begins not with managing things but with thinking ideas that release deep passions within us. "Thing" Christianity must be replaced with thoughtful Christianity. It's truth that sets us free. Every Christian, whether counselor, pastor, elder, or "mere disciple," shares in that high calling, to "truth in love." But it's hard. It's confusing. Shepherding and friendship are messy.

To shepherd souls, to connect with the reality of another person, we must aim high, bend low, and take risks. Aim high: believe that powerful engagement is possible. The laity, the people of God, must value worship that releases the church to become a community over pseudo-worship that stirs excitement without connecting souls. Bend low: move away from moralism and professionalism to face the largely uncharted territory of our own interior world and the interior world of others, with all its self-deception, self-entitlement, and self-absorption; and learn to depend on the Word and the Spirit to guide us. Take risks: get in over your head. Get involved till you feel profoundly inadequate. Then maybe we'll be humbled enough to hear the Spirit. And then the miracle of the Gospel will surface: we are indwelt by life that loves—and we can release it in each other.

Scripture Meditation

Peter was hurt because Jesus asked him the third time, "Do you love me?" He said, "Lord, you know all things; you know that I love you." Jesus said: "Feed my sheep."

—JOHN 21:17

Thought for the Day

If the Good Shepherd seeks one lost sheep, what measure of pastoral attentiveness should we have?

Prayer

Father.... may they be brought to complete unity to let the world know that you sent me and have loved them even as you have loved me.

—JOHN 17:21, 23

NOVEMBER 28: CHRISTIAN LIFE AS THE PORTRAITURE OF FAITH

Dr. Timothy George (b. 1950), dean of Beeson Divinity School, Samford University, Birmingham, Alabama, is a distinguished historical scholar of the Reformation leaders. He wrote a personal letter to the editor dated October 28, 2002.

*D*ear Jim:

As you know, I have had a lifelong interest in the genre of biography. Here at Beeson Divinity School, we have established the John Pollack

award for Christian Biography both to honor one of the great practitioners of biography writing and to encourage a flourishing of this medium
among others.

As a small boy I once read some twenty-five or thirty biographies in a
single summer. I remember being entranced by the stories of heroes and
villains of the past, each uniquely placed within the swimming river of
time, and each possessed of enormous capacities for good and evil. Some
years later, while working on a biography of William Carey, the great missionary pioneer to India, I was struck by how his life so closely paralleled
that of his near contemporary, the great explorer, Captain [James] Cook.
Both grew up in extreme poverty in landlocked counties of England.
Both had almost no formal education. Yet, each was possessed of a
remarkable genius—Cook for drawing maps and Carey for learning languages. Both gave themselves to a great dream and dared to go where no
one else had gone before. Cook expanded the horizons of European consciousness, and filled in the map of nearly one-third of the globe. Carey
overcame great obstacles to carry the gospel of Christ to India where he
planted churches, founded schools, and translated the Bible into some
forty languages and dialects of people. Both Carey and Cook were hori-
zontal figures who saw beyond the limitations others had set for them
and, despite their flaws, challenged others to follow a higher calling.

As Christians, we are surrounded by "a great cloud of witnesses." They
are given to us for a reason: to remind us of our own finitude and need
for grace, and yet to point us forward towards ever expanding horizons,
indeed towards that City with foundations, towards which we journey as
a band of pilgrims in company with all the saints.

Yours ever in Christ,
Timothy

Scripture Meditation

Remember your leaders, who spoke the word of God to you.
Consider the outcome of their way of life and imitate their faith.
Jesus Christ is the same yesterday and today and forever.
—HEBREWS 13:7–8

Thought for the Day

Live with a desire to have further vision "beyond the ranges."

Prayer

Be thou my vision,
O Lord of my heart.

—Mary E. Byrne translator, "Be Thou My Vision"

NOVEMBER 29: NO LONGER SEEING CHRISTIANITY
FROM A WESTERN MIND-SET

Professor Andrew Walls (b. 1929), the renowned professor of missiology at
Edinburgh and Aberdeen universities, wrote this letter on August 9, 2003.

*D*ear Jim,

Thank you for your very kind message. That I have taken so long to answer it is a measure, not of disregard for it, but of the difficulty of giving an adequate answer....

We are moving now from a Christian West into a post-Western Christianity. We from the West are no longer the leaders, the initiators, the norm setters. We now have to learn to be helpers, assistants, facilitators.

There is no promise of steady, resistless Christian advance; advance is often followed by recession. The spread of the Gospel does not produce the sort of gains that can be plotted on a map, only points through which Christ's influence may come to bear at the present time. Christianity is vulnerable, Christian progress fragile; the vulnerability, perhaps, of the Cross, and the fragility of the earthen vessel. We have no Mecca, no permanent centre—our new Jerusalem will come down, newly made, at the last time. Christian communities often wither in the heartlands and flower anew at or beyond the periphery. No one country, no one people, no one culture owns the Christian faith. Christian advance is serial, rooted now in one place, now in another. And the baton of leadership passes on. God has been preparing his church in many parts of the world, and in some cases testing it by fire, to carry out His mission in the new century.... And it now looks more like that multitude gathered from every tribe, tongue, nation and kindred than at any previous time in history. What an amazing time we have lived through! What an amazing time we have come to!

Scripture Meditation

The nations will walk by its light, and the kings of the earth will bring their splendor into it.... The glory and honor of the nations will be brought into it.

— REVELATION 21:24, 26

Thought for the Day

A Christian faith grounded upon the death and resurrection of Christ has no need of a "territorial imperative," west or east, north or south.

Prayer

Thy wonders wrought already / Require our ceaseless praises
But show thy power / And myriads more
Endue with heavenly graces.
But fill our earth with glory / And, known by every nation
God of all grace / Receive the praise
Of all thy new creation.

— CHARLES WESLEY

NOVEMBER 30: SEEING THE CHRISTIAN LIFE
THROUGH WIDE-ANGLED LENSES

The editor, Dr. James Houston, wrote this closing letter to address the reader.

*D*ear Reader,

It may surprise you when I admit that I really did not know how this lectionary of letters would unfold. It took on a life of its own. Yes, since ours is a historic faith, the Christian calendar fixes a sequence for its celebrations. But it is the mark of the Christian to "walk by faith and not by sight," so this collection of letters will lead us forward also circumstantially, sometimes in unexpected ways.

Certainly the letters have expanded my own horizons, more than I thought possible. Amassing this collection has been like putting on wide-angled lenses to see much wider perspectives. It has made me realize, more than ever, how cheated we are by being "modern" or even "postmodern," since these labels lack a historical perspective. When secularism—by ignoring God rather than overtly denying his existence—saturates our consciousness, we tend to ignore our rich Christian heritage. How stupid can we be to be politically correct, opening our door domestically to all the religions of the world, yet they never deny their own past, while we are ignoring or even denying our own past! Should we be surprised if one day our national apostasy is condemned when we become aliens within our own land, outvoted by those strongly faithful to their past?

Modernism also emphasizes cleverness over wisdom, in order to make technical sense of our world. The threat of being so technical, even in the life of the church, is actually the loss of our souls. These letters help us then to explore Christian personhood, as a vast, inner domain, one that has infinite potentials when God is enthroned there in his triune Being.

Despite globalization, we still tend to think too parochially of the Christian identity. Some of these letters may reflect this tendency, but today the fight is no longer between Protestant and Roman Catholic, but of all Christians—Orthodox, Roman Catholic, and Protestant—against the formidable foe of secularism. For our diverse traditions provide also complementary truths that enrich the wholeness of our Christian identity.

I have also been convicted that the Christian should never be an autonomous thinker like the Greek philosopher, Aristotle. In this regard, Nathaniel Hawthorne once described himself in a reflective letter as living like a night owl, nesting in his own darkness most of the time. No, the Hallelujah Chorus is to "the Lamb that was slain, and is alive for evermore." This requires a new genre, more expressive of the communion of saints, more like the conducting of a symphony than the isolated thoughts of the authorial "I." We have seen how significant letters are in the message of the New Testament. We have witnessed the vast range of personal circumstances, perspectives, and emotions, which even a Stoic letter writer like Seneca counted ninety-two ways of being personal with one other. Think too how some of our scholars have given us in one letter the gist of what they have spent volumes of learned discourse to unfold!

Finally, in spite of all the personal insights these letters have given us, our response may be one of discouragement, now feeling even more inadequate in our faith and life as a Christian as a result of our readings. We live in an age of superficialities, a "plastic" culture of unreflective activists. Yet enough of the letters call us to repentance, to the hope that yes, God's purpose is that we should be conformed to the image of his Son through the indwelling of the Holy Spirit. So now it is time to anticipate the Advent season once more with its challenge of renewal and transformation. Thank you for sharing this journey with me through the Christian calendar as well as through many vicissitudes of the human condition.

Scripture Meditation

By the meekness and gentleness of Christ I appeal to you.... I do not want to seem to be trying to frighten you with my letters.... What we are in our letters when we are absent, we will be in our actions when we are present.

—2 CORINTHIANS 10:1, 9, 11

Thought for the Day

May this lectionary encourage us to be a new Christian generation of reflective, loving e-mail writers!

Prayer

May the grace of the Lord Jesus Christ, and the love of God, and the fellowship of the Holy Spirit be with you all.

—2 CORINTHIANS 13:14

NOTES

1. Glenn Tinder, *The Political Meaning of Christianity* (San Francisco: Harper Collins, 1991), 83.
2. Ibid., 159.
3. Miklós Radnóti, *The Seventh Eclogue* from *Foamy Sky: The Major Poems of Miklos Radnoti* (Princeton: Princeton University, 1992).
4. Imre Kertész, *Kaddish for the Unborn Child* (London: Vintage, 2004).
5. John Sergieff, *My Life in Christ*, E. E. Goulaeff, ed. (London: Casel & Co., 1897), 8–9.

BIBLIOGRAPHY

Abbe de Tourville, *Letters of Direction, with an Introduction by Evelyn Underhill.* London & Oxford: Mowbray, 1982, 12–13, 28–30.

Adam of Perseigne. *The Letters of.* Translated by Grace Perigo. Vol. 1. Kalamazoo, MI: Cistercian Publications, 1976, 58, 59, 61.

Aelred of Rievaulx. *Treatises and Pastoral Prayer.* Kalamazoo, MI: Cistercian Publications, 1982, 3–4, 9–10, 11–12, 13–14, 15–16, 26–27, 35, 36, 38.

— — —. *A Letter to his Sister.* Translated by Geoffrey Webb and Adrian Walker. London: A. R. Mowbray & Co. Ltd., 1957, 60.

Alexander, Desmond. Personal communication.

Alexandrina of Ricci. *Letters from the Saints.* Compiled by Claude Williamson. London: Salisbury Square, n.d., 149–51.

Alphonsus of Liguori. *Alphonsus de Liguori: Selected Writings.* Edited by Frederick M. Jones. New York: Paulist Press, 1999, 228-29.

Ambrose of Milan. *Saint Ambrose: Letters 1–91.* Translated by Mary Melchior Beyenka. Vol. 26. Washington, DC: Catholic University of America, 1954, 386–91.

Anonymous. Letter of April 22, 2001 by hot-air balloon manufacturer. Reproduced by permission of Paula Glass Sevier.

— — —. Mother's letter of April 21, 2003. Personal communication.

— — —. Pastor's letter of October 7, 2002. Personal communication.

— — —. Pastor's letter of resignation on February 11, 2004. Personal communication.

— — —. *The Pursuit of Wisdom and Other Works,* Translated and edited by James Walsh. New York: Paulist Press, 1988, 166–69, 219–24.

— — —. *Stories from Rwanda.* Edited by Philip Gourevitch. New York: Farrar, Strauss & Giroux, 1998.

Athanasius, Bishop of Alexandria. *A Library of Fathers of the Holy Catholic Church: Historical Tracts of St. Athanasius.* Translated by members of the English Church. Oxford: John Henry Parker, 1843, 299–300.

— — —. *St. Athanasius: Select Works and Letters. A Select Library of Nicene and Post-Nicene Fathers of the Christian Church.* Vol. 4. Edinburgh: T.& T. Clark, 1998.

―――. *Festal Letters,* Edinburgh: T.& T. Clark, 1998, 519–20, 551–52.

―――. *The Resurrection Letters, St. Athanasius, Bishop of Alexandria, from AD 328–373.* Paraphrased by Jack N. Sparks. Nashville: Thomas Nelson, 1979.

―――. *Athanasius: The life of Antony and The Letter to Marcellinus.* Translated by Robert C. Gregg. New York: Paulist Press Inc., 1980.

Augustine of Hippo. *Letters.* Translated by Sister Wilfrid Parsons. Vols. 2, 4. New York: Fathers of the Church, 1953, 1955, 56, 78, 79, 87, 88, 94–97, 97–100, 153, 154, 155, 177.

―――. *Letter 147 to the noble lady Pauline.* New York: Paulist Press, Inc., 1965.

―――. *The Works of Saint Augustine: a Translation for the 21st Century, Letters 1–99.* Edited by John E. Rotelle, translated by Roland Teske. New York: New City Press, 2001, 110, 111, 114.

―――. "Letter to Proba." from *Letters of Saint Augustine.* Translated by John Leinenweber. Liguori, Missouri: Triumph Books, 1992, 120–29.

―――. *Saint Augustine's Enchiridion.* London: S.PC.K., 1953, 7–8.

Averbeck, Dr. Richard. Personal communication.

Barbosa de Sousa, Ricardo. Personal communication.

Barnes, M. Craig. Personal communication.

Barnett, Bishop Paul. Personal communication.

Barth, Karl. *Karl Barth: Letters, 1961–1968.* Translated by Geoffrey W. Bromley. Grand Rapids: Wm. B. Eerdmans Publishing Company, 1981, 9, 184, 267–68.

―――. *Karl Barth, A Letter to Great Britain from Switzerland.* London: The Sheldon Press, S.P.C.K., 1941, 1, 4, 5, 6, 7, 9–11, 11–13, 23–24, 25, 26.

Basil the Great. *St. Basil: Select Works and Letters.* Translated by Blomfield Jackson. Grand Rapids: Wm. B. Eerdmans Publishing Company, 1978, 194–96, 231.

Baxter, Richard. "Advice to a Young Minister." *The Congregational Quarterly,* 3 (1952): 232–35.

Begbie, Jeremy. Personal communications.

Bernard of Clairvaux. *The Letters of St. Bernard of Clairvaux.* Translated by Bruno Scott James. Kalamazoo, MI: Cistercian Publications, 1998, 137–38, 289–90, 292–93.

―――. *Five Books on Consideration: Advice to a Pope.* Translated by John D. Anderson and Elizabeth T. Kennan. Kalamazoo, MI: Cistercian Publications, 1976, 29, 37, 38, 47, 48, 52, 53, 56.

Berulle, Cardinal Pierre de. *Berulle and the French School: Selected Writings.* Edited by William M. Thompson, translated by Lowell M. Glendon. New York: Paulist Press, 1989, 183-84.

Bethge, Eberhard. "How the Prison Letters Survived," in *Friendship and Resistance.* Grand Rapids: Wm. B. Eerdmans, 1995, 38–57.

Blake, William. *The Portable Blake.* Harmondsworth, Middlesex: Penguin Books, 1981, 178–80.

Bockmuehl, Elisabeth. Personal communication.

Bockmuehl, Klaus. *Books: God's Tools in the History of Salvation.* Colorado Springs: Helmers & Howard, 1986.

Bonhoeffer, Dietrich. *Letters and Papers from Prison.* London: S.C.M. Press, 1971, 278–82.

Bossuet, Jacques-Benigne. *Oeuvres Completes de Bossuet*. Edited by F. Lachat. Vol. XXVII. Paris: Librairie de Louis Vives, 1864, 294–95.

Bowen, Stuart C. Personal communication.

Bray, Gerald. Personal communication.

Brother Lawrence. *Selections from the World's Classics*. Edited by Robert Scott and George W. Gilmore. Vol. IX. New York: Funk & Wagnalls Co., 1916, 19–21, 54–55.

Cabrini, Frances Xavier. *The Travels of Mother Frances Xavier Cabrini, Foundress of the Missionary Sisters of the Sacred Heart of Jesus, as related in several of her letters*. Exeter: Streatham Hill, 1925, 252–56.

Calvin, John. *Letters of John Calvin*. Edited by Jules Bonnett. Vol. 1. Edinburgh: Thomas Constable & Co, 1855, 16–19, 295–96, 300–301, 411–12, 413, 414.

Camus, Jean Pierre. *The Spirit of Francis de Sales*. Translated by H. L. Sidney Lear. London: Longmans, Green and Co., 1908, 11–12.

Canlis, Julie. Personal communication.

Carrouges, Michael. *Soldier of the Spirit: the Life of Charles de Foucauld*. Translated by Marie-Christine Hellin. New York: G. P. Putnam, 1956, 81, 86–87.

Catherine Benincasa. *Catherine of Siena as seen through her Letters*. Translated and edited by Vida D. Scudder. London: J. M. Dent & Co., 1906, 25–26, 27, 28, 132–33, 168.

Chalmers, James. *Autobiography and Letters*. Edited by Richard Lovett. 6th edition. London: The Religious Tract Society, 1903, 209–10, 212, 214–15.

Chan, Grace. Personal communication.

Charles Wesley's papers. Methodist Archives and Research Centre. John Ryland University Library, University of Manchester.

Constantine. *Private Letters Pagan and Christian*. London: Earnest Benn Limited, 1929, 106, 108.

Cowper, William. *The Letters of the late William Cowper, Esq. to his Friends*. London: Baldwin, Cradock and Joy, 1820, 10–11, 529–30.

Crabb, Larry. Personal communication.

Cyprian of Carthage. *Cyprian Letters 1–81, Fathers of the Church*. Translated by Sister Rose Bernard Donna. Vol. 51. Washington, DC: Catholic University of America Press, 1964, 162–63, 167–68.

Damian, Peter. *Peter Damian: Letters 1–30*. Translated by Owen J. Blum. Washington, DC: Catholic University of America Press, 1989, 109–11.

Davies, Mark. Personal communication.

de Caussade. *Abandonment to Divine Providence*. Translated by E. J. Strickland. Exeter: Catholic Records Press, 1921, 122–25, 268–69, 348–49.

— — —. *Lettres Spirituelles*. Edited by Miche Olphe-Galliard. Paris: Desclee de Brouwer, 1964, 77–78, 127–30.

— — —. *Spiritual Letters of Jean-Pierre de Caussade*. Translated by Kitty Muggeridge. Wilton, CT: Morehouse-Barlow, 1987.

— — —. *Inner Search: Letters (1889–1916)*. Translated by Barbara Lucas. New York: Maryknoll, Orbis, 1979, 84–85.

Francis de Paola. *Tradition Day by Day, Readings from Church Writers*. Villanova, PA: Augustinian Press, 1994, 116.

Derderian, Hovnan. *The Lenten Period and the Lord's Prayer.* Quebec, 1–4.

Devenyi, Eva. Personal communication.

Diewert, Dave A. Personal communication.

Doherty, Catherine de Hueck. *Dearly Beloved: Letters to the Children of My Spirit.* Vol. 1. Combermere, ON: Madonna House Publications, 1988, 171–74, 174–77, 177–78, 234–35.

Dostoyevsky, Fyodor. *Selected Letters of Fyodor Dostoyevsky.* Edited by Joseph Frank and David Goldstein. Piscataway, NJ: Rutgers University Press, 1987, 420, 420–21.

Dudden, F. Homes. *Gregory the Great: his Place in History and Thought.* Vol. 2. London: Longmans, Green, and Co., 1905, 237.

Dugalescu, Peter. Personal communication.

Elchaninov, Alexander. *The Diary of a Russian Priest.* Translated by Helen Iswolsky. London: Faber & Faber, 1967, 207–8.

Elves, Alberto. Personal communication.

Eudes, St. John. *En Tout la Volonte de Dieus: Eudes a travers ses Lettres.* Edited by C. Guillon. Paris: Cerf, 68–69.

Evagrius Ponticus. *The Pratikos. Chapters on Prayer.* Translated by John Eudes Bamberger. Kalamazoo, MI: Cistercian Publications, 1978, 12–14, 16–20.

Fenelon, Francois de la Motte. *Spiritual Letters of Archbishop Fenelon: Letters to Women.* Translated by H. L. Sidney Lear. London: Rivingtons, 1877.

— — —. *Selections from the Works of Fenelon,* London: John Chapman, 1845.

Ferrer, Vincent. *Letters from the Saints.* London: Salisbury Square, n.d., 33–35, 38, 41–42, 45–46.

Fletcher, John William. *The Posthumous Pieces of the Reverend John William de la Flechere.* Edited by Melville Horne. Albany, NY: T. Spencer and A. Ellison, 1794, 277–79, 288–90, 297–300, 305–9, 327–28.

Foley, Henry. *Records of the English Province of the Society of Jesus.* Vol. 1. London: Burnes and Oates, 1877, 338.

Fulbert of Chartres. *Tradition Day by Day, Readings from the Church Fathers.* Villanova, PA: Augustinian Press, 1994, 23.

Gay, Craig M. Personal communication.

George, Timothy. Personal communication.

Gerson, Jean. *Jean Gerson: Early Works.* Translated by Brian Patrick McGuire. New York: Paulist Press, 1998.

Gourevitch, Philip. *Stories from Rwanda.* New York: Farrar, Strauss & Giroux, 1998.

Gregory Nazianzen. *Private Letters Pagan and Christian.* London: Earnest Benn, Ltd, 1929, 143–43.

— — —. *A Select Library of Nicene and Post-Nicene Fathers of the Christian Church.* Vol. 7. Edinburgh: T. & T. Clark, 1989, 471–72.

Gregory of Nyssa. *Select Writings and Letters of Gregory, Bishop of Nyssa.* Translated by William More and Henry Austin Wilson, edited by Henry Wace. Edinburgh: T. & T. Clark, 1994, 542–45.

Groote, Geert. *Devotio Moderna: Basic Writings.* Translated by John van Engen. New York: Paulist Press, 1988, 98.

Grou, Jean Nicolas. *Selections from the World's Devotional Classics*. Edited by Robert Scott and George W. Gilmore. Vol. X. New York & London: Funk & Wagnalls, 1916, 89–90.

Hall, Bishop Joseph. *The Works of Joseph Hall*. Edited by Josiah Pratt. Vol. IX. London: Whittingham, 1808, 490–97.

Harris, Joel Chandler. *Letters of the Century*. Edited by Lisa Grunwald and Stephen J. Adler. New York: Random House, 1999, 13–14.

— — —. *Dearest Chums and Partners: Joel Chandler Harris's Letters to his Children*. Edited by Hugh T. Keenan. Athens: University of Georgia Press, 1993, 350–52.

Hatina, Tom. Personal communication.

Havergal, Frances Ridley. *Memorials, by her Sister, M. V.G. H*. New York: Anson D. F. Randolph and Co., 1880, 64, 72–73, 217, 229, 230.

Hindmarsh, Bruce. Personal communication.

Holt, Helen. Personal communication.

Ignatius of Antioch. *The Genuine Epistles of the Apostolical Fathers*. Edited by William, Lord Archbishop of Canterbury. New York: Southwick and Pelsue, 1810, 211–16.

— — —. *Early Christian Writings, the Apostolic Fathers*. Translated by Maxwell Staniforth. New York: Penguin Books, 1976, 103–7.

Ignatius of Loyola. *Ignatius of Loyola: The Spiritual Exercises and Selected Works*. Edited by George E. Ganss. New York: Paulist Press, 1991, 332–34.

Jacobs, Harriet Ann. *Incidents in the Life of a Slave Girl*. Edited by Jean Fagan Yellin. Cambridge, MA: Harvard University Press, 1987, 242.

Jagerstatter, Franz. *In Solitary Witness: The Life and Death of Franz Jagerstatter*. Edited by Gordon Zahn. Springfield, IL: TempleGate Publishers, 1964, 101, 101–2.

Jerome. *Private Letters Pagan and Christian*. London: Ernest Benn Ltd., 1929, 155–56.

John of Avila. *Letters of Blessed John of Avila*. Translated by the Benedictines of Stanbrooke. London: Burns Oates, 1904.

John of the Cross. *The Works of St. John of the Cross*. Edited by David Lewis. London: Thomas Baker, 1891, 549–50.

John of Kronstadt (John Iliytch Sergieff). *My Life in Christ*. Translated by E. E. Goulaeff. London: Cassell & Company, Ltd., 1897, 8–9, 439.

Johnson, Darrell. Personal communication.

Keble, John. *Letters of Spiritual Counsel and Guidance*. Edited by R. J. Wilson. Oxford: J. Parker, 1870, 154–57.

Keusseyan, Hacob, and Vardon Devri. *Holy Murion: the Mystery of the Holy Murion (Chrism)*. Translated by Lilith Sargissian. St. Etchmiadzin, Armenia: Holy See Press, 2001, 3–4, 11.

Kierkegaard, Søren. *Journals and Papers: Autobiographical part 1, 1829–1848*. Edited and translated by Havard and Edna Hong. Bloomington: Indiana University Press, 1978, 83, 148.

Kim, Sang-Bok. Personal communication.

Kreiner-Phillips, Kathy. Personal communication.

Lee, Michelle. Personal communication.

Leighton, Robert. *The Whole Works of Robert Leighton, D.D.* Edited by John Norman Pearson. New York: J. C. Riker, 1852, 762.

Leo the Great. *Letters*. Translated by Edmund Hunt. Vol. 34. New York: Fathers of the Church Inc., 1957, 71–72

———. *Sermons of S. Leo the Great on the Incarnation*. Translated by William Bright. London: Joseph Masters, 1862, 64–67, 70–71, 72–73, 74, 77, 78, 79.

Levine, Jerry. Personal communication.

Lewis, C. S. *They Stand Together: Letters between C. S. Lewis and Arthur Greaves*. Edited by H. W. Lewis. London: Geoffrey Bles, 1966, 303–6, 335–36.

———. *The Screwtape Letters*. London: Centenary Press, 1942, 136, 138–40.

Long, V. Philip. Personal communication.

Luther, Martin. *Luther: Letters of Spiritual Counsel*. Edited and translated by Theodore G. Tappert. Vancouver: Regent College Publishing, 1997, 98, 125–27, 129.

Macarius of Optino. *Russian Letters of Direction, 1834–1860*. Crestwood, NY: St. Vladimir University Press, 1975, 30.

MacDonald, Greville. *George MacDonald and his Wife*. London: George Allen & Unwin, 1924, 373–74.

Mackenzie, Robert. *John Brown of Haddington*. London: Banner of Truth Trust, 1964, 204–5.

Maid of Madame Guyon. *The Archbishop of Cambrai's Dissertation on Pure Love*. 3rd edition. London: Luke Hinde, 1750, 239–49.

Mann, Bart. Personal communication.

Manson, Mary. Personal communication.

Markkula, Juhana. Personal communication.

Markus, R. A. *Gregory the Great and his World*. Cambridge: Cambridge University Press, 1997, 206–9.

Martyn, Henry. *Journals and Letters of Henry Martyn*. Edited by S. Wilberforce. London: R. B. Seeley and W. Burnside, 1839, 512, 513, 514, 516, 757.

Mason, Mike. Personal communications.

Maximus the Confessor. *Centuria*. Translated by Andrew Louth. Oxford: Routledge Press, 1996, 86–87, 90.

Mihoc, Fr. Vaslie. Personal communication.

Millard, Allen. Personal communication.

Milne, Fred. Personal communication.

More, Hannah. *English Spirituality in the Age of Wesley*. Edited by David Lyle Jeffrey. Grand Rapids: William B. Eerdmans, 1987, 441–42, 442–43, 443–44.

McCheyne, Robert Murray. *Memoirs and Remains of the Rev. Robert Murray McCheyne*. Edited by Rev. Andrew A. Bonar. London: Oliphant, Anderson & Ferrier, 1892, 322–33.

Muelle, Karen. Personal communication.

Muggeridge, Malcolm. Personal communication.

Mutch, Barbara. Personal communication.

Newton, John. *The Works of the Rev. John Newton, An Authentic Narrative*. Edited by Richard Cecil. Vol. 1. Edinburgh: Thomas Nelson and Peter Brown, 1827, 1–3, 16–18, 39–41, 100–104.

Newton, Sir Isaac. *The Orthodox Churchman's Magazine and Review, a Treasury of Divine and Useful Knowledge*. Vol. X. London: J. G. Barnard, 1806, 199–202.

O'Connor, Flannery. *The Habit of Being: Letters of Flannery O'Connor.* Edited by Sally Fitzgerald. New York: Random House, 1940, 92, 99–100.

Olier, Jean-Jacques. *Oeuvres Completes de M. Olier, M. L' Abbe Migne.* Paris: J-P. Migne, 1856, 802–4, 951–53, 1050–53.

Overman, Dean. Personal communication.

Packer, J. I. Personal communication.

Palmer, Earl F. Personal communication.

Pascal, Blaise. *The Mind on Fire: Blaise Pascal.* Edited by James M. Houston. Colorado Springs: Victor, 2005, 235–43, 249–50, 253.

— — —. *Blaise Pascal, Oeuvres completes.* Edited by J. Chevalier. Cambridge, MA: Schoenhof Foreign Books Inc., 1936, 703–5.

— — —. *Selections from the World's Devotional Classics.* Edited by Robert Scott and George W. Gilmore. Vol. VI. New York: Funk & Wagnalls, 1916, 173–74.

Peterson, Eugene. Personal communication.

Pliny the Younger. *Private Letters, Pagan and Christian.* London: Earnest Benn Limited, 1929.

Powerscourt, Theodosia. *Letters and Papers of the late Theodosia A. Viscountess Powerscourt.* Edited by Robert Daly. London: G. Morrish, n.d.

Pozapalian, Nerses. Personal communication.

Priddy, Barbara. Personal communication.

Provan, Iain. Personal communication.

Pusey, Edward Bouverie. *Spiritual Letters of Edward Bouverie Pusey.* Edited by J. O. Johnston and W. C. E. Newbolt. London: Longmans, Green and Co., 1898, 251–52, 281–83.

Quek Swee Hwa. Personal communication.

Ravier, Andre. *Francois de Sales: Lettres Intimes.* Paris: Le Sarment, Fayard, 1991, 131–33, 147–51, 171–72.

Ridley, Nicholas Bishop. *The Works of Bishop Ridley.* Cambridge: Cambridge University Press, 1841, 395–418.

Robson, Ellie. Personal communication.

Rogers, Henry. *The Life and Character of John Howe, M.A. with an Analysis of his Writings.* London: The Religious Tract Society, 1863, 201–12.

Rogers, John. *The Puritans: a Sourcebook of their Writings.* Edited by Perry Miller and Thomas H. Johnson. Mineola, NY: Dover Publications, Inc., 2001, 481–82, 487–88.

Romaine, William. *Select Letters of the Rev. William Romaine.* Edited by Thomas Chalmers. London: William Collins Co., 1830, 56–59, 156–58, 276–84, 377–78.

Rosenstock-Huessy, Eugen. *Judaism against Christianity.* New York: Schocken Books, 1969, 97, 98, 99, 103, 104, 109, 111, 119, 120, 121, 122–23, 123, 124, 125, 126.

Rutherford, Samuel. *The Letters of Samuel Rutherford.* Edited by Andrew A. Bonar. 4th edition. Edinburgh: Oliphant & Ferrier, 1891, 85–87

Samway, Patrick H. *Walker Percy: a Life.* New York: Farrar, Strauss and Giroux, 1997, 300–301.

Schnabel, Eckhard. Personal communications.

Scougal, Henry. *Selections of the World's Devotional Classics.* Edited by Robert Scott and George W. Gilmore. Vol. IX. New York: Funk & Wagnalls, 1916, 54.

Simeon, Charles. *Memoirs of the Life of Rev. Charles Simeon, M.A.* Edited by William Carus. New York: Robert Carter, 1848, 303–4.

Simpson, Donald H. Personal communication.

Six, Jean-Francois. *Spiritual Autobiography of Charles de Foucauld.* Translated by J. Holland Smith. New York: Dimension, 1964, 31–32, 80–82, 108–9.

Slaymaker, Olav. Personal communication.

Smith, Rick. Personal communication.

Spilsbury, Paul. Personal communication.

Susanna Wesley's papers. Methodist Archives and Research Centre. John Ryland University Library, University of Manchester.

St. Theophan the recluse. *The Spiritual Life: How to be Attained to It.* Translated by Alexndra Dockham. Crestwood, NY: St. Xenia Skete Press, 1995, 149–50, 227–29.

Stapleton, T. *The Life and Illustrious Martyrdom of Sir Thomas More.* London: Burns Oates, 1928, 111, 115.

Stevenson, Gail. Personal communication.

Stowers, Stanley K. *Letter-Writing in Greco-Roman Antiquity.* Philadelphia: Westminster Press, 1986, 100–1, 122–25.

Suh, Robin. Personal communication.

Tarrants, Tom. Personal communication.

Tauler, Johannes. *The Sermons and Conferences of Johann Tauler.* Translated by Walter Elliott. Washington, DC: Apostolic Mission House, 1910.

Temple, William. *William Temple, Some Lambeth Letters.* Edited by F. S. Temple. London: Lambeth Palace Library, 1963, 25–26, 26–27, 40–41, 113–14, 135–38, 148, 158–59.

Teresa of Avila. *The Letters of Saint Teresa of Jesus.* Translated by E. Allison Peers. London: Sheed and Ward, 1951, 316, 317.

Tersteegen, Gerhard. *Gerhard Tersteegen, Eine Auswahl aus seinen Schriften.* Edited by Walter Nigg. Wuppertal: R. Brockhaus Verlag, 1967, 104, 105, 111–13, 115, 129–31.

Thomas a Kempis. *Thomas a Kempis and the Brothers of the Common Life.* Vol. 2. London: Kegan, Paul, Trench, & Co., 1882, 165–70.

Toews, John B. *Czars, Soviets & Mennonites.* Newton, KS: Faith and Life Press, 2004, 157–58.

Toon, Peter. *The Life, Walk and Triumph of Faith, with an Account of his life.* Cambridge: James Clarke & Co., 1970.

Torrance, Alan. Personal communication.

Twain, Mark. *Letters from the Earth. Uncensored Writings by Mark Twain.* Edited by Bernard de Voto. San Francisco: Harper Collins, 1991, 15–16, 51, 53.

Tyndale, William, *The Fathers of the English Church,* reproduced from John Fox, *The Works of Tindal, Frith and Barnes,* 1573, vol. 1. London: John Hatchard, 1807, 351–52.

van Bruggen, June. Personal communications.

van Eeghan, Ernst. Personal communication.

Venn, Henry. *The Life and a Selection of Letters of the late Rev. Henry Venn.* 4th edition. London: John Hatchard, 1836, 538–39.

Voillaume, Rene. *Brothers of Men: Letters to the Petit-Freres.* Edited by Lancelot

Sheppard. London: Darton, Longman and Todd, 1966, 132–33, 134–36, 190–91, 206–7.

von Hugel, Friedrich. *Letters from Baron von Hugel to a Niece.* Chicago: Regnery Press, 1955, 21–22, 137.

von Moltke, Helmuth James. *Letters to Freya, 1939–1945.* Edited and translated by Beate Ruhm von Oppen. New York: Vintage Books, 1995, 407–12.

Walls, Andrew. Personal communication.

Walter of Hilton. *Towards a Perfect Love: the Spiritual Counsel of Walter Hilton.* Translated by David L. Jeffrey. Portland: Multnomah, 1985, 8–12.

Waltke, Bruce. Personal communication.

Watts, Rikk. Personal communication.

Weil, Simone. *Waiting for God.* Translated by Emma Crafurd. New York: Putnam, 1950, 23, 26–27.

Wesley, John. *The Letters of the Rev. John Wesley.* Edited by John Telford. Vol. VIII. London: The Epworth Press, 1792, 264–65.

Whitfield, George. *English Spirituality in the Age of Wesley.* Grand Rapids: William B. Eerdmans, 1987, 314–15.

Whyte, Alexander. *Santa Teresa: an Appreciation.* Edinburgh: Oliphant, Anderson and Ferrier, 1897, 78.

William of St. Thierry. *The Enigma of Faith.* Translated by John D. Anderson. Washington, DC: Cistercian Publications, 1973, 35, 37, 38, 91, 92.

Williams, Roger. *The Puritans: a Sourcebook of their Writings.* Mineola, NY: Dover Publications, 2001, 486–88.

Wycliffe, John. *Writings of John Wycliffe.* Philadelphia: Presbyterian Board of Publications, 1842, 48.

Zlotnik, Michael. Personal communication.

Additional copies of *Letters of Faith through the Seasons Vol. 2*
are available wherever good books are sold.

ဆာလ၁

If you have enjoyed this book, or if it has had an impact on your life,
we would like to hear from you.

Please contact us at:

HONOR BOOKS
Cook Communications Ministries, Dept. 201
4050 Lee Vance View
Colorado Springs, CO 80918

Or visit our Web site:
www.cookministries.com

HONOR ⒣ BOOKS
Inspiration and Motivation for the Seasons of Life